Pal

Land Law

PALGRAVE LAW MASTERS

Series editor: Marise Cremona

Land Law

Fifth Edition

Kate Green
Formerly Principal Lecturer in Law, University of East London

and

Joe Cursley
Senior Lecturer in Law, University of East London

Series Editor: Marise Cremona
Professor of European Commercial Law
Queen Mary Centre for Commercial Law Studies
Queen Mary, University of London

First edition 1989
Reprinted twice
Second edition 1993
Reprinted four times
Third edition 1997
Reprinted twice
Fourth edition 2001
Reprinted once
Published 2004 by
PALGRAVE MACMILLAN
Houndmills, Basingstoke, Hampshire RG21 6XS
and 175 Fifth Avenue, New York, N.Y. 10010
Companies and representatives throughout the world

ISBN-13: 978-1-4039-1598-6

This book is printed on paper suitable for recycling and made from fully
managed and sustained forest sources. Logging, pulping and
manufacturing processes are expected to conform to the environmental
regulations of the country of origin.

A catalogue record for this book is available from the British Library.

10   9   8   7   6   5
13 12 11 10 09 08 07

Printed and bound in Great Britain by
Creative Print & Design (Wales), Ebbw Vale

Contents

Part V   Licences in Land

Table of Cases

Table of Statutes

Table of European Legislation

Preface to the Fifth Edition

The purpose of this book is to serve as an accessible introduction to land law in England and Wales and to form a foundation for the further study of the subject. As in previous editions, the intention has also been to show that land law is adaptable and rich in interest, essentially concerned with the relationships which people, organisations and the state have with each other about land – rather than a difficult, dry, abstract subject couched in arcane language and somehow detached from the reality of people's lives.

The study of land law cannot really be undertaken in isolation from other law subjects such as contract, tort and equity, to which reference is made in the text where appropriate. In addition, much of the land law which appears in textbooks on the subject, including this one, is overlaid by a statutory framework (for example, in leasehold law); readers may wish to direct themselves to relevant specialist textbooks.

Since the last edition, the Land Registration Act 2002 has come into force, abolishing the Land Registration Act 1925 with which generations of land law students were familiar. The new Act aims to simplify and rationalise the law in order to prepare the way for universal conveyancing by electronic means, and it is clear that there is no future for the unregistered system (although unregistered conveyancing continues to be covered in this edition). The Act also fundamentally changes the operation of the law of adverse possession in registered land. This edition covers the long-awaited introduction of the commonhold system that is expected in Summer 2004, when the Commonhold and Leashold Reform Act 2002, Part I, is due to come into force. Its practical effects are uncertain, however, at least in the short term. This edition also considers the developing importance on land law issues of the Human Rights Act 1998 and the European Convention on Human Rights.

The syllabus of most land law courses is covered, but there is no detailed reference to the working of the Settled Land Act or analysis of future interests and the law against perpetuities.

My thanks are due to colleagues, especially Hilary Lim, for comments on the draft of this edition. Any errors are, of course, my own.

JOE CURSLEY
January 2004

References

In addition to the Further Reading listed at the end of each chapter, reference may be made to the following texts:

Cheshire G. C., Burn E. H., *Modern Law of Real Property*, 15th edn (London: Butterworth, 2000) (referred to as 'Cheshire')

Gray K., Gray S. F., *Elements of Land Law*, 3rd edn (London: Butterworth, 2001) ('Gray and Gray')

Megarry R., Wade H. W. R., Harpum C., *The Law of Real Property*, 6th edn (London: Sweet & Maxwell, 2000) ('Megarry and Wade')

Megarry R., Oakley A. J., *A Manual of the Law of Real Property*, 8th edn (London: Sweet and Maxwell, 2002) ('Megarry')

Murphy W. T., Roberts S., *Understanding Property Law*, 3rd edn (London: Sweet & Maxwell, 1998).

Smith R. J., *Property Law*, 4th edn (Harlow: Longman, 2003).

Sparkes P., *A New Land Law*, 2nd edn (Oxford: Hart, 2003)

Thompson M. P., *Modern Land Law*, 2nd edn (Oxford: OUP, 2003) ('Thompson')

Part 1

Introduction

1   Introduction to Land Law

1.1 How to Study Land Law

Land law is an interesting and challenging subject, involving profound questions about the way we choose to live our lives, for land is vital for human life. In any society – even our technological, high-speed one – the use of land is of the utmost importance; where the supply is limited, as in England and Wales, the problems are acute. The dry and legalistic façade created by the artificial language and technical concepts of land law tends to conceal the fundamental issues: land law is really just about the sharing out of our limited island.

Land law has been developing ever since people got ideas about having rights over certain places, probably beginning with the cultivation of crops. Through the long process of development there have been periods of gradual change, and also more dramatic times such as the Norman conquest of 1066 and the property legislation of 1925. By and large, lawyers have, over the centuries, continued to use the words and ideas of their predecessors. However, although land law has kept its feudal roots and language, the substance of today's law is fundamentally changed. The law can certainly seem obscure – cloaked in the fog, rather than the mists, of time – so it is perhaps best at the start to treat it like a foreign language. The vocabulary soon becomes natural, especially through reading about the same topic in different books.

The law is often further distanced from real life by historical introductions which serve to conceal more than they reveal. Lawyers' history tends to be of the 'century per paragraph' variety and is often coloured by unspoken political opinions. Such history should be treated with caution.

As explained further below, lawyers are concerned with various rights to land, called 'interests in land'. They might talk about someone 'owning land' but really they mean someone owning *an interest in* the land; these interests are not the land itself – the earth and the buildings – but abstract concepts, like the freehold and the lease.

The first thing to do when studying any interest in land is to grasp the definition thoroughly. This helps to avoid two of the most depressing things that can happen to land law students: the first is staring at a problem without having any idea of what it is about, and the second – possibly worse – is recognising what the problem is about, but feeling incapable of writing anything down. If in doubt, start with the interests in the land.

The rules which constitute land law are like a complicated machine; moving one lever, or adjusting one valve, changes the end product. Some authors compare the subject with playing chess; there are various 'pieces' (which correspond to interests in land) and they can be moved about according to strict rules. The owner of an interest in land has limited freedom of action, and one small change in her position can affect the relative value of other interests in the land.

In practical terms, the complicated connections within the machine mean that one part of the subject cannot be fully grasped until all the others have been understood. There is no single starting place: it is necessary to watch the machine, piece by piece, until the connections become clear. It is useful, from the beginning, to ask, 'What would happen if …?'; if one lever is moved, what interests will be affected, and why?

As a consequence of the complex definitions and the interdependent rules, land law may only make sense when the course is nearly complete. However, in the meantime, it is necessary to make mistakes in order to grasp the way the rules relate to one another. It *will* eventually come together, with hard work and faith and hope: the charity, with any luck, will be provided by the teacher.

The language used by land lawyers expresses the way they think they see the world. This is a world in which people's relationships to land can only occur within the legal structure of interests in land, so lawyers squeeze the facts of ordinary life into the pre-existing moulds of 'the interests'. A land law student's job is to learn the shapes of the moulds, and imitate the squeeze; then she will be able to operate the whole machine. Finally, armed with this knowledge and skill, she may begin to question whether land law really does operate like this in practice.

1.2 **Land Law Rules**

Land law is made up of rules in statutes and cases; case law rules are further divided into legal and equitable rules. That is, the rules were created, if not by an Act of Parliament, either by a court of 'law' or by a court of 'equity'. The development of these two sets of rules is well described by others (for example, Murphy and Roberts, 1998), and is merely outlined here.

The customs which became known as the 'common law' were enforced with extraordinary rigidity by judges who followed the strict letter of the law. Aggrieved citizens – in the absence of crusading television journalists – wrote begging letters to the King. These received replies from his 'secretary', the Chancellor, who employed the King's power to override the decisions of the King's judges. Appealing to the Chancellor's conscience, to 'equity', grew in popularity and from about 1535 the Chancellor's court, Chancery, was regularly making decisions overriding the law in the King's court.

However, this new system of justice did not set out to replace the rules of law, but merely to intervene when conscience required it: *equity came not to destroy the law but to fulfil it.* The common law and Chancery courts existed separately, each with its own procedures and remedies, to the great profit of the legal profession. Eventually things became intolerably inefficient and the two courts were merged by the Judicature Acts 1873 and 1875 but, even today, lawyers keep the legal and equitable rules and remedies separate (see 1.5 below).

Many land law statutes are dated 1925, an emotive date for land lawyers. The law was actually changed by a very large Law of Property Act in 1922, but that Act was not brought into force, being divided into the various 1925 Acts. The main statutes of that year are:

1925 legislation

- Administration of Estates Act (AEA)
- Law of Property Act (LPA)
- Land Charges Act (LCA) (now 1972)
- Land Registration Act (LRA) (now abolished – replaced by LRA 2002)
- Settled Land Act (SLA) (now see Trusts of Land and Appointment of Trustees Act 1996)
- Trustee Act (TA)

The 1925 statutes contained many radical reforms and also 'wordsaving' provisions, some of which had appeared in earlier statutes. In the old days, lawyers were 'paid by the yard', so the more words they used the better for their bank balances, but Parliament ensured that many common promises in land transactions no longer needed to be spelt out in full, being implied by statute: in effect, the customs of conveyancers (lawyers who manage the transfer of land) become enshrined in statute.

One of the aims of the 1925 legislation was to make conveyancing (the buying, selling, mortgaging and other transfer of land) simpler in order to revive the depressed market in land and to make it easier to deal with commercially. It is impossible to say whether it had this effect. Certainly, the reasons for the great increase in home ownership in the twentieth century were not connected to the reforms, some of which were inappropriate to the modern world of owner-occupation.

1.3 **Land Law Today**

At the most basic level, human beings are land animals; they need somewhere to put their bodies, a piece of land on which to 'be'. On the emotional plane, humans must have contact with land, their roots in the earth. Physically, they need air to breathe and space in which to move about, food and shelter; all these are provided by land.

As a resource, land also has other special characteristics. Except in the rare cases of land falling into or being thrown up from the sea, it is geographically fixed and immoveable; it is also ultimately indestructible.

Its nature means that the boundaries between one piece of land and another are normally touching, so neighbouring owners are aware of one another's business. Further, to its occupant one piece is never exactly the same as another: each is unique – even in apparently uniform tower blocks each floor, each flat, has its own particular characteristics.

The permanence and durability of land are matched by its flexibility. It has an infinite number of layers, and is really 'three-dimensional space'. A plot of land can be used by a number of people in different ways simultaneously: one person can invest her money in it, while two or more live there, a fourth tunnels beneath to extract minerals and half a dozen more use a path over it as a short-cut, or graze their cattle on a part of it.

Land can be shared consecutively as well as simultaneously; that is to say, people can enjoy the land one after another. The great landowning families traditionally created complicated 'settlements' of their estates, whereby the land would pass through the succeeding generations as the first owner desired. Each 'owner' only had it for a lifetime, and could not leave it by will because, at death, it had to pass according to the directions in the settlement (see 12.2 below). In this way the aristocratic dynasties preserved their land, and consequently their wealth and their political power.

Each society develops its own cultural attitudes to its land. These attitudes are coloured by the kind of land (for example desert or jungle) because this determines the uses to which it can be put. The view taken of land is also influenced by its scarcity or otherwise, and by the economic system. In places where land was plentiful, it was not normally 'owned'. When European colonists arrived in America, the indigenous people believed that:

> the earth was created by the assistance of the sun, and it should be left as it was ... The country was made without lines of demarcation, and it is no man's business to divide it ... The earth and myself are of one mind. The measure of the land and the measure of our bodies are the same ... Do not misunderstand me, but understand me fully with reference to my affection for the land. I never said the land was mine to do with as I chose. The one who has the right to dispose of it is the one who created it.   (McLuhan T.C., *Touch the Earth* (Abacus, 1972), p. 54)

Similarly, native Australians regarded the land with special awe; as concluded in one of the cases about aboriginal land claims, it was not so much that they owned the land, but that the land owned them (*Milirrpum* v. *Nabalco Pty Ltd and the Commonwealth of Australia* (1971) 17 FLR 141). A traditional African view was that the land was not capable of being owned by one person but belonged to the whole tribe:

> land belongs to a vast family of which many are dead, a few are living and countless numbers still unborn.   (West African Lands Committee Cd 1048, p. 183)

In early English land law, the fundamental concept was 'seisin'. The person who was seised of land was entitled to recover it in the courts if she were disseised. Originally, 'the person seised of land was simply the person in obvious occupation, the person sitting on the land' (Simpson, 1986, p. 37). Seisin thus described the close relationship between a person and the land she worked and lived on. This simplicity was, over centuries, 'refined, modified and elaborated', and the concepts of ownership and possession took over. Nevertheless actual possession or occupation can still be of great importance in land law, for example in adverse possession (see Chapter 3).

Over the last three or four hundred years, our land law has been developing alongside the growth of capitalism and city living. There has been a huge population increase: in 1603, there were about 4 million people in Britain, while today there are about 59 million on the same area, about 235 000 square kilometres (that is, about 4000 square metres of surface area per person although, of course, most people are confined to a comparatively tiny urban space). More recently there has been an enormous increase in the number of ordinary people who own land. The percentage of households which lives in owner-occupied accommodation – a house or a flat – has more than doubled in the last 40 years, and is currently about 70 per cent of all households (source: Census 2001). It is unlikely to grow much more than this, however, as a significant part of the population either does not wish to take on the responsibilities of owner-occupation or is unable to afford it.

For the majority of owner-occupiers, the land they own (although subject to a huge debt in the form of a mortgage) is both home and investment. It is an expression of their personality and a retreat from the world; at the same time it represents a status symbol and – they hope – an inflation-proofed savings bank. For other people (for example, those who rent their home on a weekly tenancy), home ownership with its apparent psychological and financial advantages may be only a hope for the future. In the meantime, their relationship with their land may be less secure, subject to the authority of a landlady. However, in a lawyer's view, tenants are also 'landowners', in theory at least (see 1.4 below).

Some authors interpret the modern law as treating land merely as if it were money, but a law which actually dealt with land in this way would not fulfil the needs of today's society. Many of the difficult issues in contemporary land law focus on the informal arrangements of people who – unlike the landowners of previous centuries – do not see the need to transact their family business via a lawyer. Take the following situation as an example. Jane lets Raj share her house and, in exchange, he pays the mortgage. Later she sells the house to Chris. Chris wants to live there by himself, but Raj does not want to leave. This kind of problem, where a transaction between buyer and seller involves a third person's interest in land, appears in various forms throughout this book. It is a kind of eternal triangle, as in Figure 1.1.

It is often said that disputes in land law centre on the conflicting requirements of the market in land. In order to maximise the value of land, ownership must be capable of being freely and safely traded, while people who have lesser interests in the land must also feel secure.

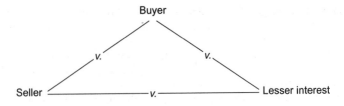

Figure 1.1   The eternal triangle

The market certainly seems to have an influence on the development of the law. One of the most influential factors in the attitudes of judges to difficult decisions is their view of the state of the market. When there was a slump at the end of the nineteenth century they tried to ensure that liabilities attached to land (that is, the lesser, third-party interests) were minimised so that the land would be attractive to buyers. In the 1970s and 1980s there were booming prices in most areas of the country, and a greater interest in the security of 'non-owners', like Raj. The falling market of the early 1990s produced its own response, significantly influenced by the interests of the building societies and banks (see Chapter 7).

1.4 'Land'

Definitions of land

At common law, 'land' means the soil, the rocks beneath and the air above (see 4.4 below). It includes things growing on the land, and buildings 'attached' to it. The general rule is that whatever is attached to the land becomes part of it. If Jane sells her land to Chris, she is selling not merely the surface, but also the grass and trees, and the bricks, tiles and chimney-pots of the house. The extent to which things fixed onto a building, or cemented into the ground, are 'fixtures', that is, part of the land itself, is a question of fact in every case.

In *Berkley* v. *Poulett* [1977] 1 EGLR 86, the eighth Earl Poulett sold his estate and took with him some pictures which had been screwed onto panelling, as well as a marble statue of a Greek god. The buyer sued him, claiming that the items were part of the land and should therefore remain. The court held that two questions had to be asked: first, to what degree was the item annexed (attached) to the land, and second, why had it been annexed? It was held (by a majority in the Court of Appeal) that the pictures were not part of the intrinsic design of the room, and the statue – unlike its plinth, which the earl had left behind – was not essential to the landscaped garden. Both had been there to be enjoyed for their own sake, and were therefore chattels – personal property – rather than fixtures.

In *Elitestone* v. *Morris* [1997] 1 WLR 687, Mr Morris lived in a rented chalet on a plot of land which Elitestone Ltd owned and wished to develop. The chalet had no intrinsic foundations, but merely rested on a number of concrete blocks. If Mr Morris could show that the chalet was land, then he would have protection under the Rent Act 1977 and Elitestone Ltd would not be able to throw him off. Because the chalet could not be removed without destroying it, the House of Lords found that it was sufficiently attached to the land as to become part and parcel of it. If it had been possible to remove the chalet without destroying it, it would probably have been considered a chattel and Mr Morris would have lost his home. *Elitestone* is an example of a modern development in the law which distinguishes between a thing which is a fixture and one which is 'part and parcel of the land' – both count as land, but the terminology makes more sense: the former is now confined to its common, everyday meaning and there is no longer any need artificially to describe a building as a fixture.

When considering whether a thing is a fixture (other than a building) or a chattel, the law nowadays probably puts greater emphasis on the purpose of annexation, that is, whether the intention was to improve the land permanently, and looks at the degree of attachment as evidence of the intention.

Land is also defined in s.205(1)(ix) LPA:

> Land includes land of any tenure, and mines and minerals ... buildings or parts of buildings ... and other corporeal hereditaments; also ... a rent, and other incorporeal hereditaments, and an easement right, privilege, or benefit in, over, or derived from land.

Thus both freeholds and leases are 'land', so a person who buys a lease (that is, becomes a leaseholder or a tenant) is a buyer of land. The term 'corporeal hereditaments' is an ancient way of referring to the land and the fixtures, while 'incorporeal hereditaments' are the invisible interests in land, such as mortgages and easements (rights of way, for example). A person who buys a right of way over her neighbour's land, therefore, is also buying land.

Types of 'land'

Since 1925 all titles to land in England and Wales are either 'unregistered' or 'registered'. Although people often refer to 'registered land', and the main statute in question is the Land Registration Act 2002 (which recently replaced the Land Registration Act 1925), technically it is a person's *title* to the land which is registered, not the land itself.

The aim of simplifying conveyancing was ultimately to be achieved by registering all titles to land in a central registry (see Chapter 11), but even now, although most titles have been registered and all land must be registered when it changes hands or is first mortgaged, about 20 per cent of titles in England and Wales are not yet registered (source: Land Registry), probably amounting to more than a third of the total area of the land (see Cahill, 2001).

The two regimes, that of registered title and that of unregistered title, have different procedures and rules, which occasionally produce different results. Therefore the very first question to ask when faced with any land law issue is:

Question 1
Has the title been registered yet?

1.5 Estates and Interests in Land

Estates and interests

It has already been mentioned that the land lawyer views every piece of land as potentially fragmented into an infinite number of interests. For historical reasons, she sees people owning an abstract estate or interest in land, not the land itself. The lesser interests are carved out of the major ones, which are called the 'estates'. This word 'estate' has a long lineage; it means 'an interest in land of some particular duration' (Megarry and Wade, 2000, p. 37), but today this definition is an academic relic of no practical importance. It is only necessary to know that there are now two estates in land – the freehold and the leasehold.

The term 'interest in land' is significant to land lawyers because it shows that the rights and duties of the people concerned are not merely personal or contractual. These rights and duties are attached to the land itself and they automatically pass to anyone who buys or inherits the land; they can therefore be transferred to other people and bind third parties. In lawyers' vocabulary, interests in land are 'property'.

On reading land law problems, it is crucial to develop an instinct for the various interests so that you can immediately say, for example, 'This looks like an easement.' The second question to ask in problem-solving is therefore:

Question 2
What interests may exist here?

Legal and equitable interests

The courts of *law* recognised various estates and interests in land and would enforce the rights of a legal owner; the courts of *equity* might override this in favour of a person with, in their view, a stronger moral right to the land. The owner of the legal interest was deemed by equity to hold it on behalf of (on trust for) the person who had the better right. Today there are many pieces of land where legal title and equitable enjoyment are divided in this way.

This can be illustrated by the well-known case of *Bull* v. *Bull* [1955] 1 QB 234. A son and mother both contributed to buying a house on the outskirts of London, but only the son's name appeared on the conveyance (the deed) so he was the legal owner. He then married and, since his wife and his mother could not get on with each other, tried to evict his mother. The Court of Appeal held that he could not simply turn her out. She had a share of the equitable title because of her contribution to the purchase, so the son held the legal title on behalf of the equitable owners (himself and his mother). Another way to express this is to say that the son is a trustee for himself and his mother; they share the 'beneficial' interest. Equity normally recognises a trust relationship like this when the apparent owner *ought* to hold the land wholly or partly for the benefit of someone else. The trust is a useful, and very common, device by which land can be shared (see Chapters 12 and 13).

There are, therefore, a number of legal interests in land and, in a kind of parallel universe, many equitable interests. As a general rule, anyone who buys or inherits land owns it subject to any interests which have been created by previous owners of the land. However, this rule has numerous exceptions.

Enforcing interests

There are two main reasons why it is still important to label interests as 'legal' or 'equitable'. The first is that equitable interests depend on equitable remedies and these depend on the court's discretion: the court of equity, being 'a court of conscience', only grants a remedy if the claimant has behaved fairly. (Legal remedies on the other hand – damages, for example – are available 'as of right'; a plaintiff is entitled to damages if her strict legal rights have been infringed, whether or not this is fair.) Thus the mother in the *Bull* case, who was relying on an equitable interest, could not have succeeded if she had been deceitful (this is expressed in the maxim, 'she who comes to equity must come with clean hands') or had delayed unreasonably, as in *Tse Kwong Lam* v. *Wong Chit Sen* [1983] 1 WLR 1349 (see 7.3 below).

The second reason to distinguish between legal and equitable interests is that the courts of equity could not bring themselves to enforce equitable rights against a completely innocent and honest legal buyer. Therefore, the rule was established that the owner of an equitable interest in land would lose it if someone paid for the legal estate, in good faith and without notice of the equitable interest. This rule about the *bona fide* purchaser is known as the 'doctrine of notice'.

The doctrine of notice

Before 1925, an equitable interest did not bind the *bona fide* purchaser of the legal estate for value without notice (actual, imputed or constructive).

Proof of any one of the three kinds of notice would mean that the buyer would be bound by the equitable interest. If she actually knew about, for example, the mother's interest in *Bull* v. *Bull* (above), or if her agent knew about it ('imputed notice'), she would step into the son's shoes and would be bound by the mother's rights. Under 'constructive notice' (also known as the rule in *Hunt* v. *Luck* [1902] 1 Ch 428), the buyer would be taken to know – whether or not she did – anything a prudent purchaser would have discovered by inspecting the land and the title deeds to the land. Any buyer of the bungalow in the *Bull* case would probably have discovered, had she looked around it carefully, that someone other than the son and his wife lived there; she would have had constructive notice of the mother's right and would have been bound by it. The 1925 legislation considerably restricted the effect of the doctrine of notice: in registered land, for example, it now 'has no application' (Mummery LJ in *Barclays Bank* v. *Boulter* [1998] 1 WLR 1 and see (2001) Law Com No 271, para. 5.16) and Chapters 10 and 11, below).

Another way to express the difference between legal and equitable interests in land is to say that legal rights are effective against anyone in the world, but equitable rights are only 'good' against certain people. The third question therefore that must be asked about a land law problem is:

Question 3

Is this interest legal or equitable?

The answer will be very important in determining the relative rights of the various parties.

Equitable interests and conveyancing

As part of the reforms directed at making conveyancing simpler, the number of legal rights to land were strictly limited in 1925; many interests could no longer be legal but could be equitable only. The section which establishes this is the 'cornerstone' of property legislation:

Law of Property Act 1925

S.1(1) The only estates in land which are capable of subsisting or of being conveyed or created at law are:
    (a) An estate in fee simple absolute in possession [a freehold];
    (b) A term of years absolute [a lease].

  (2) The only interests or charges in or over land which are capable of subsisting or of being conveyed or created at law are:
    (a) An easement, right, or privilege in or over land for an interest equivalent to an estate in fee simple absolute in possession or a term of years absolute [rights of way, for example];

    (b) A rentcharge in possession issuing out of or charged on land being either perpetual or for a term of years absolute [a periodical payment secured on land, but which does not arise out of a lease or a mortgage];

    (c) A charge by way of legal mortgage;

    (d) ... and any other similar charge on land which is not created by an instrument [effectively repealed];

    (e) Rights of entry exercisable over or in respect of a legal term of years absolute [a landlady's right to end a lease].

(3) All other estates, interests, and charges in or over land take effect as equitable interests.

Thus, whatever the historical position, since 1 January 1926 there are only two estates (freehold and leasehold), and (effectively) four interests which are capable of existing *at law*; all the rest must be *equitable*. Such equitable interests, however, would have been insecure because of the doctrine of notice – there would always be the threat of a 'purchaser of the legal estate in good faith for value without notice'. The 1925 scheme therefore provides ways to protect these equitable interests against unscrupulous legal owners (see especially Chapters 10 to 12).

It must be emphasised that s.1 LPA 1925 does not say that the estates and interests listed there *are* legal, merely that they *may* be. Whether or not an interest is legal or equitable is an interesting question: the answer will be clearer after reading the next chapter.

1.6 **Human Rights**

Most of the rights in the European Convention on Human Rights are directly enforceable under the Human Rights Act 1998, which came into force on 2 October 2000. The Act is relevant to land lawyers because the rules and practices of land law are now open to challenge if they should offend against Convention rights.

The Act requires the courts to interpret legislation 'in a way which is compatible with the Convention rights' (s.3), and is directly applicable against public authorities (s.6) which includes courts and tribunals, central and local government and any body exercising functions of a public nature. In *Aston Cantlow and Wilmcote Parochial Church Council* v. *Wallbank* [2003] 3 All ER 1213, the Wallbanks were the owners of a certain field and, as a result, owed an archaic and feudal duty to repair the chancel of their parish church. They argued that this obligation deprived them of the peaceful enjoyment of their possessions (their money) contrary to Article 1, Protocol 1 (below). The Wallbanks failed in the House of Lords, not because they were being deprived of their money, but because the Parochial Church Council was not a public authority, and therefore the provisions of the Act were unenforceable against it (see also 11.5 below).

The extent to which the Act has 'horizontal' effect – in other words, how far it is applicable in a dispute between two private individuals – is uncertain. It may be that it has wider horizontal effect than originally intended, since the s.3 requirement applies even if the parties are private individuals, and s.6 prevents the courts (as public bodies) from interpreting common law as well as statute in a way which is incompatible with Convention rights.

In the context of land law, the most important of the Convention rights are:

- Article 1, Protocol 1 – the right to peaceful enjoyment and protection of possessions;
- Article 8 – the right to respect for a person's private and family life and home;
- Article 6 – the right to a fair and public hearing;
- Article 14 – the right to enjoy Convention rights without discrimination.

Article 1, Protocol 1 guarantees a person's right to enjoy her property free from interference from the state, unless this is in the public interest and in accordance with the law. This might well allow the compulsory purchase of a person's land by a local authority, for example, and it has permitted long leaseholders to buy the freehold of their land under the Leasehold Reform Act 1967, since this is in the interests of social justice (see *James* v. *UK* (1986) 8 EHRR 123 and 5.6 below).

Under Article 8, no public authority may interfere with the exercise of the right to respect for a person's private and family life and home, except in accordance with the law and to the extent that it is necessary in a democratic society. This Article might be thought to be relevant in the context of the right of the landlady to evict a tenant for breach of covenant (see 6.5 below) and the right of a mortgage lender to re-enter the borrower's home when the mortgage debt is in arrears (see 7.3 below). However, in *Harrow LBC* v. *Qazi* [2003] UKHL 43, the House of Lords confirmed that the Article concerned rights of privacy rather than property, and that it cannot be used to defeat contractual and proprietary rights to possession:

A person's 'home' is rather the place where he and his family are entitled to be left in peace free from interference by the state or agents of the state. It is an important aspect of his dignity as a human being, and it is protected as such and not as an item of property. (Lord Millett at para. 89)

The effect of the Human Rights Act and the Convention rights it incorporates will be further discussed where relevant during the course of this book.

1.7 **Comment**

It can be seen, even from this brief introduction, that land law works within a special language, using a set of abstract interests as the basis for the ownership and enjoyment of land. The language, abstractions and interdependent rules can cause difficulties initially, but perseverance overcomes these. The fascinating history of land law can, if there is time to read in depth, provide a more profound understanding of the roles played by the law and by lawyers in relation to people sharing their space.

Summary

1.1 Land law is fundamentally about how people share land.
1.2 In your approach to land law, it is essential to grasp the language and definitions of interests in land as well as the rules about them.
1.3 'Land' means the physical land and fixtures and includes any interest in land; land may be either registered or not yet registered.
1.4 There are many interests capable of existing in a piece of land; these interests should be identified as either legal or equitable.
1.5 Historically, legal interests would bind anyone who owned the land; equitable interests would bind everyone except a buyer of a legal estate in good faith for value without notice, actual, imputed or constructive.
1.6 Land law was reformed in 1925, and the number of estates and interests capable of being legal is now limited to two estates, freehold and leasehold, and four interests.
1.7 In analysing a land law question, the following three primary questions should be asked: is the title registered or not yet registered? What interest may exist here? Is the interest legal or equitable?
1.8 The provisions of the Human Rights Act 1998 must be considered in the context of land law.

Exercises

1.1 Is an equitable interest as good as a legal interest?
1.2 Why does it matter whether land is registered or not yet registered?
1.3 Why is s.1 LPA 1925 important?
1.4 How does a lawyer define land?
1.5 Waheeda has bought Jack's house. When she first viewed the house, she was particularly taken with the garden, which contained an ornamental pond and a statue of a mermaid set on a plinth in its centre. She was also pleased that she would be getting a large garden shed which rested on a concrete base.

When she moved in, she was horrified to discover that Jack had taken away both the statue and the shed. The fitted carpets in the house had also been removed. Waheeda checked the contract for the sale, but found that it made no mention of any of these items.

Advise Waheeda, who also tells you that she cannot understand how Jack managed to remove the shed, since he would have had to dismantle it completely in order to do so.

Further Reading

Baker, *An Introduction to English Legal History*, 3rd edn (London: Butterworth, 1990)

Bright, 'Of Estates and Interests: A Tale of Ownership and Property Rights' in Bright and Dewar (eds), *Land Law Themes and Perspectives* (Oxford: OUP, 1998)

Cahill, *Who Owns Britain*, (Edinburgh: Canongate, 2001)

Haley, 'The Law of Fixtures: An Unprincipled Metamorphosis?' [1998] Conv 138

Howell, 'The Human Rights Act 1998: The Horizontal Effect on Land Law' in Cooke (ed), *Modern Studies in Property Law, Volume 1* (Oxford: Hart, 2001)

Milsom, *Historical Foundations of the Common Law*, 2nd edn (London: Butterworth, 1981)

Rook, *Property Law and Human Rights* (London: Blackstone, 2001)

Rook, 'Property Law and the Human Rights Act 1998: A Review of the First Year' [2002] Conv 316

Simpson, *History of the Land Law* (Oxford: Clarendon Press, 1986)

2 Buying and Selling Land

2.1 Introduction

This chapter explains the normal process of buying and selling land and the effects of the sale, including the rules about the creation and enforcement of contracts for the sale of land, and about deeds. These rules are crucial to land law because there may not be a contract if they are not observed, or the buyer may only obtain an equitable interest which may be insecure, as explained in 1.5 above.

First, it is important to remember that 'land' includes all interests in land (see 1.4 above) and:

> purchaser means a purchaser in good faith for valuable consideration and includes a lessee, mortgagee or other person who for valuable consideration acquires an interest in property. (s.205(1)(xxi) LPA 1925)

Therefore, the rules in this chapter control, for example, the creation of leases and mortgages, as well as the sale of freehold land and assignment of leases.

The transfer of a form of property which is financially and emotionally so important is bound to be the subject of some ritual and, therefore, of technical rules. These conveyancing rules are also, to a large extent, a recognition of the good practices of conveyancing lawyers: the roles of Parliament and the courts can often be seen as approving retrospectively the accepted practice of the experts. All land in England and Wales must now be registered on sale, transfer or first legal mortgage, and therefore every sale today is subject to at least some of the rules about registration of title (see Chapter 11).

The Law of Property (Miscellaneous Provisions) Act 1989 introduced completely new rules about how a contract for the sale of a legal interest in land must be made. The old law (including the 'written memorandum' of a contract, 'part performance', the 'subject to contract' protection, and the old definition of a deed) is now mainly of historical interest. As time passes old contracts are decreasingly likely to be the subject of legal action, although in *Lloyds Bank plc* v. *Carrick* [1996] 4 All ER 630 the Court of Appeal had to consider the status of a contract made in 1982. This chapter refers briefly to the old law but concentrates on the new.

As in all areas of land law, the rules on which this chapter focuses are affected by other rules. The most important are those about registered and unregistered land but, in addition, legal title can also be obtained by long use and equitable title by means of a trust. Given the interdependent parts of the land law machine, it is only possible fully to understand the rules about buying and selling land when the rest of land law is also understood.

2.2 **A Typical Domestic Sale**

The usual procedure

Figure 2.1 shows the important steps in a typical conveyance of freehold land. (A conveyance is a document which transfers property and includes a deed, also called a 'grant'.) The buyer's aim is to own the legal title to the house. The first step which has any binding effect takes place at exchange of contracts (see 2.3 and 2.4 below), but the buyer does not become the legal owner at this stage. In unregistered land, legal title is initially transferred by means of a deed; the new owner must then register the title at the Land Registry. If title is already registered, its transfer must be recorded at the Land Registry in order for legal ownership to be changed (see Chapter 11).

During the period of pre-contractual enquiries and negotiation, neither side can be sure of completing the sale. The buyers might fail to get their loan, or might decide that the house is too expensive; the sellers might receive a higher offer from another prospective buyer or might decide to withdraw the house from the market. Each side would like the other to be bound as soon as possible, but is wary of committing itself too soon. The delay, cost and uncertainty inherent in the current system are well known, and the present government has proposed measures to speed up the

Time	Facts	Law
About 8 weeks	Negotiation of price, fittings, etc.	None of these steps has any legal or equitable implications: there is no contract (s.2 1989 Act).
	Survey and finance arranged.	
	Draft contract prepared by seller.	
	Local authority searches by buyer.	
	Buyer checks details of property.	
	Contract agreed by buyer.	
	Deposit paid by buyer and contracts containing all the terms agreed by the parties are signed by both sides and exchanged.	The contract is made: equitable title passes to buyer.
About 4 weeks	Pre-completion searches of title.	
	Purchase deed prepared.	
	Completion by execution of the deed and payment of the balance of the purchase price.	Legal title is transferred to buyer in unregistered land (s.52 LPA).
	Land transfer received by the Land Registry.	Legal title is transferred to buyer in registered land.

Figure 2.1   The main stages in the purchase of a house

process. The main proposal will require the seller to provide potential buyers with an information pack containing a copy of the title documents, results of search enquiries, a report on the condition of the property and a draft contract of sale.

2.3 Transfer of the Equitable Interest

Fortunately, the parties to a sale of land can usually feel secure some time before the final transfer of legal ownership. The rules of equity provide that the contract may be specifically enforced before the deed is executed. The remedy is available because 'equity looks on that as done which ought to be done'. Since specific performance is an equitable remedy, it is discretionary and will only be ordered if the claimant has behaved properly.

If equity is prepared to grant specific performance of the contract, the sellers become, effectively, trustees for the new equitable right of the buyers to become the legal owners when the contract is completed. This trust relationship between the buyers and the sellers allows the sellers to retain some rights to enjoy the land – they can remain in possession of the land and exclude the buyers but they must take care to keep the land in the same condition as it was when contracts were exchanged and the buyers became the equitable owners.

The case of *Walsh* v. *Lonsdale* (1882) 21 Ch D 9 (see also 5.5 below) is an example of the rule that an equitable interest in land is created as soon as there is a contract. In this famous old case, Lonsdale made a contract to grant a seven-year lease of a mill to Walsh, but the parties never completed the deed necessary for transfer of the lease, the legal estate. Jessel MR said:

> The tenant holds under an agreement for a lease. He holds therefore under the same terms in equity as if a lease had been granted, it being a case in which both parties admit that relief is capable of being given by specific performance. (at p. 14)

A written contract for the sale of land is, therefore, an equitable interest in land (called an 'estate contract'). Walsh had a seven-year equitable lease, and one might have expected him to be delighted with this result. Unfortunately for him it meant that he had to observe all the terms of the lease, including payment of rent in advance: he owed Lonsdale £1005.

2.4 Enforcing the Contract

Under the old rules, replaced by the Law of Property (Miscellaneous Provisions) Act 1989, a contract for the sale of any interest in land was not enforceable until there was some evidence of it either by writing, or by part performance. The original rule that contracts for the sale of land had to be evidenced in writing originated from s.4 Statute of Frauds 1677, designed to reduce the 'frauds and Perjuryes' committed by people trying to enforce alleged oral contracts. In 1925, the old section was restated in s.40(1) LPA which applies to all agreements for the sale of any interest in land made before 27 September 1989, but is irrelevant to any contract made on or after that date.

The wording of s.40(1) was clear but somewhat misleading:

> No action may be brought upon any contract for the sale or other disposition of land or any interest in land, unless the agreement upon which such action is brought, or some memorandum or note thereof, is in writing, and signed by the party to be charged or by some other person thereunto by him lawfully authorised.

There did not need to be what most people would think of as a memorandum or note; not all the terms had to be written down; it did not need the actual signature of the party to be charged (usually the defendant or his agent) although it is likely that the signature would be there. On the other hand, case law spelt out the implicit need for the writing to show that a contract had been made. The modern requirements of s.40(1) were: (a) writing (possibly in several different but related documents); (b) details from which the essential terms of the contract could be ascertained; (c) some form of acknowledgement by the defendant; and (d) an indication that an agreement had been reached. The essential terms of the contract usually included: the identities of buyer and seller, the property, and the price, and, in the case of a lease, the beginning and ending of the term. However, it was not actually necessary for all to be written in full. It was enough to satisfy the statute if the essential terms could be deduced from the written description without relying on oral evidence, and this was a question of fact in every case.

Modern requirements for the contract

The world of buying and selling land is today very different from that of 1677, but the aim of the modern law is still to ensure that ordinary people's expectations are fulfilled, and that they are not caught out by legal technicalities. The 1987 Law Commission Report No. 164 ('Formalities for Contracts for Sale etc. of Land') concluded that special formality is appropriate for transfer of property, both in order to avoid the inadvertent transfers which could arise under s.40 and to ensure that people do not unfairly escape their moral obligations. However, the Law of Property (Miscellaneous Provisions) Act 1989 does not match exactly the recommendations of the Commission and its Report cannot therefore wholly be relied on in deciding what the new law means.

Section 2 of the Act states :

> A contract for the sale or other disposition of an interest in land can only be made in writing and only by incorporating all the terms which the parties have expressly agreed in one document or, where contracts are exchanged, in each.

(Note the exceptions to the requirement for writing, below.)

> **Most section 2 contracts require:**
>
> All the terms expressly agreed:
>
> - to be in writing;
> - in one document (or two identical documents, as is usual);
> - and signed by both buyer and seller.

In brief, under s.2 there is no contract at all until there is a signed document containing all the agreed terms. It is no longer a question of a contract being merely unenforceable (as under the old s.40(1)) without written evidence; now, there *cannot be any contract without writing*. Further, the requirements of the new statute are far stricter than the old law.

Section 2, inevitably, induced an increasing flow of case law, much of which involves the same problems as those which faced the courts under s.40. Initially, the judges appeared reluctant to find that an apparent agreement was not, under s.2, a 'contract', and sought to hold people to their word; later, a stricter view seemed to be emerging, in which the courts were more ready to find that there was no contract because of a failure to comply with s.2.

Very soon after the section came into force, in *Tootal Clothing Ltd* v. *Guinea Properties Ltd* (1992) 64 P & CR 452, the Court of Appeal held that s.2 does not apply to contracts which have already been completed. In this case, where a long lease had already begun, s.2 could not be invoked to make the lease non-existent.

Another early case on s.2, *Spiro* v. *Glencrown Properties* [1991] 2 WLR 931, concerned an option to purchase land and raised the question of whether the letter giving notice that the buyer was going to exercise the option and buy the land had to satisfy the section by containing also the seller's signature. Hoffmann J held:

> Apart from authority, it seems to me plain enough that section 2 was intended to apply to the agreement which created the option and not to the notice by which it was exercised ... The exercise of the option is a unilateral act. It would destroy the very purpose of the option if the purchaser had to obtain the vendor's countersignature to the notice. (p. 933)

The only document which required both signatures was the contract creating the option and, since this had been signed by both parties, the buyer was entitled to demand enforcement of the contract.

Several Court of Appeal cases were concerned with the question of the circumstances in which more than one document could satisfy s.2. The section states that the terms must be 'contained in one document, or, where contracts are exchanged, in each'. Further, in s.2(2), the terms may be contained in a separate document from the one that is signed by both parties, but then the signed document must refer to the document containing the terms. In *Hooper* v. *Sherman* [1994] NPC 153, it was held that the exchange of two informal letters between the parties' solicitors, each containing the terms and signed by the sender, could amount to 'an exchange of contracts'. Here, as part of a separation agreement, Hooper agreed to transfer his share of a house to Sherman in exchange for her paying the mortgage. Due to the building society's delay in approving this arrangement, Hooper tried to get the house sold to someone else, claiming that s.2 was not satisfied so there was no contract preventing him. The majority in the Court of Appeal held that the letters could be joined together and thus satisfy the section; all the terms were in writing and signed by both parties. Morritt LJ dissented, however, on the ground that, although these letters would have been enough for s.40, they were not sufficient for the clear terms of the new law.

Soon afterwards, the parties in *Commission for New Towns* v. *Cooper (GB) Ltd* [1995] Ch 259 (and see Thompson [1995] Conv 319) were in dispute as to the terms of payment for building work as part of a complex arrangement of various land agreements. They reached an agreement, subject to the approval of the plaintiff's directors, the terms of which were included in an exchange of faxes. One side claimed that this amounted to an 'exchange of contracts' for s.2, but the Court of Appeal unanimously held that it did not, because 'exchange of contracts' in the section refers to the exchanging of identical documents, a formal process which indicates the intention to enter a contract:

> where there has been a prior oral agreement, there is only an 'exchange of contracts' when documents are exchanged which set out or incorporate all of the terms which have been agreed and when, crucially, those documents are intended, by virtue of their exchange, to bring about a contract to which section 2 applies. (Evans LJ at p. 295)

The Court decided that for procedural reasons *Hooper* was not binding. The Law Commission had proposed that a valid contract could still arise through exchange of correspondence ((1987) Law Com No 164, para. 4.15), but s.2 as enacted is clearly substantially different. *Commission for New Towns* v. *Cooper* effectively puts an end to the argument that a contract for the sale of land can arise through such an exchange.

In *Firstpost Homes* v. *Johnson* [1994] 4 All ER 355, Mrs Johnson orally agreed to sell some farm land to the claimant. The buyer drafted a letter which had his name typed on it as addressee and contained the terms of the contract to sell the land 'shown on the enclosed plan'. He signed the plan but not the letter, and sent both documents to Mrs Johnson, who signed and dated them both. She then died, and the buyer sought to enforce the agreement. However, Mrs Johnson's personal representatives claimed there was no contract because s.2 was not satisfied. On appeal it was held that the two documents could not be joined as one, since the plan – the only document signed by both parties – did not incorporate the letter merely because it had been in the same envelope. In fact, it was the letter which incorporated the plan and therefore should have been signed by both parties; the buyer's typed name on the letter did not amount to his signature. The judges thus refused to follow the old cases on s.40 which suggested that this could be enough; indeed, Peter Gibson LJ remarked that he did not think it right to 'encumber the new Act with so much ancient baggage', suggesting that s.2 should be read in its own, radical, terms.

Section 2 poses problems for conveyancers since, as is clear from the cases above, conveyancing is not always as tidy an operation as the legislation suggests and contractual terms are often agreed and added over a period of time. The Law Commission Report which preceded the 1989 Act suggested that the solution to this gradual agreement of terms could lie in the doctrine of 'collateral contracts' (contracts 'on the side'):

> A collateral contract is, as its name suggests, a separate contract which is in some way related to the main contract. It must be a true contract, that is, there must be an agreement supported by consideration and it must be intended to be binding. Often the consideration will be that, without the promise contained in the collateral contract, a party would not enter into the principal contract ... The collateral contract seems to us to be a useful conceptual tool to assist in analysing what may be a complicated situation. ((1987) Law Com No 164, para. 5.8)

This is what happened in *Record* v. *Bell* [1991] 1 WLR 853. Here contracts had been signed but then an additional term was agreed in another document. In this second document, the seller, Record, promised that there were no unforeseen burdens in the Land Register (this was necessary because of delays in the Registry). After this the buyer, Bell, then changed his mind about buying the house, and argued that there was no contract under s.2 since all the terms were neither written nor incorporated in one document. The seller, however, claimed that the additional term was a collateral contract and asked for specific performance of the original agreement of sale.

Judge Baker QC held that the additional term was indeed a collateral contract; there was an original contract for sale and an additional one, under which the buyer had effectively agreed to complete the original contract in exchange for the seller's extra promise. This was therefore not a case where the writing failed the s.2 test, and Bell was bound to complete his purchase (and see Smith (1992) 108 LQR 217). Under the old law too, Bell would probably (depending on the operation of 'subject to contract') have been liable to complete the contract.

The question of terms not included in the exchanged documents also arose in two subsequent cases. In *Wright* v. *Robert Leonard Developments Ltd* [1994] EGCS 69, contracts were exchanged for the sale of a show flat, but they omitted the term that the furnishings would be included in the sale (they were not fixtures, see 1.4 above). It was held by the Court of Appeal that the exchange of contracts did not satisfy s.2 since an expressly agreed term had been omitted, and therefore, it would appear, there was no contract. However, the Court agreed that the document could be rectified to include the term, thus satisfying the statute – s.2(4) recognises that the equitable remedy of rectification will, on occasion, be needed (and see Thompson [1995] Conv 484).

This convenient escape from the rigours of s.2 was not available in the second case, *McCausland* v. *Duncan Lawrie Ltd* [1997] 1 WLR 38. Here the exchanged contracts set completion of the contract for a Sunday and then, by an exchange of letters between the solicitors, rearranged it for the preceding Friday. Completion did not take place, and the Court of Appeal held that s.2 was not satisfied here and there was therefore no contract. The correct completion date was an essential term and it was fatal to the failed contract that it had not been included in the exchanged contracts:

> The choice lies between permitting a [later, oral] variation, however fundamental, to be made without any formality at all and requiring it to satisfy s.2. In my view it is evident that Parliament intended the latter. There would be little point in requiring that the original contract comply with s.2 if it might be varied wholly informally. (Morritt LJ at p. 49)

Where writing is not necessary

The previous section considered the strict requirements of s.2 and examined the body of case law which surrounds it. However, not all contracts for the sale of land need be in writing. Under s.2(5) of the 1989 Act, the following contracts do not need to be made in writing:

1 contracts to grant leases of three years or less which take effect in possession and are at the market rent (see s.54(2) Law of Property Act and 2.7 below); and
2 contracts made in a public auction (because the public nature of the agreement is sufficient evidence); and
3 contracts regulated under the Financial Services Act 1986 (which governs investments such as shares, which may include interests in land).

The rule that there is no need for writing for a contract for a short lease is a new one, to tidy up the old law which was anomalous and illogical, since s.40(1) had required written evidence of a contract for a lease which, by s.54(2), was itself legal even if created orally.

In addition, under s.2(5)(c), s.2 has no effect 'on the creation or operation of resulting, implied or constructive trusts' (see Chapter 13). This provision was unnecessary under s.40 which relied on part performance to mitigate the writing rule, but the new, stricter requirements may now be mitigated in some cases by the creation of a constructive trust through proprietary estoppel (see 2.6 below).

Remedies

If there is a valid contract, then the buyer or the seller will be entitled to specific performance if the other party defaults, provided that damages would be an insufficient remedy (which will usually be the case, given the unique nature of land). If the plaintiff, however, does not come with clean hands, specific performance may be denied. In *Wilkie* v. *Redsell* [2003] EWCA (Civ) 926, the Court of Appeal declined to grant a rogue specific performance of his contract to buy land, since firstly there was no evidence that he would be able to pay the purchase price and thus complete his side of the bargain, and secondly he had 'abused the facilities of the court in relation to the very matter in respect of which he [sought] relief' (para. 34) and so did not have clean hands.

Even if a person is entitled to specific performance, the court may award damages instead if it would be fairer: for example, where the land has now been sold to a third party. Under the Law Society's Standard Conditions of Sale, if the buyer refuses to complete, the seller may retain the deposit, a powerful incentive for the buyer.

Other remedies for the buyer include suing for the restitution of a lost deposit, or for misrepresentation. In *McMeekin* v. *Long* (2003) 29 EG 120, buyers of a house were awarded £67000 damages for fraudulent misrepresentation when the sellers deliberately failed to disclose a dispute with their neighbours.

2.5 The Intervention of Equity – Part Performance

Within ten years of the Statute of Frauds 1677, it was apparent that the statute, far from preventing fraud, merely provided a different loophole for liars. Whereas, before 1677, a rogue could unfairly force a sale by buying witnesses to give false evidence of an oral contract, after that date he could unfairly escape a contract if there was no writing to satisfy the statute. Therefore the court of equity provided a remedy on the basis of the maxim, 'equity will not allow a statute to be made an instrument of fraud'.

Equity would accept evidence that the plaintiff had performed a part of (or had done some other act showing the existence of) the unwritten contract and that the defendant knew of this. This 'part performance' of the contract by the plaintiff enabled a court of equity to enforce it although there was nothing in writing to satisfy the statute, for otherwise the defendant would be using the statutory rule in order to cheat. This equitable doctrine was expressly preserved in 1925 by s.40(2) Law of Property Act but is effectively repealed by the 1989 Act: there can be no part performance of a non-existent contract.

An uncontroversial example of the old doctrine is *Rawlinson* v. *Ames* [1925] Ch 96. Mrs Rawlinson was converting a large house into flats and Miss Ames orally agreed to buy a 21-year lease of one of them. She sent a letter which would have been sufficient for s.40(1) except that it did not specify the starting date of the lease. Mrs Rawlinson carried out Miss Ames's substantial and detailed construction and decoration requirements but then Miss Ames changed her mind. The construction and decoration at her request were held to be acts of part performance by Mrs Rawlinson who was therefore entitled to an order of specific performance to enforce the contract.

Generally, however, the courts had great difficulty with the doctrine and the Law Commission had no hesitation in recommending its abolition, since it envisaged that the existing equitable doctrine of proprietary estoppel could supplement s.2 to prevent rogues taking unfair advantages.

2.6   Equity Intervenes Again – Proprietary Estoppel and Constructive Trusts

The essence of proprietary estoppel is that a court will stop someone enforcing a legal right to land if to do so would be unfair on the claimant who has acted to his detriment as a result of the other person's actions. In relation to s.2, the argument is that, although there is no contract because of the absence of the signed document, for reasons of conscience one party should be prevented from relying on his strict legal rights not to continue with the agreement.

Although the Law Commission expected part performance to be replaced by proprietary estoppel, it did not anticipate frequent resort to equity:

> In putting forward the present recommendation we rely greatly on the principle, recognised even by equity, that 'certainty is the father of right and the mother of justice'. ((1987) Law Com No 164, para. 4.13)

Some judges have found difficulty in applying the doctrine of proprietary estoppel in the context of a failed s.2 contract on the grounds of public policy: if Parliament requires strict formalities to be observed in order to effect a valid contract, then estoppel should not be used to make such a failed transaction valid (see Halsbury Laws of England, 4th edition, para. 962). An alternative is the use of the constructive trust, which is closely related to estoppel and also requires an element of unconscionability. (Proprietary estoppel and constructive trusts are considered in more detail in Chapter 13.)

In *Yaxley* v. *Gotts* [2000] Ch 162, a builder, Yaxley, orally agreed with a friend that he would take the ground floor of a house that his friend was about to buy, in return for renovating and rebuilding the house as a number of flats. In fact, the house was bought by the friend's son and Yaxley carried out the work as he had promised. A few years later, Yaxley fell out with the father and son who barred him from the premises and denied that he had any right to the ground floor of the house. At first instance, Yaxley, having relied on the father's oral promise (which had apparently been adopted by the son), successfully claimed an interest in the house by virtue of proprietary estoppel and was awarded a 99-year lease of the ground floor. On appeal, Robert Walker LJ was reluctant to find an estoppel in Yaxley's favour because of the public policy reason discussed above, although he was not prepared to rule out the possibility of estoppel never being appropriate in circumstances in which s.2 had not been complied with. Instead, he imposed a constructive trust on Gotts. He felt able to do this because of the provision in s.2(5)(c) that the creation or operation of constructive trusts is not affected by s.2. Beldam and Clarke LJJ, while agreeing with the imposition of a constructive trust, also supported the first instance judge's finding of proprietary estoppel, both being persuaded that the views of the Law Commission should be taken into account, particularly since the Act was based on the Commission's Report.

In *Lloyd* v. *Dugdale* [2002] 2 P & CR 13, Dugdale was promised a long lease of commercial premises by the owner, Ingham. There was no written contract, however, and Ingham, who had assured Dugdale that 'his word was his bond', eventually decided not to proceed because he had received a better offer for the land. He then began an action for possession against Dugdale. Although the provisions of s.2 were not mentioned, the Court of Appeal found that Dugdale, having relied to his detriment on Ingham's promise to grant him a lease, had established an estoppel in his favour which would have bound Ingham. Unfortunately for Dugdale, Ingham died before the case was over, and his successor in title, Lloyd, was able to take the land free of Dugdale's estoppel interest under the rules of registered land, since, on the facts, Dugdale was deemed not to have been in actual occupation at the time of the sale (see 11.5 below).

2.7 Transfer of the Legal Interest

The deed

As mentioned already, a deed is normally necessary to transfer a legal estate or interest. (When the land is registered the deed is a Land Transfer form from the Land Registry.) Section 52(1) LPA states:

> All conveyances of land or of any interest therein are void for the purpose of conveying or creating a legal estate unless made by deed.

Before 31 July 1990, a deed was a document that was 'signed, sealed and delivered'. Now, the ancient requirement for a seal is replaced by the need for a witness. The requirements for a deed are defined in s.1 Law of Property (Miscellaneous Provisions) Act 1989.

A deed is a document which:
- makes clear on its face that it is a deed;
- is signed and witnessed;
- is delivered.

Signature and witnessing

The signature must be by the person who is 'executing' (that is, making) the deed, and in this case the signature must be in the presence of one witness who also signs. Alternatively, the deed can be signed 'at his direction and in his presence' by another person, and in this case there must be two witnesses present who also sign the deed.

Delivery

A deed is 'delivered' when the 'grantor' (the person executing the deed) does or says something to 'adopt the deed as his own'. In practice, solicitors usually treat a deed as delivered at the moment they add a date to a document which has already been signed and witnessed; this is said to show that they adopt it.

Where a deed is not needed

There are a number of circumstances where a legal interest can be obtained without a deed.

1 *Short leases* (defined in s.54(2) LPA, and see 2.4 above): by s.52(2)(d), a lease is legal without any formality (even writing) if it does not exceed three years, the tenant moves in straight away (that is, the lease 'takes effect in possession') and it is at a market rent. There is no need for any special formality for this kind of short lease because there is little risk that a buyer of the property will be caught unawares – the tenant will be present on the property and paying rent. In addition, the expense and delay in conforming to the formality requirements of ss 1 and 2 of the 1989 Act would be bound to inhibit the creation of these commonly found leases or would lead to non-compliance. However, somewhat illogically, a deed is still needed to *assign* any lease (to transfer the whole of the legal interest to another person, as opposed to creating a sublease), as shown in *Crago* v. *Julian* [1992] 1 All ER 744 (see 5.5 below).
2 *Long use:* in unregistered land, using someone else's land for a minimum of 12 years can ensure that the user cannot be defeated by anyone; effectively, he becomes a legal owner (see Chapter 3). Long use of an easement or profit (for example a right of way or a right to fish) can create a legal right by 'prescription' (see 8.5 below).
3 *Personal representatives' assent* (s.36(1) AEA 1925): if a landowner dies, his land automatically goes to ('vests in') his legal representatives. When they have completed their administration of the estate, they transfer the land to the heir(s). Writing, but no deed, is necessary to do this; it is called an 'assent'.
4 *Trustee in bankruptcy's disclaimer:* where a landowner becomes bankrupt, the land automatically vests in his trustee in bankruptcy. If the land is more trouble than it is worth (for example a lease with a high rent) the trustee can disclaim it in writing; a deed is not necessary.
5 *Court order:* a court can order land to be transferred.

The effect of a deed

The deed not only transfers the interest but also any advantages which belong to the land, unless the parties show that they intend otherwise; s.62 LPA states:

> A conveyance of land shall-be deemed to include and shall by virtue of this Act operate to convey, with the land, all buildings, erections, fixtures, commons, hedges, ditches, fences, ways, waters, watercourses, liberties, privileges, easements, rights, and advantages whatsoever, appertaining or reputed to appertain to the land, or any part thereof, or, at the time of conveyance, demised, occupied, or enjoyed with, or reputed or known as part or parcel of, or appurtenant to, the land or any part thereof.

Thus, a buyer of land may, by s.62, get the right enjoyed by his predecessor to park his car in his neighbour's drive (see 8.5 below). Sections 78 and 79 ensure that he will automatically have the right to enforce, and will be bound by, any valid restrictive covenant over the land (see 9.2 below). (These three sections are some of the 'wordsaving provisions' mentioned in 1.2 above.)

Where the formalities of the deed have not been complied with

The formalities described above are necessary for the valid execution of a deed. However, in the recent case of *Shah* v. *Shah* [2002] QB 35, a person was induced to rely on what appeared on the face of it to be a deed. A later representation by the executor of the deed that it was invalid since it had not been properly witnessed was unsuccessful, and the executor was estopped from relying on his strict legal rights.

2.8 Comment

The rules relating to the buying and selling of interests in land are, in general, formalistic and detailed, but, in an area where the law is seeking to achieve a simple and certain resolution of complicated and dynamic human relationships, this is hardly surprising. Cases on s.2 suggest that not all the problems have been solved by the 1989 Act, but the courts now recognise that it is a radical departure from the old s.40 LPA, and enforce it more strictly.

In the compromise between the need for a clear rule, and the need to make sure people do not unfairly take advantage of one another, there is a tendency towards a more ruthless simplicity, but this may change according to the state of the property market, and according to the attitude adopted by the courts towards proprietary estoppel and constructive trusts. In any event, despite the nature of the rules, many hundreds of thousands of interests in land are successfully conveyed each year; the state of the property market is far more important to most non-lawyers than the technical rules.

In the future, the law will increasingly have to come to terms with developments in new technology. The Electronic Communications Act 2000 and the Land Registration Act 2002 provide the statutory framework for the 'move to electronic conveyancing over the coming decade – the most revolutionary change ever to take place in conveyancing practice' ((1998) Law Com No 254, *Land Registration for the Twenty-first Century*, p. 1). In order to be effective, contracts and deeds will eventually have to be created, signed and communicated to the Land Registry by electronic means (for more detail on this, see Chapter 11). The intention is that paper will become obsolete in the conveyancer's office of the future, along with the 1989 Act and its rules on land contracts and deeds. Whether this means that there will be no longer be room for the 'do-it-yourself' conveyancer remains uncertain.

Summary

2.1   The normal procedure for buying and selling interests in land is governed by rules relating to the need for formality in land contracts, by writing and by deeds, and is supplemented by equity.

2.2   As soon as there is a contract for the sale of an interest in land, the buyer effectively becomes the equitable owner of the land, provided the discretionary remedy of specific performance is available.

2.3   In order for there to be a contract for the sale of an interest in land, normally all the terms must be in writing and signed by both sides.

2.4   If there is no contract under statute, equity may nevertheless enforce the 'agreement' by finding a constructive trust or under the doctrine of proprietary estoppel if it would be unconscionable for the defendant to deny that he made a promise to transfer the interest, provided that the plaintiff acted to his detriment in reliance on the promise.

2.5   A deed, signed, witnessed and delivered, is now normally necessary to create or transfer a legal interest in land. It also transfers benefits attached to the land.

2.6   Some legal leases not exceeding three years (or a contract to grant one) may be created, but not assigned, without any formality.

Exercises

2.1   When did ss 1 and 2 Law of Property (Miscellaneous Provisions) Act 1989 come into force? Why does it matter?

2.2   At what stage in the conveyancing process is the equitable interest in land transferred?

2.3   What are constructive trusts and the doctrine of proprietary estoppel? How are they relevant to the rules for buying land?

2.4   What is a deed? Why is the definition significant?

2.5   William owned the freehold of a rather dilapidated house. He agreed to sell it to Ajay for £150 000 and, once contracts were exchanged, Ajay began work on the repairs. Due to a change in his circumstances, William has decided he no longer wishes to sell the house to Ajay. William's solicitor has told him that, since no deed has yet been executed, William can withdraw from the arrangement. It also turns out that Ajay never signed his copy of the contract. Advise Ajay.

Further Reading

Critchley, 'Taking Formalities Seriously' in Bright and Dewar (eds), *Land Law Themes and Perspectives* (Oxford: OUP, 1998)

Mason and Bohm, 'The Signature in Electronic Conveyancing: An Unresolved Issue' [2003] Conv 460

Moore, 'Proprietary Estoppel, Constructive Trusts and Section 2 of the Law of Property (Miscellaneous Provisions) Act 1989' (2000) 63 MLR 912

Smith R. J., 'Contracts for the Sale of Land: Collateral Contracts' (1992) 108 LQR 217

Thompson, 'Contracts by Correspondence' [1995] Conv 319

Thompson, 'Blowing Hot and Cold' [1995] Conv 484

3   Adverse Possession

3.1 Introduction

The last chapter explored the rules governing the formal transfer of interests in land, and was concerned with land which clearly belonged to a particular person. This chapter investigates the issues which arise when the owner's title is challenged because she has not been in possession of her land for many years. A typical example might concern a narrow strip of land between two houses, perhaps where one householder has failed to take care of her boundaries and the other has encroached.

Adverse possession is part of the general law of limitation of actions, now contained in the Limitation Act 1980 and also, where title to the land is registered, in the Land Registration Act 2002. The basic principle is straightforward and quickly grasped: through adverse possession, a person can effectively become the legal owner of land solely because of her occupation of it. After a certain length of time, a person using land may have a better title to it than anyone else, including the real or 'paper' owner, simply because the law will not permit anyone to remove her.

The statutes provide the structure of the rules, but the cases are of great importance because the essence of adverse possession is a question of fact: it is necessary to examine carefully all the details of each individual story in order to decide whether a person has adversely possessed the land for the limitation period. The cases also help in grasping the way the judges see the issues: they are concerned to do justice in disputes between neighbours and at the same time to satisfy the various demands of public policy.

3.2 The Basic Issues

In cases where the title to the land is not yet registered, a traditional justification for the rule that actions to recover possession may not be brought after a certain length of time (they become 'time-barred') is that, in the interests of certainty and the market in land, there must be an end to 'stale claims'. In addition, deeds can get lost and people can forget what they own, but the land itself remains. If the law did not provide for cases where there is no formal proof of title, areas of land would be 'outside the law' and unmarketable. Adverse possession thus provides a way of curing defective titles in unregistered land since, after the required period of possession, the squatter cannot be evicted by the paper owner.

In registered land, the justifications for retaining rules on adverse possession are different but no less compelling. Here, title is not based on possession, as it is in the unregistered system, but on the fact that ownership has been recorded at the Land Registry, which guarantees the title (see Chapter 11). If the registered owner cannot be found, or if there has been a failure to comply with the formalities for the transfer of land so that the Register does not reflect the real position, or if the paper owner sleeps on her rights, adverse possession is a means by which the land becomes marketable.

If it were not for adverse possession, many pieces of land would be waste, forgotten by the paper owner and worthless to anyone else. However, the law of adverse possession inevitably causes problems for people who think that legal title to land – private property, for which the owner has probably 'paid good money' – ought to be protected by the law, come what may: the idea that people can be deprived of their land in such a way certainly raises issues under the Human Rights Act, (see 3.6). In real life, few unregistered titles are perfect and innumerable difficulties arise when a title needs to be traced to its origin. In *Johnston* v. *O'Neill* [1911] AC 552, a case involving eel-fishing rights, title to land in Northern Ireland had to be traced back to 1605. Lord Macnaghten said:

> My Lords, I will not weary you by recapitulating or reviewing what has been called the paper title ... Infinite labour and excellent learning have been expended on the law relating to grants from the Crown, on patents, on commissions, and on inquisitions ... I must say I am rather surprised to find the title as complete as it is. At the same time, I have no doubt that lawyers less learned than those to whom we have had the pleasure of listening would not have much difficulty in picking holes in it here and there, either because there may be something missing which cannot be supplied after the lapse of centuries, or because it is not proved that formalities, adjudged necessary in other cases, have been duly observed in this. (p. 580)

If the land has not yet been registered, it is nowadays normally sufficient to prove a good title (the 'root of title') going back only 15 years to satisfy a purchaser of land (s.23 Law of Property Act 1969, and see Dockray [1985] Conv 272).

It is unusual to see Parliament and the judges helping a person who in some lights appears to be a common thief, but there are good reasons to do so. The main practical reasons have been discussed above, but there is also the ethical issue of the neglectful owner belatedly trying to evict an industrious and careful squatter. Since land is, after all, a national resource, should the law protect the title rights of the paper owner against someone who has invested her labour in improving the land? It may be argued that the public interest lies in encouraging the efficient use of land resources (see *Hounslow LBC* v. *Minchinton* (1997) 74 P & CR 221). Clearly, protecting private ownership is only one of the policy considerations.

The case of *Williams* v. *Usherwood* (1982) 43 P & CR 235 illustrates the interplay of the various policies behind the law. Here, adjoining suburban houses, which were built in 1934, shared a drive; the legal arrangement was that each owner had title to the half running alongside her house and an easement over (a right to use) the other's half of the drive. For convenience, the fence between the houses was built close to Number 33, and it therefore looked as if the drive belonged to Number 31. As it happened, the owner of Number 33 never did use the drive and, from 1952, never even had access to her strip. The people who bought Number 31 in 1962 paved it and used it for parking their cars.

In 1977, the Williams family moved into Number 33 and decided to pursue their apparent legal right, as the 'paper owners', to half the width of the drive. They lost. The owners of Number 31 successfully argued adverse possession (by earlier owners of the house) so that the Williams family could not enforce any remedy against them. In this case, the land was registered and therefore, under the old rules for adverse possession in registered land, it was necessary for the judge also to order that the Land Register should be corrected to show the owners of Number 31 as owners of the whole drive (see 11.8 below).

The argument in favour of the Williams family was that they were the legal owners of the strip of land – the original title deeds stated it clearly – and they ought therefore to have been entitled to legal protection against trespassers. From their point of view, the law of limitation of actions was a 'cheat's charter' (McCormick [1986] Conv 434). On the other hand, the earlier owners of their house had 'slept on their rights', even later acknowledging that they did not think they owned the strip of land, whereas the owners of Number 31 had used it and repaved it 'at some expense, which went beyond any normal maintenance requirements'. The Court of Appeal was not prepared to allow the Williams family years later to resurrect a stale claim.

3.3 **The Basic Rules**

Before discussing the meaning of adverse possession, it is necessary to consider how the rules operate. Before 13 October 2003, they were in many respects similar in both registered and unregistered land. In its 1998 Consultation Paper, the Law Commission recognised that many of the traditional justifications for adverse possession discussed above hold no relevance in a regime where title to land is registered and, in the course of a radical reappraisal of the registered land system, proposed fundamental changes to the operation of the principles of adverse possession within that system (see (1998) Law Com No 254, Part X). These were then enacted in the LRA 2002. Bear in mind, then, that although the kind of conduct which will amount to adverse possession is the same whether title to the land is registered or unregistered, the operating rules are now very different.

Unregistered Land

Section 15(1) Limitation Act 1980 provides:

> No action shall be brought by any person to recover any land after the expiration of twelve years from the date on which the right of action accrued to him, or, if it first accrued to some other person through whom he claims, to that person.

The section states clearly that the paper owner cannot bring an action if 12 years have passed since the right to do so arose: that is, since the squatter – by definition, a trespasser – moved onto the land. The statute does not operate to transfer the paper owner's title to the adverse possessor but, by refusing any remedy, merely ensures that no one can remove her.

Not only can the paper owner not bring an action to recover possession after 12 years, her title to the land is extinguished after that period (s.17 Limitation Act).

By s.38 Limitation Act, 'land' means more than just the legal freehold; it includes, for example, equitable freeholds and legal and equitable leases. It is possible therefore to obtain title to a long lease as well as to freehold land (see 3.5 below).

There are special rules for adversely possessing Crown land and for special classes, such as between trustees and their beneficiaries (s.21 Limitation Act). In *Pollard* v. *Jackson* (1994) 67 P & CR 327, the heir of a freeholder returned from Canada to claim her inheritance – 15 years after the death of her father. She found that the tenant of the ground floor flat in the house had taken over the whole of the house when the old man, who lived upstairs, had died, and was claiming adverse possession of it. In her claim for possession, she argued, among other things, that the tenant had become a constructive trustee (see Chapter 13) of the freehold since he knew that the land must, from the time of the death, be held on trust. As a constructive trustee, she said, he could not deny her beneficial right to possession of the land. However, the Court of Appeal rejected this argument because it would mean that in any case where a paper owner died during the 12-year period, and the squatter knew of the death, adverse possession would be impossible.

It is important to remember that, as the squatter herself is not a 'purchaser' of land, like someone who simply inherits land she is bound by all earlier interests in the land, whether they are legal or equitable, and whether or not they were protected by registration or she had notice of them.

Registered land

Where the title to the land was registered, the old rules again prevented the registered owner from bringing an action to evict the squatter after 12 years. Unlike the position in unregistered land, however, her title was not extinguished; instead, she held it on trust for the squatter (s.75(1) LRA

1925). The squatter could also, if she wished, apply to the Land Registry to become the registered proprietor after 12 years (s.75(2) LRA 1925).

In accordance with the view that the role of adverse possession in registered land should be more restricted, the new rules, in force from 13 October 2003, have made it much more difficult for a squatter to obtain title. The Land Registration Act 2002, Schedule 6, para. 1, states that, in most cases, a squatter may apply to the Land Registry to be registered as owner of the land after ten years' adverse possession (60 years in the case of the foreshore owned by the Crown). Under para. 2, the Land Registry will inform the registered proprietor, any owner of a registered charge on the land (such as a mortgage lender) and, if the land is leasehold, the proprietor of the freehold, of the application. If no response has been received by the Registrar within three months, the adverse possessor becomes the new registered proprietor.

However, if there is an objection within that period, the application will automatically be rejected unless one of three conditions applies (para. 5). The first is that the paper owner has acted unconscionably and is estopped from denying title. This would not include a situation where the applicant is on the land with the permission of the owner, since such occupation could not amount to adverse possession (see 3.4), but it could arise where a person has developed land thinking it belonged to her, and the paper owner, aware of the true position, has allowed this to happen. It could also happen where a buyer of land has paid the purchase price but there has been no s.2 contract and thus no transfer of the equitable title. The second condition is where the adverse possessor is for some reason other than adverse possession entitled to be registered as the owner – under a will, perhaps, or where, although a valid contract might exist for the sale of the land to the adverse possessor, there had been a failure to transfer the legal title to her (see Chapter 2). The third is where the disputed land is next to land already owned by the adverse possessor, the boundary between the two plots is unclear and she has occupied the land for ten years, thinking it belonged to her. (On these three special cases, see (2001) Law Com No 271, paras 14.36–14.52.)

If the squatter's application is rejected and none of the conditions in para. 5 applies, she may make a further application to have title to the land transferred into her name if she has not been thrown off the land after a period of two years from the date of the original rejection (unless possession proceedings are in the process of being taken against her, or unless judgment has already been given against her (para. 6)). Following this second application, she is entitled to be registered as the new proprietor with the same class of title as that of the paper owner she has dispossessed (see 11.4, below).

These new reforms in registered land mean that the paper owner cannot automatically lose her right to evict a trespasser after 12 years' adverse possession, as formerly, but will be warned by the Registry that a squatter is attempting to gain title to her land. However, she may not continue to sleep on her rights, since if she does nothing to regain possession of the land, she will lose it.

Dispossession

In order for time to start running in the squatter's favour, the paper owner must either have been dispossessed of the land or have discontinued possession (Limitation Act 1980, Schedule 1, para. 1). It is now clear, following the leading case of *Pye* v. *Graham* [2003] 1 AC 347, that all that is required is for the squatter to take possession of the land. Possession cannot be shared between the paper owner and the squatter so, if the squatter is in possession, the paper owner cannot be.

If a tenancy is an oral periodic tenancy (see 5.3 below), time can begin to run in favour of the tenant from the time she stops paying rent, since the tenancy is then deemed to have ended (Limitation Act 1980, Schedule 1, para. 5(2)). In *Hayward* v. *Chaloner* [1968] 1 QB 107, a quarter of an acre of land was let as a garden on such a tenancy to whomever was the rector of a small village, but for some 25 years from 1942 no rent was paid and there was no acknowledgement of the paper owners' title. The then rector decided to sell the land as his own and the paper owners decided to fight him; they had failed to collect the rent, not because they forgot, but because of 'their loyalty and generosity to the church'. The rector won by a majority decision in the Court of Appeal, although all the judges regretted it:

> The generous indulgence of the plaintiffs and their predecessors in title, loyal churchmen all, having resulted in a free accretion at their expense to the lands of their church, their reward may be in the next world. But in this jurisdiction we can only qualify them for that reward by allowing the [Rector's] appeal. (Russell LJ, pp. 123-4)

No concealment or fraud

Under s.32 Limitation Act, the adverse possessor must prove that she did not deliberately conceal her activities or keep her possession through fraud. If there is any deception, time starts to run from the date when the paper owner 'could with reasonable diligence have discovered it'. Concealment was argued in *Rains* v. *Buxton* (1880) XIV Ch D 537; the adverse possessor had occupied an underground cellar, and the paper owner – 60 years later – said that the possession had been concealed. However, as the door to the cellar was clearly visible from the basement area and was used without secrecy, this argument was rejected. The squatter here obtained title to a layer of the land – the cellar – leaving the paper owner's rights above undisturbed.

Continuous possession

The squatter must prove that she has been in continuous possession throughout the required period. Any interruption to her possession means that the period must begin again. The adverse possession need not have been by one squatter. In *Williams* v. *Usherwood* (see 3.2 above), there were several different owners of Number 31 who, in succession, adversely possessed the land continuously for the period.

The simple position regarding successive squatters has been modified in cases where a claim is made under the LRA 2002. Schedule 6, para. 11, provides that a valid claim to the Land Registry may be made in the following situations, as long as the total consecutive period amounts to ten years: firstly, where the applicant is the successor in title of the first squatter, having bought the land from her or having inherited it, and then moved into possession; and secondly, where the applicant was the original squatter, was dispossessed by another squatter but then was able to regain possession. However, no valid claim may be made by a squatter who is merely the last of a succession of squatters until she herself has been in possession for ten years; this is different from the rules in unregistered land.

How the Paper Owner Can Stop Time Running

If the squatter leaves the land before she has completed the necessary period of adverse possession or if the paper owner physically re-enters the land before the end of the period, then the squatter's right to the land is lost. The adverse possession will also cease if the squatter acknowledges in writing the title of the paper owner (ss 29–31 Limitation Act). In *Edgington* v. *Clark* [1967] 1 QB 367, the claimant had occupied bombed land in the East End of London for about seven years and then offered to buy it from the owner. No sale followed and, after a further ten years, he claimed adverse possession. It was held that the offer to buy was an acknowledgment of the owner's title and that therefore the squatter's possession was interrupted.

An interesting question arises if the paper owner merely writes to the squatter, granting her a licence to use the land. On the face of it, since the squatter now occupies the land with permission, the possession can no longer be adverse. Indeed, in *BP Properties* v. *Buckler* (1987) 55 P & CR 337, a case which has been subject to some criticism (see Wallace [1994] Conv 196), the paper owner wrote to the squatter, giving her permission to remain on the land for the rest of her life. Although the squatter did not respond to the letter, the paper owner was deemed to have ended the adverse possession. Of course, in such situations it is always open to the squatter to reject the licence.

A much more certain approach is for the paper owner to bring an action for possession within the limitation period. Of itself, this does not 'stop time running' but simply means that the paper owner is not time-barred. She must, therefore, pursue the action and bring it to a successful conclusion (*Markfield Investments Ltd* v. *Evans* [2001] 1 WLR 1321).

3.4 What is the Nature of Adverse Possession?

The most difficult issues in this area of law arise when the courts have to consider what the squatter must do if she is to show that she actually was in adverse possession of another person's land. In *Pye* (3.3 above), the House of Lords identified two fundamental elements.

The requirements of adverse possession:

- The possession must be real (or 'factual') – the squatter must act as owner, showing an 'appropriate degree of physical control'.
- The trespasser must have an intention to possess the land (*animus possidendi*).

Factual possession

The case of *Buckinghamshire County Council* v. *Moran* [1990] Ch 623, illustrates the sort of behaviour required from the trespasser if she is to be able successfully to claim adverse possession. From 1971, Moran had used as an extension to his garden a patch of land owned by the council which they intended to use for a future bypass; his predecessor had probably done the same since 1967. Moran built a new fence, enclosing the land, and added a new gate and a lock. The council finally noticed him in 1985 and sued for possession. In its analysis of the sort of acts required to constitute factual possession, the Court of Appeal quoted with approval from the first instance judgment by Slade J in *Powell* v. *McFarlane* (1979) 38 P & CR 452:

> Factual possession signifies an appropriate degree of physical control ... The question of what acts constitute a sufficient degree of exclusive physical control must depend on the circumstances, in particular the nature of the land and the manner in which land of that nature is commonly used or enjoyed. (p. 470)

Physical control can be shown if the squatter encloses the land or improves it in some way, but trivial acts performed on the land will generally be insufficient to establish factual possession. In *Pye* (3.3 above), Mr Graham was a farmer who had occupied some 57 acres of Pye's land under a grazing licence. Pye refused to renew the licence because it wanted vacant possession of the land in order to get planning permission to develop it. The Grahams continued to occupy the land, keeping animals on it all year round, maintaining and improving it, and excluding everyone from it. An occupying owner could not have done more, and the House of Lords found that Mr Graham had clearly been in factual possession of the land.

What acts are required to show 'an appropriate degree of physical control' of residential property such as a house or flat? In *Lambeth LBC* v. *Copercini*, unreported, 1 March 2000, a housing co-operative had squatted in a council-owned property for many years. The judge found clear evidence of factual possession, since the co-operative had decided who should live there, had arranged lettings, funded repairs and maintenance and 'without doubt ... treated the property as their own'. In *Lambeth LBC*

v. *Blackburn* (2001) 82 P & CR 39) the squatter moved into a council flat which had been damaged by fire. He replaced a padlock with a new Yale lock, repaired and decorated the flat and lived in it as his home. The Court of Appeal found that these acts were sufficient to amount to factual possession.

The intention to possess (*animus possidendi*)

Exactly what constitutes the necessary intention to possess the land has been a contentious issue until recently. It might be thought that a trespasser must show that she intends to become the owner of the land but, although this may have been the case in the past, it clearly no longer is. In *Powell* v. *McFarlane* (above), Slade J stated that *animus possidendi*:

> involves the intention, in one's own name and on one's own behalf, to exclude the world at large, including the owner with the paper title … so far as is reasonably practicable and so far as the process of the law will allow. (p. 471)

At first instance in *Moran* (above), Hoffmann J observed that what is required is 'not an intention to own or even an intention to acquire ownership but an intention to possess' ((1988) 56 P & CR 372 at p. 378).

It is rare that the court will have direct evidence of an intention to possess the land and exclude the world, but the intention can be inferred from the acts of the trespasser, such as the enclosure in *Moran*, or through otherwise controlling access. Lord Browne-Wilkinson, who gave the leading speech in *Pye*, stated that 'intention may be, and frequently is, deduced from the physical acts themselves' (para. 40).

Depending on the facts, a person may be deemed to have sufficient intention to possess the land even if she were prepared to accept a licence or a lease from the paper owner, so her claim to adverse possession could still succeed if the licence was not in the end forthcoming. In *Pye*, Mr Graham had admitted that he would have accepted a licence from the paper owners if one had been offered. This was an admission that Lord Diplock thought 'any candid squatter hoping in due course to acquire a possessory title would be almost bound to make' (*Ocean Estates Ltd* v. *Pinder* [1969] 2 AC 17, p. 24) and did not prevent him from being in possession.

There is a clear difference, though, between a squatter's willingness to recognise the title of the paper owner if asked to do so, and the squatter's written acknowledgment of that title, perhaps through asking for a lease or a licence which, as indicated above, is enough to stop time running in the squatter's favour.

Must the possession be adverse to the paper owner?

Possession clearly cannot be adverse if it is enjoyed with the paper owner's permission. However, a difficulty has arisen in cases where the paper owner intends to use the land in the future for some particular purpose, but has no present use for it. In the past, the courts have used the doctrine of the implied licence to show that the possession is not adverse. In *Wallis's Cayton Bay* v. *Shell-Mex and BP* [1975] QB 94, a petrol company bought a garage by a proposed new road with the intention of extending the garage if the new road were to be built. Wallis's farmed this land and then used it to enlarge their holiday camp business. Their use of the land totalled just over the necessary 12 years and they claimed adverse possession of it. They lost by a majority decision in the Court of Appeal. Lord Denning stated:

> When the true owner of land intends to use it for a particular purpose in the future, but has no immediate use for it, and so leaves it unoccupied, he does not lose his title to it simply because some other person enters on it and uses it for some temporary purpose ... his user is to be ascribed to the licence or permission of the true owner. By using the land, knowing it does not belong to him, he impliedly assumes the owner will permit it: and the owner, by not turning him off, impliedly gives permission. (p. 103)

This heresy, had it been allowed to stand, could have spelled the end of adverse possession in cases where the paper owner had in mind a future use for the land, or at least severely limited its effect. The doctrine of the implied licence was examined by the Law Reform Committee (Cmnd 6923, 1977) and, as a result, the Limitation Act 1980, Schedule 1, paragraph 8(4) states that the law will not automatically imply a licence simply because the trespasser's use of the land is not inconsistent with the paper owner's present or future enjoyment of it. The courts will find an implied licence only on the rare occasions where the facts suggest it.

3.5 Leases and Adverse Possession

The rules about leases and adverse possession can be complex and, again, the results may differ depending on whether title to the land is registered or unregistered.

If a squatter takes possession of land subject to a lease, the possession is adverse to the tenant; that is, it is the tenant who is liable to lose her interest in the land, not the landlady. This is because it is the tenant who is entitled to possession; the landlady is entitled only to the rent. The landlady has no right to possession until the lease ends, and it is also at that time that the squatter's period of adverse possession against the landlady begins.

An interesting situation arises if the tenant (of an unregistered 99-year lease, let us say), against whom a squatter has been in adverse possession for 12 years and who therefore could now look forward to many more years of possession, surrenders her lease to her landlady (below, 5.6). (There is little point in the tenant continuing with the lease, since she now has no cause of action against the squatter.) Following the tenant's surrender of the lease, the landlady can bring an action for possession against the squatter (*Fairweather* v. *St Marylebone Property Co Ltd* [1963] AC 510). Having evicted the squatter, there is then nothing to prevent the landlady from granting a new lease to her former tenant.

Under the old rules for registered land, the position was different. In *Central London Commercial Estates Ltd* v. *Kato Kagku Ltd* [1998] 4 All ER 948, a squatter had adversely possessed registered land against the tenant for more than 12 years, but had not made an application under s.75(2) LRA 1925 to be registered as proprietor (3.3 above) when the tenant surrendered the lease to the landlord. Applying s.75(1) LRA 1925, Sedley J held that the tenant was trustee for the squatter, who was now entitled to remain on the land for the remaining term of the lease. This decision effectively prevented a tenant of registered land from surrendering her lease once the 12-year period of adverse possession had been completed.

It is unlikely that this situation will arise under the new rules contained in the LRA 2002. The tenant will have no need to surrender the lease to the landlord since either she will object to the squatter's application and subsequently gain possession, or the squatter will succeed in her application, with the result that the squatter's name will be registered at the Land Registry with the title of the former tenant (3.3 above). This means that she will now be subject to the covenants in the lease and failure to comply with them may result in forfeiture of the lease by the landlady (see 6.5 below).

3.6 Adverse Possession and Human Rights

In *Pye* (3.3 above), the question was raised as to whether the use of the Limitation Act to deny a landowner the right to bring an action to recover her land amounted to a breach of Article 1, Protocol 1 of the European Convention on Human Rights (depriving a person of her property without compensation). Although the action was between private individuals, the deprivation of the property resulted from statutory authority, thus allowing the Convention to be invoked.

In the Court of Appeal, Mummery LJ was of the opinion that the Limitation Act did not amount to:

> a deprivation of possessions or a confiscatory measure for which the payment of compensation would be appropriate: it is... simply a logical and pragmatic consequence of the barring of [the paper title owner's] right to bring an action after the expiration of the limitation period (para. 43.2)

Even if that were wrong, the provisions of the Act were not disproportionate and were:

> reasonably required to avoid the real risk of injustice in the adjudication of stale claims, to ensure certainty of title and to promote social stability by the protection of the established and peaceable possession of property from the resurrection of old claims (para. 43.3)

These views had not been shared by Neuberger J in the High Court who found Pye's loss of potentially very valuable development land to be 'disproportionate' and 'draconian'. This was supported by some of the judges in the House of Lords, although nothing turned on the human rights point since by this time it had become clear that the Human Rights Act had no retrospective effect and so did not apply in *Pye*.

The new provisions in the LRA 2002, Schedule 6 are less likely to be open to challenge under the Human Rights Act, since all owners with registered title will have warning of the potential loss of their land, along with the opportunity to prevent it.

3.7 **Comment**

The traditional justifications for retaining adverse possession in a private system of unregistered title to land remain as convincing as ever. In unregistered land, titles to land are relative and an English court will assist the party with the better claim to possession. However, in a public system of registered land, where title is absolute and guaranteed by the state, some of the traditional justifications are not so persuasive. The new law on adverse possession in cases where title to the land is already registered is intended to allow adverse possession of registered land only in order to ensure that the land remains marketable and in order to prevent injustice.

It is evident that the new scheme in registered land will make it much more difficult for a squatter to gain title to the land and, as a result, may well also provide an incentive for the owners of unregistered titles to apply for voluntary registration in order to protect themselves from being dispossessed by a squatter of whose presence they may be unaware.

Summary

3.1 In unregistered land, adverse possession allows a weak title to be cured as time passes and prevents ancient claims being revived.

3.2 In unregistered land, twelve years' unconcealed adverse possession, without interruptions, prevents the paper owner repossessing the land.

3.3 In registered land, the registered proprietor is given warning of the threat to her land and has two years to evict the squatter.

3.4 The squatter's possession must be real, with intent, and without the permission of the paper owner.

Exercises

3.1 How can a landowner get rid of a trespasser?

3.2 In unregistered land, when does the trespasser become the owner of the land?

3.3 How easy is it for a registered proprietor to lose her land to a trespasser?

3.4 What intention is required by an adverse possessor?

3.5 In what ways is the nature of the piece of land relevant to an adverse possession dispute?

3.6   When may an apparently successful adverse possessor lose the land?

3.7   Olwen owns a 300-year lease in Animal Farm, the freehold owner of which is a pension company called Trusties. Neither the leasehold nor the freehold titles are registered. At one corner of the farm lies a small triangle of woodland of about one-third of an acre. Here Kate, an eccentric old woman, lives in a barrel with her tame goat, Peter, who finds his food in the wood. She moved into the barrel when Tony Blair became Prime Minister, just after the death of her friend Mumtaz, who had lived in the barrel, so he had claimed, since well before 1970. Mumtaz had originally been a weekly tenant but had never paid rent after the first week.

Olwen has just been offered an excellent price for her lease, if she can deliver vacant possession. She wishes to sell but Kate refuses to leave. Olwen claims that, although she never gave permission for anyone to live there, she did not really mind as it was so far from the house. She had no particular use for the woodland although, if she could have got a grant, she would have cut down the trees and erected battery hen units. Kate says that it is her woodland now and points out that her boundary was marked out by large boulders and electric cable (hung between the trees) by Mumtaz. She claims that Olwen has not been allowed in the woodland for years and years.

In an action for possession, who will win? Who should win? Would your answers be different if Olwen's leasehold title were registered?

Further Reading

Curwen, 'The Squatter's Interest at Common Law' [2000] Conv 528

Davis, 'Informal Acquisition and Loss of Rights in Land: What Justifies the Doctrines?' [2000] Legal Studies 198

Dixon, 'Bringing Home Another's Rights' [2001] Conv 276

Dockray, 'Why Do We Need Adverse Possession?' [1985] Conv 272

McCormick, 'Adverse Possession and Future Enjoyment' [1986] Conv 434

Rhys, 'Adverse Possession, Human Rights and Judicial Heresy' [2002] Conv 470

Tee, 'A Harsh Twilight' [2003] CLJ 36

Thompson, 'Adverse Possession: The Abolition of Heresies' [2002] Conv 480

Wallace, 'Limitation, Prescription and Unsolicited Permission' [1994] Conv 196

Part II

The Estates and Interests

4 Freehold Land

4.1 Introduction

In English land law, the predominant method of owning land is to hold the 'freehold estate'. At this point, the ancient historical roots of modern English land law show through the ground: the origins of freehold land can take lawyers straight back to the conquest of England by William of Normandy in 1066. In theory, all the land in England and Wales is still owned by the Crown, with individuals holding interests in the Queen's land.

There used to be many different legal estates, with different rules about inheritance and transfer, but only two of these remain: *freehold* is a holding for an indefinite period (providing there is someone able to inherit the land under a will or through the rules of intestacy on the freeholder's death), and *leasehold* is a holding for a fixed time. Because of the reforms of 1925, the legal freehold estate is the basic concept of landownership but, in registered land, the 'registered proprietor' holds a new kind of title, the statutory equivalent of the legal freehold (see 11.3 below).

4.2 Definition of the Freehold Estate

The fee simple is the only surviving legal freehold estate; its proper name is *fee simple absolute in possession*. Each of these words has a particular significance.

Fee: This word comes from 'fief' (*feudum* in Latin), the basic concept of the feudal system. By the sixteenth century a fee had come to be recognised as an estate which could be inherited because it did not automatically return to the feudal landlord when the tenant died.

Fee simple: The fee is 'simple' because it does not suffer from the complications of the other fee, the fee tail or 'entail', which has to go to a particular kind of heir when the owner dies. The fee simple can be inherited by anyone the owner wishes, but the fee tail has to pass to a direct descendant (child, grandchild and so on), and it could be restricted to, for example, a male child (a 'tail male'). In modern times, the use of the fee tail has fallen into obsolescence and it has not been possible to create new entails since 1997 (Trusts of Land and Appointment of Trustees Act 1996, Schedule 1, para. 5). Entails created before 1997 remain valid.

Fee simple absolute: The word 'absolute' is used to distinguish this fee simple from others which are limited in some way. For instance, there is a 'fee simple upon condition'; an example is where a mother gives land to her son *but if* he marries a solicitor, the land will go to his cousin. This must be distinguished from the 'determinable fee simple', which is created by words such as '*until* he marries a solicitor': a very subtle difference. It is important because, although in 1925 only the fee simple absolute could be a legal estate (s.1(1) LPA, see 1.5 above), a special exception was made in 1926 for conditional fees simple (s.7(1) LPA, as amended): these can now be legal, but the other limited fees simple (including determinable fees) must be equitable.

Fee simple absolute in possession: All interests in land can be 'in possession', 'in remainder' or 'in reversion'. In possession means that the owner is entitled to enjoy the interest *now* (occupy the land or collect the rent and so on); the other two mean that the owner will have the right to enjoy the interest after another interest (for example an interest for life) has ended. In the example above, therefore, the son has a conditional fee simple in possession, and the cousin has a fee simple absolute in *remainder*. However, if it were settled that the land was to go back to the mother if the son did the unthinkable, the mother would have a fee simple absolute in *reversion*.

4.3 **Legal and Equitable Freeholds**

Out of all the possibilities raised in the sections above, only the fee simple absolute in possession can be a legal estate (subject to the exception for conditional fees), because of s.1 LPA (see 1.5 above). The fee tail, therefore, can only be equitable, held behind a trust.

4.4 **The Rights of the Freeholder**

In theory, at common law the owner can do whatever he likes with his land: he owns everything under, above and on his land, down to the centre of the earth and up to the heavens.

In 1885, Challis wrote that ownership of the fee simple 'confers ... the lawful right to exercise over, upon, and in respect of the land, every act of ownership which can enter into the imagination' (Challis H.W., *The Law of Real Property, Chiefly in Relation to Conveyancing* (London: Reeves and Turner, 1885).

However, even then this was not true because the law of tort could be used (in nuisance, for example, to prevent a landowner unreasonably interfering with his neighbour's enjoyment of his land). Today, legislation has imposed great limitations on the owner of land, so that, for instance, he cannot prevent aeroplanes from flying above his land, may not mine coal, demolish a listed building, kill protected species or pollute water; he must also observe building regulations and licensing laws.

The Town and Country Planning Acts impose probably the best known limitation on landowners. When the first was passed, in 1947, it was suggested by some that the fee simple had been destroyed by the powers taken by the government to control land use. Few people would say so now, since most landowners appreciate the fact that the value of their land is maintained for them by the local authority, which can forbid their neighbours to open an amusement arcade or a garage, for example.

4.5 Comment

This chapter has given a glimpse of the ancient law hidden within the modern rules; even the basic concept of today's law, the fee simple, can only be explained by reference to events which took place nearly 1000 years ago. However, although we may use the same words as lawyers in the eleventh or fifteenth centuries, the meaning and context are quite different: our forebears might recognise the terms but they would not understand our law.

Part of the fascination of the history of land law is the tracing of threads which link us to very different worlds. Many people find the history interesting for its own sake but the methods of historians can also be used to illuminate our own world: historians explain changes in land law by reference to the political, economic and social events of the time, and modern cases and statutes, which appear as merely technical rules, should be viewed in the same light (see for example Anderson [1984] CLP 63).

Summary

4.1 The basic unit of ownership in modern land law is the legal fee simple absolute in possession which originates in the feudal system imposed after 1066.

4.2 'Fee simple absolute in possession' means an interest in land which can be inherited by anyone, is not restricted by some future event and which is enjoyed at the moment.

4.3 Although it has been asserted that the owner in fee simple absolute in possession has unlimited powers over his land, both common law and statute have greatly restricted his freedom of action.

Exercises

4.1 Does the history of land law matter?
4.2 Which is more important, planning law or the doctrine of estates?
4.3 What is special about a fee simple upon condition?
4.4 What is an entail? Can it be legal?

Further Reading

Anderson, 'Land Law Texts and the Explanation of 1925' [1984] CLP 63

5   The Leasehold Estate

5.1 Introduction

By s.1 LPA 1925 (see 1.5 above), the freehold (the fee simple absolute in possession) and leasehold are the only estates in land which can be legal. A lease was originally a contract for the occupation of land, and it was only in the sixteenth century that leases were recognised as interests in land, so that the rights and duties of the parties were no longer merely contractual, but became attached to the land. However, much of the law of leases is still based on contract law, albeit with overarching statutory provisions controlling residential, business and agricultural tenancies.

The commercial advantages of the lease are obvious. A landowner can let other people use her land for a certain period of time – to farm, mine for gravel, or live there – in exchange for a regular income. She can make rules about the kinds of things that are – or are not – to be done on the land and, at the end of the period, she will get the land back. The wealth of the powerful land-owning families came, to a large extent, from rental income. Great cities like London were developed in the eighteenth and nineteenth centuries through building leases. The ancestors of the Duke of Westminster owned large estates in London and granted long leases to speculative builders, subject to strict rules about the density and type of housing. The builders made their profit, the Dukes enjoyed the rent, and at the end of the period the valuable housing estates reverted to the descendants of the first Duke. Thus London and other cities grew through the carefully planned, high quality developments of far-sighted land-owners – and also, of course, through get-rich-quick rented slums.

Today, leasehold arrangements are still very important. In financial terms, the most significant use of leases is in the business world, for office blocks and factory units, for example. In addition, most flats are bought on long (often 99-year) leases (see 6.4 below). One of the problems with long leases is that they are a diminishing asset, so statute has intervened – not particularly successfully so far – to allow the owners of long residential leases either to extend the period of their leases or to buy the freehold. The introduction of the commonhold scheme designed to avoid some of the difficulties associated with leases is considered in 6.6 below.

There are also many other tenants, those who are unable to or do not wish to climb on to the so-called 'property ladder', with much shorter leases. Short leases for housing have been greatly affected by Acts of Parliament since 1915 because of the social and economic importance of decent housing for the community as a whole. Statutes on rent control, security and repairs were intended to protect poor tenants with little bargaining power against more powerful landladies. However, much of this protection, latterly found in the Rent Act 1977, has been removed in recent years (especially by the Housing Act 1988) in order to provide realistic commercial opportunities for landladies. The detail of this area of the law is usually outside the scope of land law courses and is referred to only occasionally in this chapter.

5.2 The Vocabulary of Leases

There are several words to describe a lease, including tenancy, letting, demise and term of years absolute (see 5.3 below). All these words have the same meaning, but lawyers tend to use 'tenancy' and 'letting' for a short period and 'lease' or 'demise' for a long one.

The following story is typical of leases: Louise let the basement flat in her house to Teresa, for three years at £500 per month. Teresa decided to live elsewhere and sold ('assigned') her lease to Ahmed who then rented the flat to Sam for six months. Then Louise decided to move, and sold her whole house (including the freehold, the 'reversion', of the flat) to Robert.

This story could be continued indefinitely, but thus far it illustrates the possibilities of leases, and is shown diagrammatically in Figure 5.1. (These diagrams are very useful for sorting out the characters in a problem on leases; leases are always shown as vertical lines and assignments as horizontal lines and, as in real life, the landlady is always on top.) Louise owned the freehold; she is the original landlady (lessor, owner of the freehold, owner of the leasehold reversion). Robert is the new landlord (lessor, landlady's assignee, assignee of the reversion). Teresa is the original tenant (lessee, owner of the lease). Ahmed is the current tenant (lessee, owner of the headlease, tenant's assignee, assignee of the headlease). He is also the landlord in the middle, the *mesne* (pronounced 'mean') landlord. Sam is the subtenant (sublessee, owner of the sublease).

The difference between an assignment and a sublease is important. Teresa assigned her lease when she sold the whole of her remaining interest to Ahmed. Ahmed created a sublease when he sold Sam a lesser period than he himself owned.

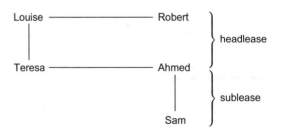

Figure 5.1 Leasehold relationships in diagram form

5.3 **Definition of a Lease**

The term of years absolute

This is the phrase adopted in the 1925 legislation and is defined at great length in s.205(1)(xxvii) LPA 1925. Essentially:

A term of years absolute has:

- a fixed beginning and a fixed end, and
- gives exclusive possession to the tenant.

(For more on exclusive possession see 5.4 below.)

The period can be anything from a few hours to thousands of years. The beginning and end must be stated at the outset but the lease may end ('determine') earlier (see 5.6 below).

Some leases do not state a fixed beginning and a fixed end but the facts nevertheless may be fitted into the definition of a 'term of years absolute', as in *Prudential Assurance Co Ltd* v. *London Residuary Body* [1992] 3 WLR 279. Here, a London council in 1930 let some land until it was needed for widening a road. Confirming previous authorities such as *Lace* v. *Chantler* [1944] KB 368, the House of Lords held that there was insufficient certainty about the date of the end of the lease and therefore it could not be a valid term of years absolute. However, they agreed instead that this was a lease 'from year to year' (a periodic legal tenancy: see below) which the council's successor in title could end by giving six months' notice (as is usual under a yearly tenancy).

This rule on the need for there to be certainty in the duration of a lease may be due for some reconsideration. Lord Browne-Wilkinson said:

> This bizarre outcome results from the application of an ancient and technical rule of law which requires the maximum duration of a term of years to be ascertainable from the outset. No one has produced any satisfactory rationale for the genesis of this rule. No one has been able to point to any useful purpose that it serves at the present day. (p. 287)

However, no statutory change has yet been proposed.

Within the definition of a lease as providing a fixed period and exclusive possession, there is a great range of types of leases. The start can be set for a date in the future, but it must start within 21 years (s.149(3) LPA); this is called a reversionary lease.

A lease for a specific period such as a week, which can be continually repeated until one side gives notice, is called a periodic tenancy. A weekly or monthly period is common for furnished accommodation and a yearly period for agricultural tenancies. If a person uses land and regularly pays money to the owner, then – providing the tenant has exclusive possession (see 5.4 below) – the common law implies a periodic tenancy unless the parties intended something else. The period of the tenancy is decided by the period by which rent is assessed, not by the period of payment; thus, if the rent is '£1000 per year, payable monthly', there is an implied legal yearly tenancy.

Another lease which continually repeats itself is the perpetually renewable lease. It is different from the periodic tenancy because here the landlady cannot give notice; the lease continues as long as the tenant chooses. This kind of arrangement was common in agricultural lettings with absentee landladies. They were anomalous within the 1925 structure of landownership, so s.145 LPA 1922 automatically converts them into a lease for 2000 years, with special rules for giving notice. At first the courts interpreted the section literally and a landlady who had carelessly drafted the lease agreement might suddenly find herself saddled with a 2000-year lease and the consequent loss in value of her freehold reversion. The judges now lean against this literal interpretation and attempt to discover the intentions of the parties.

Leases for life

Before 1925 there were two types of lease: the term of years absolute and the lease for life (or until marriage), and both could exist as legal estates. By s.1 LPA, only the first of these can now be legal, but because some people with legal leases for life or marriage would have suddenly found themselves to be merely equitable lessees on 1 January 1926, s.149(6) LPA converts their interests into legal leases for 90 years, providing rent is payable. Such a lease can be determined by one month's notice following the death or marriage.

5.4 Leases and Licences

Normally, if a person occupying another's land does not have exclusive possession (the right to keep the owner out), she is not a tenant under a lease but only a lodger, or a licensee. The word 'licensee' describes anyone who has a permission to be on land, such as readers in a library; these 'non-interests-in-land' are discussed in more detail in Chapter 14. A licence can be created by contract, with a regular payment of what looks like rent, and then it may closely resemble a lease. However, leases are interests in land, while licences are merely personal rights: they cannot usually be transferred and will probably not bind a buyer of the land.

The difference between a lease and a licence is 'notoriously difficult' (Bridge [1986] Conv 344); there are hundreds of pages of judgments devoted to explaining the difference. Historically, the distinction was very important because many residential tenants had, through the Rent Act 1977 or its equivalent, statutory protection of their occupation and could claim a fair rent, while 'mere licensees' enjoyed neither of these statutory protections (but see also 14.4 below for terms implied into licences). However, this difference is no longer of such importance. Landladies are unlikely now to try to create a licence rather than a lease, since, with effect from 15 January 1989, the Housing Act 1988 created the form of short-term residential tenancy known as the 'assured shorthold' tenancy, which allows landladies to receive a market rent and considerably limits a tenant's security. The case law nevertheless remains relevant to commercial agreements, to any occupation agreements made before that date and in cases where an occupier must hold a lease in order to gain the benefit of a statute (see, for example, *Bruton* v. *London and Quadrant Housing Trust* [2000] 1 AC 406, below).

The decision of the House of Lords in *Street* v. *Mountford* [1985] AC 809 was a milestone in the case law on the lease/licence distinction. Mr Street (a solicitor) let Mrs Mountford live in his house in return for a weekly payment. In a written agreement, headed 'Licence', she accepted rules about visitors and heating, and eviction if the 'licence fee' was more than a week late. Mr Street reserved the right to enter the house to inspect it. Such agreements had formerly been assumed to be licences, since this seemed, on paper, to be the clear intention of the parties. However, the House of Lords held that this was a weekly tenancy, thus allowing Mrs Mountford to claim the protection of the Rent Act.

Lord Templeman was clear that an occupier of residential land must be either a tenant or a licensee, and that:

> A tenant armed with exclusive possession can keep out strangers and keep out the landlord. (p. 816)

The normal test of a tenancy is the factual question of 'exclusive possession'; the expressed intention of the parties is irrelevant:

> The occupier is a lodger [licensee] if the landlord provides attendance or services which require the landlord or his servants to exercise unrestricted access to and use of the premises ... If on the other hand residential accommodation is granted for a term at a rent with exclusive possession, the landlord providing neither attendance nor services, the grant is a tenancy ... The manufacture of a five-pronged implement for digging results in a fork even if the manufacturer, unfamiliar with the English language, insists he intended to make, and has made, a spade. (Lord Templeman at pp. 817–18, 819)

The case was held to apply to all occupation agreements, including shops and agricultural land. It soon became clear, however, that multiple occupation, as is common in rented flats, posed different problems. In *A.G. Securities* v. *Vaughan*; *Antoniades* v. *Villiers* [1990] 1 AC 417 the House of Lords held, in the first of this pair of cases heard together, that a group of four people who shared a flat could not be tenants because they did not fulfil the requirements of a 'joint tenancy', the only way by which people can legally share land (see 12.5 below). They did not all arrive at the same time, and so they did not share 'unity of title': they were merely licensees. In the second case, however, a 'Licence Agreement', which seemed to give the owner the right to sleep in the tiny flat with a cohabiting couple, was held to be a tenancy; the term looked as if it denied exclusive possession to the couple but it was held to be a sham, inserted into the agreement merely in order to avoid giving Rent Act protection to the occupants, and it therefore had no effect.

These cases, and the many subsequent decisions, cannot provide all the answers. Essentially, the question is whether the agreement itself gave exclusive possession to the tenant (or the tenants jointly) so that they had the right to keep the owner out. However, it is often impossible to decide what the agreement means or whether a term in it is a sham without looking at the facts of the whole case. Thus, the House of Lords decided in *Westminster City Council* v. *Clarke* [1992] 2 AC 228 that a person given temporary accommodation by a local council did not have a tenancy but only a licence. Lord Templeman held that this was 'a very special case' (p. 703), quite different from private lettings. He held that there was no exclusive possession here because of the purpose of this agreement: a term that the occupant could be moved at any time to another room was not a sham because the council needed it in order to fulfil its statutory duty to vulnerable people.

The decision in *Clarke* may be compared with *Bruton* v. *London and Quadrant Housing Trust* (above), a case in which the Trust had given Mr Bruton a weekly 'licence' to occupy short-life accommodation. Despite the very clear wording of the licence agreement and the fact that the Trust was itself a licensee, the House of Lords found that Mr Bruton had exclusive possession of his flat, was thus a tenant and not a licensee. He was therefore able to bring an action against the Trust under s.11 Landlord and Tenant Act 1985 for breach of the implied repairing obligations (see 6.2 below) which a landlady may owe to a tenant but not to a licensee. Lord Hoffmann stated:

> There is nothing to suggest that he was to share possession with the trust, the council or anyone else. The trust did not retain such control over the premises as was inconsistent with Mr Bruton having exclusive possession, as was the case in *Westminster City Council* v. *Clarke*. The only rights which it reserved were for itself and the council to enter at certain times and for limited purposes. As Lord Templeman said in *Street* v. *Mountford* ... such an express reservation 'only serves to emphasise the fact that the grantee is entitled to exclusive possession and is a tenant'. ([2000] 1 AC 406 at 413, 414)

The Court was clear that exclusive possession for a term was sufficient to create a lease. This was so, even though the lease might be personal only and not amount to an estate in land, as in this case, since the Trust itself held no estate out of which to carve a leasehold estate for Mr Bruton (the principle is *nemo dat quod non habet* – no-one can give something which they do not have).

5.5 The Creation of Leases

Legal formalities

The rules for the creation of legal interests in land were set out in Chapter 2. Briefly, a deed is necessary to *create* a legal lease, unless it is within the exception in s.54(2) LPA for short leases (see 2.7 above). A deed is always required to *assign* a legal lease (see *Crago* v. *Julian* [1992] 1 All ER 744, 2.7 above). When the land is registered, special rules apply to leases over seven years (see 11.4). If there is no deed where one is needed (or the registered land procedure is not followed), then only an equitable interest may be created or transferred.

Equitable leases

Between the original landlady and tenant, an equitable lease is probably as good as a legal lease. It will be recalled that in *Walsh* v. *Lonsdale* (2.3 above), there was an equitable seven-year lease of a mill. Since the tenant had moved in and was paying a yearly rent, there was also an implied legal periodic yearly tenancy. The Judicature Acts of 1873 and 1875 (now see s.49(1) Supreme Court Act 1981) required that where the rules of equity and the common law conflicted on the same matter, the equitable rules should prevail. The landlord of the mill was therefore able to enforce the 'rent-in-advance' term in the equitable seven-year lease against the tenant.

An equitable lease can be converted into a legal lease through the equitable remedy of specific performance (2.4 above) but it should be remembered that, while the behaviour of a claimant is not relevant if she is seeking a legal remedy, equitable remedies are discretionary and are unlikely to be available if she has behaved badly and does not come to equity 'with clean hands'. It follows, therefore, that if the remedy of specific performance is not available, no equitable interest will have been created.

Walsh v. *Lonsdale* was followed in the recent case of *R* v. *Tower Hamlets LBC, ex parte von Goetz* [1999] 2 WLR 582. Miss von Goetz had a ten-year assured shorthold tenancy of a house. Although a written contract had been agreed (so the requirements of s.2 Law of Property (Miscellaneous Provisions) Act 1989 were satisfied), no deed had ever been executed. The council argued that this equitable lease could not attract a renovation grant under the Local Government and Housing Act 1989, since, in its view, such leases had to be legal. In rejecting the council's appeal, Mummery LJ stated that Miss Goetz had:

> for all practical purposes an interest as good as a legal interest ... [and that] if she asked the grantors for a deed to perfect the legal title, there is no ground on which that could be refused. (pp. 585, 587)

As indicated above, the terms in the equitable lease will normally prevail as between the original parties. However, this may not be the case if either the lease or the freehold is assigned. The most important rule here is that legal interests bind the world, but equitable interests are subject to the doctrine of notice and its statutory replacements (see the rules in Chapters 10 and 11 on the protection of estate contracts). In addition, depending on the date of its creation, the rights and duties in an equitable lease may not pass with the land (see 6.4 below). Whether an equitable lease is as good as a legal lease is an ancient essay question; a useful discussion on this issue is provided in Cheshire, 2000, pp. 405–8.

Statutory conditions

When choosing a tenant, the owners of property may not discriminate on the grounds of sex, race or disability (s.30 Sex Discrimination Act 1975; s.21 Race Relations Act 1976; ss 22, 23 Disability Discrimination Act 1995). The only common exceptions concern small houses or flats where the landlady lives on the premises. Such discrimination is a tort and the victim can take action for damages, an injunction and/or a declaration.

5.6 Determination of Leases

Since all leases must be only for a limited period, sooner or later they must end ('determine'). This happens through:

1 *Forfeiture* (where the landlady repossesses the land following the tenant's breach of covenant – see 6.5 below).
2 *Expiry* (when the period ends).
3 *Notice* (for example, a month's notice for monthly period tenancies, half a year's notice for yearly tenants, or as specified in the lease).
4 *Surrender* (where the tenant gives up the lease with the agreement of the landlady – there can be no unilateral surrender).
5 *Frustration* (very rarely: for example where there is some physical catastrophe). For discussion of the principles involved, see *National Carriers Ltd* v. *Panalpina (Northern) Ltd* [1981] AC 675.
6 *Repudiatory breach* (rarely, but where the landlady is in fundamental breach of her obligations under the lease, it may be possible for the tenant to accept this breach and walk away from the lease – see *Hussein* v. *Mehlman* [1992] 2 EGLR 87 and 6.5 below).
7 *Merger* (where the tenant obtains the freehold). Certain tenants have the right under statute to extend their long lease or to buy their freehold – the right-to-buy scheme for local authority tenants is one example. Another example is long leases at a low rent; when a number of his tenants exercised their rights under the Leasehold Reform Act 1967 to claim the freehold of their leases, the Duke of Westminster in *James* v. *UK* (1986) 8 EHRR 123 (see 1.6 above) argued unsuccessfully that his rights to his property under ECHR, Article 1, Protocol 1, had been violated. The European Court of Human Rights found that the provisions of the 1967 Act, intended to provide a measure of protection for certain tenants against the diminishing value of their leases (see 5.1 above), were not disproportionate.

5.7 **Some Odd Kinds of Leases**

Tenancy at will

This is, in some respects, similar to a licence; the 'tenant' has exclusive possession of the land but either side can end the arrangement at any time. It is not an estate in land.

Tenancy at sufferance

This arises if a tenant remains in occupation ('holds over') after the lease has expired, without the landlady's agreement. The landlady can evict the tenant at any time, but if she accepts rent, the tenant becomes a tenant at will or even a periodic tenant.

Tenancy by estoppel

If a person attempts to grant a lease which she could not grant because she had no title, she is estopped from denying her tenant's rights against her. This is part of the ordinary principle of estoppel. Such a tenancy is personal and does not create an estate in land. However, if the landlady subsequently gains the legal title, then the tenant is automatically 'clothed' with the legal lease (this is known as 'feeding the estoppel'). For recent judicial comment on tenancies by estoppel, see *Bruton* v. *London and Quadrant Housing Trust* (5.4 above).

Lease of the reversion

Where a landlady creates a lease of her remaining interest, she is leasing the reversion; it is also called a concurrent lease. The tenant of the reversion has the right to collect rent and enforce other covenants against the tenant of the lease. (Compare the reversionary lease explained in 5.3 above.)

5.8 **Comment**

Despite all its faults, the lease is an instrument of enormous flexibility. Leases can control housing development, providing both long-term and short-term housing; they provide for the changing needs of businesses and are a common means of holding agricultural land; they allow land to be used to provide an income and raise capital.

The post-war consensus about the need to protect the security of private residential tenants ended in the 1980s: their statutory protection was reduced, partly in order to revitalise the private rented sector. Public authorities became less able to provide adequate housing for those excluded from home-ownership, and the responsibility in this area was transferred mainly to housing associations.

In its recent Consultation Paper ((2002) Law Com No 162), the Law Commission considers abolishing the present complicated statutory regime of residential tenancies in favour of a much simpler system of tenancies which would no longer be estates in land but merely consumer contracts, as in much of the rest of Europe. One effect of this would be the removal of the distinction between the lease and the licence, since both would become consumer contracts. Issues such as those discussed in *Bruton* (5.4 above) would be irrelevant.

Summary

5.1 A lease must have a fixed beginning and a fixed end and the tenant must have exclusive possession.

5.2 In deciding whether an arrangement is a lease or a licence, the court looks to the substance of the agreement, not the name given to it.

5.3 No formalities are required to create a lease not exceeding three years, providing it is at a market rent and takes effect in possession.

5.4 An equitable lease may be as good as a legal lease between the original parties but, once the lease or reversion is sold, an equitable lease may be less secure.

Exercises

5.1 How certain must a 'term of years absolute' be?

5.2 What is the difference between a lease and a licence?

5.3 Pilbeam owns a house in London which he converted into three one-bedroomed flats some years ago. He granted Yasmin a lease of Flat 1 until she got married. The tenant of Flat 2 is Javed, who was told by Pilbeam that he could have a lease until his parents come over from Pakistan. Six months ago, Pilbeam rented Flat 3 to Brenda on a one year 'licence agreement' in which Brenda agreed that Pilbeam could sleep there whenever he stayed in London. The three occupants all pay their rent monthly.

Advise Pilbeam whether Yasmin, Javed and Brenda have leases of their flats and, if so, what kind of leases.

Further Reading

Ball, 'Renting Homes: Status and Security in the UK and France – A Comparison in Light of the Law Commission's Proposals' [2003] Conv 38

Bridge, '*Street* v. *Mountford* – No Hiding Place' [1986] Conv 344

Bright, 'Uncertainty in Leases – Is it a Vice?' [1993] Legal Studies 38

Bright and Gilbert, *Landlord and Tenant Law: The Nature of Tenancies* (Oxford: Clarendon Press, 1995)

Morgan, 'Exclusive Possession and the Tenancy by Estoppel: a Familiar Problem in an Unusual Setting' [1999] Conv 493

Pawlowski, 'Occupational Rights in Leasehold Law: Time for Rationalisation' [2002] Conv 550

Smith P. F., 'What is Wrong with Certainty in Leases?' [1993] Conv 461

6 Leasehold Covenants

6.1 Introduction

The last chapter examined the characteristics of different kinds of leases and how they may be created and ended. This chapter considers the contents of a lease – more specifically, the obligations of the landlady and the tenant. A properly drafted business lease or long residential lease will be lengthy and detailed, and probably devoted mostly to the obligations of the tenant. On the other hand, some short leases, especially of residential tenancies, may not even be in writing and any express agreement may have gone no further than to stipulate the amount of rent payable and the frequency with which the tenant should pay it. Even the simplest of leases, however, will contain many more terms than this, and it is fundamental that the parties should understand their obligations under the lease, whether assignees are bound by or can enforce these obligations, and the remedies which are available for either party in case of the other's breach.

6.2 Commonly Found Covenants

'Covenant' is the general name given to promises in contracts concerning land; they may be express (written or spoken) or implied (either by common law or by statute). The following covenants are commonly found in leases:

Common leasehold covenants

By the lessor

- not to derogate from her grant
- to allow the lessee quiet enjoyment
- to repair

By the lessee

- to pay rent (sometimes also land taxes and/or a service charge)
- to repair
- to permit the lessor to enter to inspect (or repair)
- to insure
- not to alter the structure
- not to assign or sublet without permission
- to use the premises only for a specific purpose (such as a dwelling)
- not to deny the landlady's title

The most important are explained here.

Covenants for quiet enjoyment and non-derogation
These are the essence of the lease, the counterpart of the tenant's right to exclusive possession. If they are not expressed in the lease, they are implied by common law. First, the landlady promises not to interfere with the tenant's enjoyment of the land: this does not mean keeping quiet, but refers to the tenant's right to take possession as promised and to be able to enjoy all aspects of her possession without interference. Second, the landlady promises not to take back what she has given. These two promises are very closely connected and whether or not the covenants have been breached is a question of fact.

In *Browne* v. *Flower* [1911] 1 Ch 219, the tenants of a ground-floor flat complained that a new outside staircase, which ran alongside their bedroom windows, invaded their privacy and breached the covenants. As regards the covenant for quiet enjoyment, Parker J said:

> there must be some physical interference with the enjoyment of the demised premises and ... a mere interference with the comfort of a person using the demised premises by the creation of a personal annoyance such as might arise from noise, invasion of privacy, or otherwise is not enough. (p. 228)

On non-derogation, he held that a breach only occurs if property is 'rendered unfit or materially less fit to be used for the purpose for which [it was] demised' (at p. 226). The tenants here lost both arguments; after all, the rooms could still be used as bedrooms if they drew the curtains.

The nature of the covenant for quiet enjoyment was considered by the House of Lords in *Southwark LBC* v. *Mills* [2001] AC 1. The tenants in a local authority block of flats complained that, due to inadequate sound insulation, they could hear all the sounds made by their neighbours and that this was causing them tension and distress. Lord Hoffman said:

> The flat is not quiet and the tenant is not enjoying it. But the words cannot be read literally ... The covenant for quiet enjoyment is ... a covenant that the tenant's lawful possession of the land will not be substantially interfered with by the acts of the lessor or those lawfully claiming under him. (p. 10)

When the flats were built in 1919 there had been no statutory requirement that they should be soundproofed; the tenant had accepted the flat in the physical condition she had found it, and subject to the rest of the building being used as flats. There had been no substantial interference with the tenant's possession – her ability to use the flat in an ordinary lawful way – and thus no breach of the landlord's covenant to allow her quiet enjoyment. In addition, the resource implications on the local authority would have been unsustainable had the House of Lords found in favour of the tenants, since it would have cost over a billion pounds to bring all their premises up to modern building standards.

Two examples of the covenant of non-derogation are given here. In *Aldin* v. *Latimer Clark, Muirhead & Co* [1894] 2 Ch 437, land was let for use as a timber yard and included a shed used for drying timber and therefore requiring a free flow of air through it. The landlord built on neighbouring land he owned in such a way as to obstruct the free flow of air, and thus prevented the timber merchant from using the land for the purpose for which he had leased it. The landlord's activities amounted to breach of his covenant not to derogate from his grant.

Similarly, in *Harmer* v. *Jumbil (Nigeria) Tin Areas Ltd* [1921] 1 Ch 200 land was leased expressly for the storage of explosives and then the landlord decided to build on his neighbouring land, which would have made the storage illegal. The tenant was able to prevent the building.

These common covenants are reinforced by s.1 Protection from Eviction Act 1977, amended by s.29 Housing Act 1988. The section allows a local authority to prosecute a landlady for the crime of harassment where she 'does acts likely to interfere with the peace or comfort of the residential occupier' or refuses any facilities (such as the electricity supply) knowing or believing that this will discourage the occupier from enforcing her rights. (This section protects residential licensees as well as tenants.)

An example is *Cardiff City Council* v. *Destrick*, unreported, 14 April 1994. A landlord cut off the gas and electricity of a flat rented by a couple with a young baby. He was charged with the offence of doing an act with intent to cause the occupier to leave (s.1(3)), and also with doing an act which was likely to make the occupier leave (s.1(3A)), but was acquitted of both charges. He had argued that he had no intent to force them out (it was summer, not winter), and, further, that it was reasonable (under s.1(3B)) to act as he did because the tenants were behind with their payments. The magistrates agreed with him. On appeal, the judges recognised that Parliament's intent was to protect residential tenants by ensuring that if a landlady wants an eviction, she must go to court and may not rely on self-help or 'indulge in harassment'. However, they found that the magistrate's decision had not been so irrational that it should be overruled. This case may have opened a useful escape route for lessors, but it will be a question on the evidence of the reasonableness of the lessor's conduct in every case.

Section 27 Housing Act 1988 also creates a tort of unlawful eviction with the potential for substantial damages to be awarded against the landlady. *Tagro* v. *Cafane* [1991] 2 All ER 235 is 'a cautionary tale for landlords who are minded unlawfully to evict their tenants by harassment or other means' (Lord Donaldson MR at p. 236). The landlord here harassed the tenant and eventually 'totally wrecked' her room and possessions. The tenant won £31 000 damages, assessed on the difference between the value of the premises with the tenant in occupation and their value with vacant possession (s.28). The recent trend is towards the award of much lower damages, perhaps reflecting the landlady's ability more easily to end her tenants' possession lawfully under the assured shorthold regime.

Covenants to repair .

At common law, a furnished dwelling must be fit for habitation at the start of the lease (although no such covenant is implied into leases of other kinds of property). A well known breach of this implied covenant occurred in *Smith* v. *Marrable* (1843) 11 M & W 5, where a house was leased and found to be full of bugs.

The only statutory provision which requires a landlady of a dwelling to keep it fit for human habitation at the start and throughout the lease is s.8 Landlord and Tenant Act 1985. However, the section applies only to tenancies let at a very low rent and, since there are probably very few of these tenancies left, it is nowadays very much a dead letter.

The covenant to repair the property is fundamental to the lease of a building or part of a building. Whether the burden of this covenant falls on the landlady or the tenant will depend on the kind of property and the length of the lease. If there is nothing expressed in the lease, under common law a periodic tenant with a year's term or less probably just has to use the premises in a 'tenant-like manner'. This is a vague expression but Lord Denning MR has given some examples. A weekly tenant must, for example, clean windows and unblock sinks:

> In short, he must do the little jobs about the place which a reasonable tenant would do. In addition, he must, of course, not damage the house ... But ... if the house falls into disrepair through fair wear and tear or lapse of time, or for any reason not caused by him, then the tenant is not liable to repair it. (*Warren* v. *Keen* [1954] 1 QB 15, p. 20)

Sections 11–14 Landlord and Tenant Act 1985 impose a duty on the landlady of any dwelling (for a term granted for less than seven years) to keep the external structure in repair, and certain items in proper working order, including installations for the supply of water, gas and electricity and for sanitation and space and water heating. This is a complex area of law, but the courts have tended to interpret these requirements as not putting an obligation on the landlady to correct some design defect in the building's structure which, for example, might have caused excessive condensation and thus made the premises unfit for human habitation, so long as the structure was not itself in a state of disrepair. However, if the various installations do not perform as they should, they are not in proper working order and the landlady is liable. In *O'Connor* v. *Old Etonian Housing Association* [2002] Ch 295, water pipes which had been working properly failed to provide a proper supply when the water pressure dropped. The Court of Appeal held that the Housing Association would be in breach if the drop in pressure had been foreseeable, unless the reason for it was temporary and external, such as a drought.

The landlady's liability under ss 11–14 is subject to her being given notice that remedial work is needed and having a reasonable opportunity to carry it out (*O'Brien* v. *Robinson* [1973] AC 912).

Covenant not to assign or sublet

Theoretically, tenants have an unlimited right to assign or sublet. In practice, a tenant often covenants not to assign or sublet, since the landlady needs to be able to protect her reversionary interest against unsuitable assignees or subtenants. This covenant may be 'absolute', in which case the landlady can prevent the tenant from assigning or subletting, however unreasonable this may be. If the covenant is 'qualified' – in other words the tenant may not assign or sublet without the landlady's consent – s.19(1) Landlord and Tenant Act 1927 provides that the consent cannot be unreasonably withheld, 'notwithstanding any provision to the contrary'. The Landlord and Tenant Act 1988, s.1, places the burden of proof on the landlady to show that her refusal of consent was reasonable.

The Landlord and Tenant (Covenants) Act 1995, s.22 amended these rules for new commercial leases. It inserted a new s.19(1A) into the 1927 Act, which provides that, in the case of non-residential leases made after 1 January 1996, lessors and lessees may agree the circumstances under which consent to assignment may be given or refused, and in such cases the courts may not inquire into the reasonableness of a refusal. This provision is likely significantly to alter commercial negotiations for future leases, but has not affected non-business or pre-1996 leases.

If the consent is withheld, the tenant is placed in a difficult position. She can take a chance that the refusal is unreasonable and assign or sublet regardless, but if she wrongly assigns or sublets, she may lose her lease (see 6.5 below). If she is not sure whether the landlady is being reasonable, she can go to court for a declaration, but the delay may lose her the prospective assignee or subtenant.

By statute, it is unreasonable to refuse consent on the grounds of a person's sex, race or disability unless the landlady lives on the premises (s.31 Sex Discrimination Act 1975; s.24 Race Relations Act 1976; ss 22(4), 23 Disability Discrimination Act 1995).

Otherwise, whether a refusal is reasonable is a question of fact in every case. As Lord Denning MR remarked:

> No one decision will be a binding precedent as a strict rule of law. The reasons given by the judges are to be treated as propositions of good sense – in relation to the particular case – rather than propositions of law applicable to all cases. (*Bickel* v. *Duke of Westminster* [1977] QB 517, p. 524)

A useful test can be found in *International Drilling Fluids Ltd* v. *Louisville Investments (Uxbridge) Ltd* [1986] Ch 513, where it was said to be a question of whether the lessor's decision was one 'which might be reached by a reasonable man in the circumstances', providing the refusal was connected to the lessor/lessee relationship. Reasonable refusals include the unsatisfactory references of the proposed tenant and the fact that the subletting would create a tenancy protected by statute.

The Court of Appeal was faced with an interesting issue in *Olympia and York Canary Wharf Ltd* v. *Oil Property Investments Ltd* [1994] EG 121 where the lessor refused leave to an assignee of the lease who wanted to sell it to the original tenant. The reason for refusal was that the original tenant had the personal right to end the lease (and this would reduce the value of the lessor's interest by £6 million). The Court held that this was a reasonable ground to refuse consent to assignment.

In *Jaison Property Development Co Ltd* v. *Roux Restaurants* (1997) 74 P & CR 357, Aldous LJ quoted with approval from the judgment of Warrington LJ in *Houlder Bros* v. *Gibbs* [1925] Ch 575:

> When you look at the authorities ... this, at any rate, is plain, that in the cases to which an objection to an assignment has been upheld as reasonable it has always had some reference either to the personality of the [proposed] tenant or to his proposed user of the property. (p. 585)

In *Ashworth Fraser* v. *Gloucester CC* [2001] 1 WLR 2180, the House of Lords considered the status of a landlord's refusal to consent to an assignment where the landlord thought that the proposed assignee would probably be in breach of a user covenant in the lease. Approving the approach in *International Drilling Fluids Ltd*, the Court held that reasonable lessors:

> need not confine their consideration to what will necessarily happen ... they may have regard to what will probably happen. (Lord Roger at para. 70)

6.3 The 'Usual Covenants'

The phrase 'usual covenants' is a technical expression, quite different from the list of common covenants above. This set of covenants is implied into a lease if the lease states that the parties will be bound by the 'usual covenants', or if the lease is silent as to most matters (as is common in short periodic tenancies). These usual covenants are also implied in a contract for a lease, unless the parties intend otherwise.

The usual covenants

By the landlady

- quiet enjoyment and non-derogation from grant
- right of re-entry for non-payment of rent

By the tenant

- to pay rent
- to pay land taxes
- to repair (or to allow access to the landlady to repair)

Other covenants may be 'usual' in the circumstances, for example, because of local or trade customs.

6.4 The Transfer of Rights and Duties under a Lease

It is the automatic transfer of both parties' rights and duties under the lease (the fact that covenants 'run with the land') which makes leases so useful; anyone who buys either the lease or the reversion takes the benefits and burdens of covenants in the lease. ('Benefit' means a right to sue and 'burden' a liability to be sued.) Thus, a person who buys the freehold and becomes the new landlady can sue for the rent; one who buys the lease can sue for repairs. This is also the main reason why almost all flats in England and Wales are sold by means of leases, rather than freehold. Only certain (negative) freehold covenants are enforceable against successors in title of the original covenantor (see Chapter 9). Mortgage lenders would be unlikely to lend money to buy a flat or a maisonette if it were not possible to force the owners of the neighbouring flats to maintain their premises, thus ensuring the continuing value of the lender's security.

The Landlord and Tenant (Covenants) Act 1995 has revolutionised this area of the law for leases granted after 1995, but the old rules still apply to the thousands of leases (and contracts for leases) made before that date.

The old law for pre-1996 leases

Under the old law, the original parties to the lease are bound by their contract and, with some exceptions in the case of the landlady, remain liable for the whole period of the lease, whether one month or 99 years. Once the lease is assigned, however, the benefit and the burden of the leasehold covenants will pass to the new tenant providing there is 'privity of estate' between the parties and the covenant 'touches and concerns' the land (*Spencer's Case* (1583) 5 Co Rep 16a).

Privity of estate means that there is a current legal relationship of landlady and tenant between the parties. A sign of privity of estate is that one person pays rent to the other, so there is therefore no privity of estate between head landlady and subtenant.

The phrase 'touches and concerns' originates from the sixteenth century and is used by the courts to decide whether promises ought, as a matter of public policy, to be attached to the land. The test is easy to explain but harder to apply; the basic question is whether the promise really affects the parties in their roles as landlady and tenant, or whether it affects them in their personal capacity. In Cheshire's terms, the promise must be 'reasonably incidental to the relation of landlord and tenant' (Cheshire, 2000, p. 477). In *P & A Swift Investments* v. *Combined English Stores Group plc* [1989] AC 632, the test was explained in the following terms: whether the covenant benefits the landlady for the time being but would cease to do so if it were separated from her ownership of the land; whether it affects the nature, quality or value of the land, or the way the land is used; or whether it is expressed to be a personal covenant (in which case it could not touch and concern the land, of course). All the commonly found covenants in 6.2 above do touch and concern the land. In Cheshire, 2000, pp. 477–8, there are long lists of covenants which do, and do not, touch and concern the land.

Where the freehold reversion is sold, by s.141 LPA 1925 the new landlady will be able to enforce the benefit of all the covenants which 'have reference to the subject matter of the lease' (which means exactly the same thing as 'touch and concern the land'). By s.142, she will be bound by the burden of all covenants which 'have reference to the subject matter of the lease'.

As already indicated, the original landlady and tenant have promised to obey the covenants for the whole lease and, in theory, through the doctrine of privity of contract, they may be able to sue – and may be liable – for the whole period; of course, they are unlikely to sue once they have parted with their interests, but the liability to be sued for unpaid rent can be a continuing worry for the original tenant of an expensive commercial lease.

The rules differ somewhat between the original lessor and the original lessee. If the *original lessor* assigns the reversion, because of the wording of ss 141 and 142, she can sue and be sued only by the original lessee and not by any other holder of the lease. The *original lessee*, however, can sue and will be liable to any assignee of the freehold, providing there is privity of estate between them and the covenant touches and concerns the land. Unlike the original landlady, therefore, the original tenant remains liable when she sells her interest: any owner of the reversion can choose to sue the original tenant of a lease rather than the present one for any breach of leasehold covenant.

The question may arise as to whether the original tenant is liable for subsequent variations or extensions of the lease. In *City of London Corporation* v. *Fell* [1994] 1 AC 458 the House of Lords offered 'a meagre crumb of comfort to the unfortunate original tenant' (Bridge [1994] CLJ 28), in this case a firm of solicitors. It held that the original tenant was not liable for rent unpaid by a later assignee of the lease in the case of a tenancy which was extended after the end of the term under the provisions of Part II of the Landlord and Tenant Act 1954. The Court of Appeal in *Friends' Provident Life Office* v. *British Railways Board* [1996] 1 All ER 336 found that an original tenant was not bound by later variations of the lease between the landlady and an assignee of the lease unless the variation had been envisaged in the terms of the original lease (such as a rent review clause).

The potential difficulties faced by the original tenant in leases created before 1 January 1996 have been addressed to some extent by the Landlord and Tenant (Covenants) Act 1995. The decision in *Friends' Provident* is now translated into a statutory provision (s.18) which applies to all leases. By s.17 of the Act, the landlady of any lease (again, whenever created) must give a 'problem notice' to the original tenant if she is planning to sue her for money unpaid by the current tenant. If the original tenant pays the sums due, she is now entitled by s.19 to an 'overriding lease' which places her between the landlady and the current tenant, thus gaining some potential relief in exchange for her liability. If no s.17 notice was given, the original tenant escapes all liability for that debt.

If the original tenant is sued, the common law provides that she can claim an indemnity from the current tenant (*Moule* v. *Garrett* (1872) LR Ex 101). If the present tenant is not worth suing (as is likely), under s.77 LPA (implied into all leases since 1925) the original tenant can choose to sue the person to whom she assigned her interest. As a further protection, when a business lease is assigned, the landlady will probably insist that the proposed new tenant obtain a guarantor (a 'surety'). If the new tenant fails to pay the rent, the guarantor may also be sued for it.

There are different rules for equitable leases because in such cases there is no privity of estate, since this depends on a *legal* relationship. Due to the wording of ss 141 and 142, the benefits and burdens of all covenants which touch and concern the land pass to any landlady, whether legal or equitable. As far as the equitable tenant is concerned, the benefit of covenants which touch and concern may pass, but it seems that the burden may not (but see below for equitable leases made after 1995).

The operation of the old rules for pre-1996 leases

Take the following leasehold story: Alpha Co granted a 99-year lease of the top floor flat in a large block to Bella in 1928. Alpha covenanted to keep the roof in repair and Bella covenanted to pay £500 per year rent and to use the premises as a private dwelling house only. There was a provision for forfeiture for breach of any covenant. Alpha went into liquidation and the reversion was conveyed to Bravo Co and then to Charlie Ltd. Bella sold the lease to Gerald who then sold it to Dino. The roof is now leaking badly. Dino is running an umbrella repairing service from the flat, and is in arrears of rent. The lease and all assignments were made by deed (see above for equitable leases).

The rights and duties of the various people in this tale obviously change as time passes. The present situation is as shown in diagram form in Figure 6.1.

1   As regards the leaking roof, there is privity of estate between Dino and Charlie and the covenant to repair touches and concerns the land: Dino can sue Charlie because the covenant was breached as soon as the roof leaked.

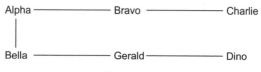

Figure 6.1

2   As regards the arrears of rent and the umbrella business, there is privity of estate and the covenants touch and concern the land: Charlie can sue Dino. Alternatively, Charlie could sue Bella as the original tenant – but only so long as a problem notice is served in respect of the unpaid rent. Bella, if liable, could sue either Gerald (s.77 LPA) or Dino (common law). (The original tenant's liability is only likely to arise in practice when money is a suitable remedy; an injunction against the business use of the flat would not be granted against the original tenant because she is no longer in control of the flat.)

Once Alpha and Bravo have assigned the lease they cannot be sued by anyone. If there were a subtenant, in theory she could neither sue Charlie Ltd (the head lessor) nor be sued by them because there would be no privity of estate between them. However, a head landlady may be able to sue a subtenant for breach of a restrictive (negative) covenant under the rule in *Tulk* v. *Moxhay* (1848) 2 Ph. 774 (see Chapter 9). Thus, in *Hemingway Securities Ltd* v. *Dunraven Ltd* (1995) 71 P & CR 30 a landlord company was able to prevent a subtenant from taking a sublease in breach of a covenant between the company and its tenant. In addition, by s.1 Contracts (Rights of Third Parties) Act 1999, a third party can enforce a term in a contract if there is express provision for her to do so, or if the term purports to confer a benefit on her and nothing in the contract rebuts this presumption, as long as she is named in the contract or can be identified from it. If Dino had a subtenant who breached a covenant in the sublease, and this covenant was made for the benefit of Charlie or whomever was for the time being the owner of the freehold reversion, Charlie or Charlie's assignee could enforce the covenant against the subtenant (see also *Amsprop Trading Ltd* v. *Harris Distribution Ltd* [1997] 2 All ER 990 and 9.3 below).

The law for leases granted after 1995

On 1 January 1996, the Landlord and Tenant (Covenants) Act 1995 came into force. Described as 'a statute without precedent ... [which] will have an untold impact on ... commercial leases in this country' (Bridge [1996] CLJ 313), the Act was passed as a result of a Law Commission Report ((1988) No 174), the commitment of a single MP, and the lessor and lessee lobbies (see Davey (1996) 59 MLR 78). The Act contains a number of highly detailed and complex provisions for the new regime which will no doubt keep lawyers busy for many years to come. The negotiations around the new law resulted in a series of hurriedly drafted provisions to effect compromises between the lessor and lessee lobbies.

In the application of the rules for leases granted after 1995, there is no distinction made between legal and equitable leases (s.28). The Act abolishes the test of 'touch and concern' (s.3), so that all landlord covenants and tenant covenants (the obligations of whomever is the landlady and the tenant at the time) automatically pass when the lease or freehold is assigned, unless they are specifically expressed to be 'personal'. In *BHP Petroleum* v. *Chesterfield Properties* [2002] Ch 194 the question arose as to whether the original landlord or its assignee should be liable for carrying out remedial work on defects on the premises. Since the covenant was, on the facts, a personal obligation on the part of the original landlord, the liability did not pass to the assignee, and the original landlord was held liable for the duration of the lease.

In order to rectify the fundamental injustice of the continuing liability of the original tenant under the previous regime, s.5 of the Act has abolished this liability for leases granted after 1995. However, in leases where the landlady's consent to an assignment of the lease is required, the assigning tenant only escapes liability until the end of the lease in exchange for the possibility of having to guarantee the performance of the lease by the next tenant (s.16) – an *authorised guarantee agreement*. The *BHP Petroleum* case, however, serves as a reminder that a personal covenant will continue to be binding throughout the term of the lease, and this applies to tenants as well as landladies.

When a landlady assigns her leasehold reversion, under s.6 of the Act she must still perform her covenants under the lease. However, in order to avoid this liability she may obtain from the current lessee a release under s.8 from her obligations (unless, of course, they are personal) and, if the lessee refuses her consent, the former landlady may apply to the court. It is important that the lessee should have some say in this, since an insolvent or reluctant landlady would be less likely to be able to carry out her repairing covenant, for example, and in such circumstances the lessee would probably want the existing landlady to continue to be bound.

Section 3(5) allows head lessors to enforce restrictive covenants relating to the use of the land against subtenants without the need to resort to equity and the rule in *Tulk* v. *Moxhay*, and without the need to bring themselves within the Contracts (Rights of Third Parties) Act.

The practical effect of many of these new rules will depend on the relative negotiating strengths of the parties, themselves influenced by the state of the property market. If the lease between Alpha and Bella (Figure 6.1) were made in 1996, the position might therefore depend more on negotiations between the parties. However, Charlie could no longer sue Bella, the original tenant, for rent unpaid by Dino.

6.5 Remedies for Breach of Covenant

The important question for a practical lawyer is always, 'What remedy is available?'. A lease is a contract and, in general, contractual remedies are available. There are also remedies particular to leases. The rules are complicated and only the briefest details of the main remedies are given here. For historical reasons there are differences between the landlady's remedies for the tenant's breach of the covenant to pay rent and her remedies for the tenant's breach of other covenants. First, however, it is necessary to distinguish between covenants and conditions.

If a promise in a lease is called a 'condition', or is clearly intended to be a condition of the lease, then the landlady can automatically take possession of the land if the condition is broken. This is called repossession (or re-entry, or forfeiture). If the promise is not a condition, but merely a covenant, there is no such automatic right and the landlady can forfeit the lease (re-enter) or give notice to quit only if there is a clause to that effect.

If the usual covenants (see 6.3 above) are implied, then there will be a provision for forfeiture for non-payment of rent but not for breach of any other covenant.

It is important to be aware of the doctrine of waiver. If a landlady accepts rent knowing of a breach of covenant or condition, she will be taken to have waived her right to take action for the breach. Any lessor wishing to enforce a forfeiture must avoid any action by which she indicates to the tenant that the lease will continue, but there is no waiver if the lessor did not know of a breach when she indicated the continuance of the lease.

Non-payment of rent

The possible remedies are an action for recovery of rent, distress and forfeiture. The landlady can only choose one of these at a time.

An action for recovery
An action can be brought for recovery of arrears of rent. Only the last six years of rent can be recovered (s.19 Limitation Act 1980).

Distress
Since 1066 a landlady has been able to enter the premises between sunrise and sunset and 'levy distress': she, or a certified bailiff, may take the tenant's belongings and sell them if the rent is not paid within five days. Many items are supposed to be exempt from distress, for example bedding and clothes. The rules are technical and complicated but have an advantage for the landlady in that she may be able to avoid the difficulties and delay in bringing a possession action in the courts. It may be that simply the threat to distrain goods will in some cases result in the arrears being paid off.

In its Report No 194 (1991), the Law Commission concluded that distress for non-payment of rent is 'wrong in principle', and recommended its abolition.

Levying distress may prove to be unlawful under the Human Rights Act 1998 which, under ECHR, Article 1, Protocol 1 gives individuals positive rights to the peaceful enjoyment of their possessions, under Article 6 to a fair trial and under Article 8 to respect for private and family life and the home (see 1.6 above). In *Fuller* v. *Happy Shopper Markets Ltd* [2001] 1

WLR 1681, Lightman J stated in his conclusion that lessors must be certain that tenants have no rights such as set-off (see below, p. 75) since:

> the human rights implications of levying distress must be in the forefront of the mind of the landlord ... and he must fully satisfy himself that taking this action is in accordance with the law. (para. 27)

In its recent Consultation Paper 'Distress for Rent' (May 2001), the Lord Chancellor's Department analysed the advantages and disadvantages of the remedy, including the human rights issues, and recommended the abolition of distress for rent arrears in residential properties and a modified procedure for its use in commercial tenancies.

Forfeiture (the right of re-entry)

The right to re-enter makes it sound as if the landlady can just barge in, but, although she may physically re-enter commercial property, such re-entry must be peaceable and without the use of force, or she will commit an offence under s.6 Criminal Law Act 1977, as amended. The House of Lords in *Billson* v. *Residential Apartments* [1992] 2 WLR 15 criticised the use of this self-help remedy, and it may be safer for the landlady to go to court for an order for possession, particularly in the light of potential claims under the Human Rights Act. Where the premises are residential and the tenant is in occupation, under s.2 Protection from Eviction Act 1977 the landlady *must* apply to the court for a possession order before re-entering.

However, before the landlady may proceed to forfeit the lease for non-payment of rent, she must issue a formal demand for payment, although most carefully drafted leases will contain a term permitting the landlady to forfeit the lease for non-payment of rent 'whether formally demanded or not'. If the lease contains such a term, or if the rent is six months or more in arrears, no formal demand is necessary before seeking to forfeit the lease.

Once the landlady has gone to court, the tenant might be able to claim 'relief' against forfeiture for non-payment of rent under s.212 Common Law Procedure Act 1852 (in the High Court) or s.138 County Courts Act 1984 (in the County Court). This is exactly what it sounds like: very simply, if the tenant pays the arrears and costs, she may be reinstated. (The rules here are intricate and somewhat illogical because of the interplay of equity, common law and statute.)

Breach of other covenants

General remedies for breach of a tenant's covenant are forfeiture or damages or an injunction; a tenant may only be able to obtain damages or an injunction but, although she cannot forfeit the lease when the landlady is in breach, there is a suggestion (in *Hussein* v. *Mehlman* [1992] 2 EGLR 87, and see below p. 75) that a tenant might be able to use contract law to repudiate a tenancy where the landlady is in fundamental or repudiatory breach of her repairing covenant.

Forfeiture

If there is a forfeiture clause, the landlady must give notice to the tenant by s.146 LPA.

The s.146 notice must specify:

- the breach; and
- the remedy (if the breach is capable of remedy); and
- the compensation (if appropriate or required).

(Section 146 notices do not apply in respect of non-payment of rent.)

The purpose of the s.146 procedure is to give tenants an opportunity to remedy their breach, if this is possible, so that they do not lose their lease through forfeiture. It is, therefore, important to know which breaches can be remedied and which cannot.

The traditional view had been that the breach of a positive covenant could be remedied by the tenant simply performing whatever it was the lease required her to do, and some negative covenants could be remedied by ending the activity which was causing the breach and promising to comply with the lease thereafter. The issue of remediability was examined in *Expert Clothing Service and Sales Ltd* v. *Hillgate House Ltd* [1986] Ch 340. In this case it had been agreed that the tenant should convert the premises but, because of lack of money, the tenant had not even begun the work by the date by which it should have been completed. Expert Clothing issued a s.146 notice, claiming that the breach was irremediable. The Court of Appeal stated that the purpose of s.146 was to give the tenant 'one last chance', and that whether a breach was capable of remedy depended, not on the nature of the breach but rather on the nature of the harm caused to the landlady and whether financial compensation would be sufficient.

In *Savva* v. *Hussein* (1997) 73 P & CR 150, the tenants were in minor breach of covenants not to put up signs or to alter the premises. On the question of whether such breaches were capable of remedy, Staughton LJ stated:

> When something has been done without consent, it is not possible to restore the matter wholly to the situation which it was in before the breach. The moving finger writes and cannot be recalled. That is not to my mind what is meant by a remedy; it is a remedy if the mischief caused by the breach can be removed. In the case of a covenant not to make alterations without consent or not to display signs without consent, if there is a breach of that, the mischief can be removed by removing the signs or restoring the property to the state it was in before the alterations. (p. 154)

It appears, therefore, that only a few breaches are now considered to be irremediable: a wrongful subletting is irremediable, and using the premises for immoral purposes in breach of covenant may well be, since this activity might cast a stigma on the premises which could only disappear with the removal of the tenant (*Rugby School* v. *Tannahill* [1935] 1 KB 87). In *Glass* v. *Kencakes Ltd* [1966] 1 QB 611 the tenant's breach was remediable, since he himself had committed no immoral act on the premises and had taken the appropriate action against his immoral subtenant by evicting her.

If the tenant does not, or cannot, remedy the breach within a reasonable time, the landlady can go to court for a possession order. Again, the tenant (or subtenant) can apply for relief under s.146(2) LPA, even if the breach is considered irremediable. The House of Lords held in *Billson* (above) that a tenant can apply for relief whether or not the landlady has actually re-entered the land, providing there is no final court order granting possession. Here the tenant was carrying out building work in breach of covenant so the landlord served a s.146 notice and then re-entered by changing the locks. Since there was no court order granting possession at this stage (these were not residential premises, so there had been no breach of the criminal law – see 6.2), the House of Lords sent the case back to the trial court for a decision as to whether relief was to be granted.

If the lease is forfeit, any sublease will also disappear since its existence depends on the headlease. Therefore, s.146(4) LPA allows the subtenant to apply for relief and, if she is successful, she steps into the shoes of the tenant but cannot gain a term longer than her original sublease.

In an attempt to prevent abuse of the s.146 procedure by landladies, especially when attempting to forfeit the lease against leaseholders who are unable or unwilling to pay unreasonable service charges, ss 168, 169 Commonhold and Leasehold Reform Act 2002 prevent a landlady of most residential leases over 21 years from issuing a s.146 notice unless either the leaseholder has admitted the breach of covenant or the landlady has established the breach to the satisfaction of a leasehold valuation tribunal. If the breach consists of arrears of service charges, the landlady must also show that the charges are not excessive. Even if the tribunal is satisfied as to the breach, the leaseholder may not be served with the s.146 notice for a further 14 days.

Damages, injunctions and specific performance

Damages and/or an injunction may be appropriate remedies for some breaches, and are available to both lessor and lessee. Specific performance was thought, until recently, to be available only to the tenant in cases of the landlady's breach of her repairing covenant, but *Rainbow Estates* v. *Tokenhold* [1999] Ch 64 has extended this remedy to the landlady 'in appropriate circumstances', although these will be rare – in this case the lease had no provision for the landlord to forfeit the lease for the tenant's breach or even to enter the premises to carry out the repairs himself. Specific performance will not usually be available if damages are an appropriate remedy, but here the property was a listed building in serious disrepair and the condition of the premises was continuing to deteriorate; an award of damages would not have helped the landlord. The traditional reason for the courts' reluctance to order specific performance in these circumstances, that the order would need continuing supervision by the court, was not seen as presenting a difficulty if there was a clear definition of the work to be done.

The House of Lords took the orthodox approach to specific performance in *Co-operative Insurance Society Ltd* v. *Argyll Stores (Holdings) Ltd* [1998] AC 1, in which it refused to make an order preventing Safeway from closing one of its stores, despite the company having contracted with its landlord, the owner of a shopping mall, to keep it open. Lord Hoffmann distinguished the performance of repairing obligations in a lease from the obligation to continue in a business relationship.

At present, tenants often have very serious problems in persuading their landladies to carry out repairs; one rationale for the introduction of 'commonhold' has been the need to address the problems faced by tenants in rundown mansion blocks (see 6.6 below). Although tenants can seek the remedies discussed above, if they hold a comparatively insecure assured shorthold tenancy, they may often be reluctant to bring an action against their landlady knowing that renewal or extension of their tenancy would probably be unlikely. An alternative remedy could be to pay for the repairs themselves and deduct the cost from the rent without becoming liable for non-payment (a 'right of set-off' – see *Lee Parker* v. *Izzet* [1971] 1 WLR 1688).

In *Hussein* v. *Mehlman* (above p. 72), a rented house was uninhabitable due to the lack of repair; the tenant not only won damages but was entitled to end the lease because of the fundamental nature of the landlord's breach of covenant. *Hussein* was a first instance decision in the County Court, but several subsequent cases, including the Court of Appeal decision in *Chartered Trust plc* v. *Davies* [1997] EGLR 83, have accepted that repudiation by a tenant can be appropriate. This is a welcome extension of contractual principles but, although appearing similar to the landlady's remedy of forfeiture, by its very nature it is clearly limited to cases where the landlady has breached a fundamental term of the lease. Nor is it likely to be available for the landlady in the case of a tenant's repudiatory breach, since that would mean that the statutory and common law protection available to tenants could be avoided by an uncompromising landlady.

The number of dwellings which are unfit for human habitation has decreased considerably in recent years. Even so, in the private rented sector, in 2001 some 11% were unfit, and half were not considered to be in a 'decent' state (source: English Housing Condition Survey 2001). In 1996, the Law Commission published a Report ((1996) Law Com No 238) recommending new implied terms in residential leases to the effect that lessors of seven years or less of residential property should be responsible for maintaining the premises in a fit state throughout the period. This recommendation has not been taken up by the government.

Instead of relying on contractual provisions within the lease, sometimes the tenant's best solution is to get the local authority to take action. Under s.604 Housing Act 1985 a local authority has the power to declare a dwelling unfit for human habitation and to issue a notice to the landlady requiring her to remedy the defects. If she fails to do so within the specified time, the local authority can do the work itself and recover its expenses from the landlady. The Housing Bill 2003 contains provisions which are intended to replace the existing fitness standards contained in s.604 and to provide a 'more effective basis for enforcement against unacceptable housing conditions'.

6.6 Commonhold

If someone wants to buy a flat rather than merely rent one on a short-term basis, the only way to do so up to now has been through buying a long lease on it, frequently by means of a mortgage. As will become evident (see Chapter 9, below), in freehold land it is frequently not possible to enforce covenants against successors of the original covenantor. However, this is precisely what the owner of a flat in a mansion block, for example, might wish to do. In order to protect the structural integrity of her own property, she or her landlady might have occasion to seek to enforce a repairing covenant against her neighbour. The only answer has been for all the flats in the block to be held on long leases, since, as we have seen, leasehold covenants are enforceable against successors in title.

However, there are difficulties with the use of the lease in such situations. The most obvious is that a lease is a diminishing asset and, eventually, will disappear (see 5.1 above). Even before that happens the lease will become unmarketable, since mortgage lenders are unwilling to lend on leases with less than 60 years to run. A further difficulty may be the inability of the tenants to get the landlady to manage the building and carry out her obligations to repair and maintain the common parts while keeping the tenants' financial contributions at a reasonable level. These problems have been addressed at various times by Parliament, but no entirely satisfactory solution has been found. The latest statute, the Commonhold and Leasehold Reform Act 2002, Part 2, contains further provisions for allowing qualifying tenants of long residential leaseholds the right to take over management of the property from the landlady, even if the latter is not at fault.

For about twenty years, there have been discussions on proposals to introduce a new form of land holding called 'commonhold', based to some extent on strata title in Australia and condominium title in the United States. After a good deal of uncertainty and procrastination, these proposals have been enacted in the Commonhold and Leasehold Reform Act 2002, Part 1, which is due to come into force in 2004. Commonhold is intended to avoid the problems with long leaseholds mentioned above.

A property to be owned on a commonhold basis (for example, a block of flats or an industrial estate) is registered at the Land Registry by the freehold owner as a 'freehold estate in commonhold land'. The property is divided into 'units', each held by the unit owner on a freehold basis. The owner of each unit becomes a member of the Commonhold Association, a private company limited by guarantee, which owns and has responsibility for the upkeep of the common parts of the building. Under the regulations in the Commonhold Community Statement (CCS), each unit owner has obligations (for example to maintain her unit in good repair and to contribute to the commonhold expenditure), binding on her successors and enforceable by the Association – a kind of private local community law. The enforcement of the rules in the CCS takes place initially through an internal complaints procedure, then, depending on Regulations introduced through secondary legislation, through some form of mediation or arbitration or through an Ombudsman, before finally moving towards formal legal proceedings.

The advantage of the commonhold scheme is that all the obligations in the CCS are binding on all unit holders at all times, so that there is no longer any need to use the unsatisfactory device of a long lease in order to buy an interest in a shared building. The scheme should also remove the associated problems of 'unreasonable and oppressive behaviour by unscrupulous landlords' (Commonhold and Leasehold Reform Consultation Paper, Cm 4843, 2000, p. 107) and the difficulties of getting mortgage finance in the later years of a lease. Of course, as the Law Commission has remarked, the scheme will not by itself solve the problems: neighbours will not always co-operate, and buildings cannot be repaired for ever. Nevertheless, commonhold gives land developers a new flexibility when building new blocks of flats or developing industrial areas.

However, the new Act does little to help those tenants who currently hold long leases on residential flats and who may wish to convert to commonhold, since the consent of all the long leaseholders (those with leases over 21 years) must be obtained, and it is thought unlikely that this will be feasible in practice. Most commonholds, therefore, will be the result of new property developments.

For commentary on and further criticism of the new law, see Clarke [2002] Conv 349.

6.7 **Comment**

The law on leasehold covenants is complex and extensive with many detailed rules, areas of uncertainty and a lack of proportionality in the remedies available to landladies and tenants. To some degree, the history of the law demonstrates the failure of legislators and judges to resolve political, social and economic problems in this field. It has never been easy to balance the varying interests of landladies, tenants and society in general – the passage of the Landlord and Tenant (Covenants) Bill 1995 is an example of the operation of the powerful interests and lobbies which influence the making of new laws.

The Law Commission has recognised the need for reform, particularly in regard to forfeiture (see, for example *Landlord and Tenant Law: Termination of Tenancies Bill*, (1994) Law Com No 221), and formal proposals are awaited. The last chapter referred to the possibility of residential leases eventually having the status of consumer contracts (see 5.8 above) and this would result in residential tenants receiving the benefit of consumer remedies against their landladies, considerably strengthening their position.

Much is expected of the new commonhold regime, but its effectiveness may well depend on the willingness of property developers to engage with this novel form of land holding.

Summary

6.1 Commonly found leasehold covenants include: the landlady's covenants for quiet enjoyment and non-derogation from grant; covenants to repair; the tenant's covenant not to assign or sublet without consent.

6.2 In leases made before 1996, a covenant automatically runs with the land if there is privity of estate and the covenant touches and concerns the land; the original tenant remains liable on all the covenants but may claim an indemnity from her assignee or the current tenant; the original tenant is entitled to an overriding lease when she has paid money due by the current tenant.

6.3 In leases made after 1995, all covenants run with land unless expressed to be personal; the original tenant ceases automatically to be liable for any breach after assigning the lease (but can be liable under an authorised guarantee agreement) but the original landlady may remain liable, unless she obtains a release from the current tenant or from the court.

6.4 Remedies for non-payment of rent are normally forfeiture, distress or an action for recovery.

6.5 Remedies for breaches of other covenants include forfeiture, damages and injunction; breach of the landlady's repairing covenant may involve local authority powers or a tenant's right to repudiate the lease.

6.6 The procedures for forfeiture for breach of the covenant to pay rent and forfeiture for other breaches are different.

6.7 A new form of landownership – commonhold – is due to be introduced in 2004.

Exercises

6.1 What is the difference between 'common covenants' and 'usual covenants'?

6.2 When is a landlady liable for repairs under a lease?

6.3 Under what circumstances may a landlady repossess her land?

6.4 Will the introduction of commonhold be an improvement on the use of the lease for long-term occupation of shared buildings?

6.5 Four years ago, Ronald granted a six-year lease of a house to Alan. Alan covenanted that he would pay the rent on time, would paint the exterior every three years and would not use the premises for illegal or immoral purposes. Ronald reserved the right to re-enter the premises for breach of any covenant.

  The following year, Ronald sold his freehold reversion to Keegan. Two years ago Alan assigned his lease to Jane.

  Keegan has found out that Jane has been smoking cannabis in her house, that she has allowed her friend Sally to use it for prostitution, much to the annoyance of the next door neighbour, and that she has not painted the house at all. She is five months in arrears with her rent. Four months ago, the roof began to leak badly whenever it rained and the bedroom ceiling has collapsed as a result. Keegan has steadfastly refused to carry out any repairs, and Jane is obliged to live on the ground floor.

Jane wants to know what she can do about the state of the house and whether she can be evicted by Keegan. Advise her.

Further Reading

Bridge, 'Former Tenants, Future Liabilities and the Privity of Contract Principle: The Landlord and Tenant (Covenants) Act 1995' [1996] CLJ 313

Bright and Gilbert, *Landlord and Tenant Law: The Nature of Tenancies* (Oxford: Clarendon Press, 1995)

Clarke, 'The Enactment of Commonhold – Problems, Principles and Perspectives' [2002] Conv 349

Davey, 'Privity of Contract and Leases – Reform at Last' (1996) 59 MLR 78

Pawlowski, 'Acceptance of Repudiatory Breach in Leases' [1995] Conv 379

Roberts, 'Commonhold: A New Property Term – But No Property in a Term' [2002] Conv 341

Samuels, 'The Tenant Seeks Consent for Assignment: Is the Refusal of the Landlord Reasonable?' [2002] Conv 307

Walter, 'Landlord and Tenant (Covenants) Act 1995: a Legislative Folly' [1996] Conv 432

Walton, 'Landlord's Distress – Past Its Sell By Date?' [2000] Conv 508

7 Mortgages

7.1 **Introduction**

Most of the rules in the law of mortgages are relatively straightforward and conform with common sense. However, the language and the concepts are not quite as they might appear at first sight. It used to be said that a mortgage deed was 'a suppression of truth and a suggestion of falsehood', and this mismatch of expectation and theory can at first be disconcerting: it is essential to keep hold of the rules while exploring the theory. As far as the language is concerned, perhaps the easiest way to assimilate the technical terms is to try and explain them to your most tolerant friend.

The word 'mortgage' is used in two senses by lawyers; first, it is a relationship between a landowner and a money-lender: the landowner creates a charge over the land in favour of the lender (see 7.2 below). The second use of the word is as a way of referring to the interest – the charge – granted as security. Contrary to the way most people talk, the mortgage is the interest in the land exchanged for the money: a mortgage is not borrowed money. When the letter arrives to say that a bank or a building society will lend the money to buy a house, the pedantic borrower should not say, 'They're giving me a mortgage!', but rather, 'They're letting me grant them a mortgage.' Thus, the mortgagor (the borrower) grants a mortgage to the mortgagee (the lender) (see Figure 7.1).

Mortgage relationships have existed since Anglo-Saxon times but their form has changed a good deal since then. Since the seventeenth century, the harsh common law approach has been softened by equity which intervened in contracts between borrowers (typified as the poverty-stricken sons of the aristocracy) and money-lenders. The basic principle behind equity's intervention in mortgages is that one party (the lender) should not take an unconscionable advantage of the other (the borrower). In more recent times, Parliament has intervened to offer some measure of statutory protection to borrowers, and the courts now generally recognise the commercial and contractual reality of mortgage agreements while at

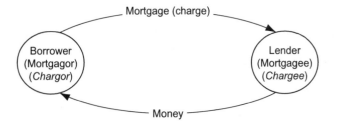

Figure 7.1 A mortgage agreement

the same time attempting to preserve equity's protection for the vulnerable.

This area of land law illustrates very clearly the way in which land simultaneously fulfils several functions. With the development of capitalism, land was seen as an asset to be mortgaged in order to raise finance for commercial enterprise and this is very much the case today – for example, many small businesses are financed by means of a mortgage on the home of the owner of the business. The mortgage is also the device by which many people become landowners – the bank or the building society lends money to buy land which itself provides the security for the loan. Such mortgages are known as 'acquisition mortgages'. The land is used as a home by the borrowers and – they hope – it is at the same time an investment, an appreciating asset, although the assumption that land would always increase in value was shaken by the slump in property values in the early 1990s, with many borrowers finding themselves in negative equity – having a debt larger than the value of their home.

Because of the many functions which land fulfils – shelter, security, direct or indirect investment – it can be difficult to untangle the financial interests when there is a dispute. Some cases, for example, concern the lender coming into conflict with an owner of a beneficial interest in land subject to a trust where the trustee has mortgaged it without declaring the beneficial interest. Where the courts decide against the lender, the burden is widely shared; where they decide against the beneficiary, he alone bears the cost.

There may be several mortgages created over one interest in land. Also, mortgages may be granted on any interest in land; thus, mortgages are frequently granted on leases, although a lender would tend to consider that only a long lease provides sufficient security (see 6.6 above). Mortgages of other property, such as company shares, can be created and the same general rules apply. Some of the commercial cases in this chapter concern such mortgages.

7.2 The Creation of Mortgages

Legal mortgages

The mortgage by legal charge (s.87 LPA 1925) is nowadays the customary means of creating a legal mortgage and, indeed, is now the only way of mortgaging registered land (s.23(1)(a) Land Registration Act 2002). It is simple, is created by the execution of a deed and can be used for mortgages of either freehold or leasehold land.

Under s.85 LPA 1925, it is possible to mortgage unregistered freehold land by granting the lender a long lease (perhaps 3000 years) containing terms setting the date for the money to be repaid (the contractual date of redemption) and for the lease to be surrendered to the borrower when the mortgage is redeemed (the mortgage money is repaid). This latter term is known as a provision for cesser on redemption. In a similar way, by s.86 a long lease of land with unregistered title can be mortgaged by the creation of a sublease. However, since these two methods of creating a mortgage are more complex than using the charge and are now restricted to unregistered titles, they are probably more or less obsolete.

Equitable mortgages

It is important to know whether a mortgage is legal or equitable because, as well as the lesser security of equitable interests if the land is sold, the remedies of the lender may be different. Equitable mortgages or charges may arise in three situations:

1   Where the borrower has only an equitable interest in the land, such as a beneficial interest under a trust (see Chapter 12). This equitable interest is mortgaged by assigning it in writing to the lender who will promise to re-assign it when the debt is repaid. (Before 1925, this was the means by which legal estates were mortgaged; this is now impossible at law, although any attempt to do it with a legal interest in unregistered land will create a 3000-year lease (or a sublease) instead (ss 85, 86 LPA 1925).)

2   Where, in unregistered land, there has been an attempt at creating a legal mortgage by means of a forgery. The mortgage will only be effective against the equitable interest of the forger and not against the interests of any innocent co-owner – see *First National Securities Ltd* v. *Hegarty* [1984] 1 All ER 139.

3   Where there is a contract for a legal mortgage under s.2 Law of Property (Miscellaneous Provisions) Act 1989, or by estoppel. An equitable mortgage, therefore, will come into existence before its conversion into a legal mortgage through the execution of a deed (see Chapter 2). Before 1989 an equitable mortgage could be created by depositing the title deeds or land certificate with the lender in exchange for the loan, since this was seen as part performance of an oral contract, but now that part performance has been abolished this method of creating a mortgage is obsolete, as confirmed by *United Bank of Kuwait plc* v. *Sahib* [1997] Ch 107 (and see Robinson (1997) 113 LQR 533).

7.3 The Position of the Lender

The legal lender

The lender (mortgagee) has remedies to enforce the payment of the money due to him (1–6 in the following list) and certain other rights. The legal mortgagee may:

1   take possession of the property;
2   sell the property;
3   appoint a receiver;

4   foreclose;
5   sue on the personal covenant;
6   consolidate;
7   hold the title deeds (or, in registered land, the charge certificate, if there is one);
8   exercise rights in connection with a series of mortgages ('tacking').

The lender does not have to choose between the remedies: he can pursue several at the same time. They were developed when mortgages were not so commonly used for home buying and have been adjusted by statute to protect the security of home buyers, just as tenants' security has been protected to some extent by modern legislation.

The issues which arise where there are several mortgages on the same land are referred to later in this section and in 7.6 below. Some of the other rights are examined here, but first it is necessary to examine a problem which can particularly affect the rights and remedies of the lender: 'undue influence'.

Avoiding undue influence
The question of undue influence in mortgages has recently been raised in a large number of cases – a symptom of the increase in family home repossessions which occurred in the early 1990s when interest rates were high and the value of property was falling. In a typical undue influence case, a lender seeks to repossess a home because of arrears, and one of the joint borrowers then claims to have signed the mortgage deed or stood surety for the loan under the undue influence of the other, claiming that she (generally) was unaware of the implications of her actions. In this situation, the question for the court is not whether one party acted towards the other unconscionably or in breach of trust; it is whether the lending institution had notice of the undue influence or was in some other way responsible for it. If the lender did not take steps to ensure that the signature was properly obtained without any undue influence, the mortgage will be void as far as the injured party is concerned.

The facts of two House of Lords cases are typical of the kind of situations where a lender might be fixed with the undue influence of the borrower. In the first of the cases, *Barclays Bank plc* v. *O'Brien* [1994] 1 AC 180, Mr O'Brien was the sole legal owner of the matrimonial home, but his wife had an equitable share in it. He told her he was borrowing £60 000 on a mortgage for three weeks to save his business, so she signed all the surety forms at the bank without reading any of them and without any independent advice. In fact, the loan was for £135 000; within six months the repayments were seriously in arrears and the bank sought possession. Mrs O'Brien successfully argued that the mortgage had been induced by her husband's undue influence and that the bank had constructive notice of this, giving rise to her right to set the mortgage aside.

In the second case, *CIBC Mortgages* v. *Pitt* [1994] 1 AC 200, the facts were fairly similar but here Mrs Pitt, the wife, was a joint legal owner of the home. As joint legal owner she could be presumed, on the facts, to be benefiting financially from the mortgage loan (its purpose was expressed to be to pay off an outstanding mortgage and to buy a second home, but the husband really wanted the money in order to play the stock market) and therefore the bank was not put on notice to take steps to protect her position.

Following *O'Brien* and *Pitt*, and after a series of undue influence cases which have exercised the minds of the judges in recent times, the House of Lords, in what is now the leading case on undue influence, *Royal Bank of Scotland* v. *Etridge (No. 2)* [2002] 2 AC 773, had another opportunity to review the law in this area. The issues were these: firstly, under what circumstances is a lender put on notice that there may have been undue influence; and secondly, if the lender is on notice, what steps must it take to avoid any subsequent claim by the innocent joint borrower or surety. Until *Etridge*, a lender would be placed on inquiry in situations where the surety trusted the debtor to deal with her financial affairs or where both were living together in a close emotional relationship. For the future, however, the lender will be on inquiry in all cases where the relationship between the debtor and the surety is non-commercial.

In such circumstances:

[t]he furthest a bank can be expected to go is to take reasonable steps to satisfy itself that the wife has had brought home to her, in a meaningful way, the practical implications of the proposed transaction. This does not wholly eliminate the risk of undue influence or misrepresentation. But it does mean that a wife enters into a transaction with her eyes open so far as the basic elements of the transaction are concerned. (Lord Nicholls at para. 54)

The bank will be considered to have taken these reasonable steps if it tells the wife or other person in a non-commercial relationship to the debtor that it requires a solicitor of her choice (who may be the family solicitor, but who must be acting for her) to confirm in writing that she has had the documents and the practical implications of the arrangement explained to her – that she risks losing her home if the mortgage payments are not met – so that at a later stage she cannot complain that she is not legally bound. The bank must provide the necessary financial information to allow the solicitor properly to advise the wife; if the debtor will not allow such confidential information to be passed on, the transaction will not be able to proceed. Finally, if the bank has reason to believe that the wife is not acting of her own free will, it must inform the solicitor of this.

This complex area of mortgage law indicates the sort of policy tensions which can arise in land law and how the courts deal with them; it is important that lenders are able to lend money on the security of property without being concerned that their security will be lost, and at the same time it is just as important that the rights of more vulnerable owners are protected (see also, for example, *Williams & Glyn's Bank* v. *Boland* [1981] AC 487, *City of London Building Society* v. *Flegg* [1988] AC 54, Chapter 11).

Taking possession

In theory, because he either has a lease or, if the mortgage has been created by a charge, he is treated as though he has a lease (s.87(1) LPA 1925), a lender has the right to 'go into possession before the ink is dry on the mortgage', although generally he will promise not to take possession unless the borrower fails to pay. It might seem extraordinary that the lender has the right to move in as soon as the mortgage deed is signed but, although it was common in the past, in practice this only happens nowadays if the borrower defaults. The lender will then probably want to sell the property with vacant possession (but see below for other remedies) and will generally obtain a court order before taking possession, although this is not strictly necessary providing there is no breach of s.6 Criminal Law Act 1977 which makes it an offence to use or threaten violence to gain entry into premises.

Where the property is (or includes) a home, s.36 Administration of Justice Act 1970 (as amended by s.8 Administration of Justice Act 1973) gives the court the discretion to postpone an order giving the lender possession if the borrower is likely to be able to pay his arrears 'within a reasonable period'. In the harsh economic climate of the late 1980s and early 1990s, repossessions increased in frequency – doubling between 1989 and 1991 – and affected the whole market in land. A number of cases have therefore focused on the issue of when the court might exercise its s.36 discretion; some have concerned the defaulting borrower's likelihood of finding employment and repaying arrears, and others on the chances of his being able to sell the land within a reasonable period.

The Court of Appeal stated in *Cheltenham and Gloucester Building Society* v. *Norgan* [1996] 1 All ER 449 that, although a 'normal' period of two years had become fairly established in judgments, 'a reasonable period' was not limited to any particular length of time. In *Norgan*, the mortgage term was to end 13 years from the time of the claim for a possession order, and the Court held that this could be a reasonable period within 'the logic and spirit of the Act'; they effectively asked the lower court to decide whether it could reschedule the debt over the whole repayment period. In future cases, such a rescheduling from the outset of the mortgagor's difficulties might avoid the continuing struggle and repeated orders and delays in repossession proceedings.

On the rare occasion that the lender enters into lawful possession without a court order, perhaps because by now the property is standing empty, the borrower in arrears will be unable to apply for relief under s.36, since that section only applies if an action for possession has been brought. This was confirmed 'reluctantly' by the Court of Appeal in *Ropaigealach* v. *Barclays Bank plc* [2000] 1 QB 263, but this might now be open to challenge under Articles 6 and 8 and Article 1, Protocol 1 of the European Convention on Human Rights (see Rook, 2001, p. 199).

Sale

If the mortgage is made by deed, and unless there is a term to the contrary in the contract, the power of sale arises as soon as the contractual date for redeeming the mortgage has passed (s.101 LPA 1925). On most domestic mortgages, the contractual date of redemption is usually set six months after the creation of the mortgage in order to allow the lender to realise its security if this becomes necessary.

However, by s.103 LPA 1925, the lender cannot exercise the power unless one of the conditions listed in the box is satisfied:

The power of sale becomes exercisable if:

- the default continues three months after a notice requiring payment is served; or
- interest is two months in default; or
- the borrower has broken another term of the mortgage.

Although he only has a charge (or a long lease or sublease), the lender may sell the borrower's whole interest as soon as one of these conditions has been fulfilled (ss 88–9). He does not need a court order (but he usually has one granting possession). The exercise of the power of sale against the family home can have distressing effects on the family, but any attempt to invoke ECHR Article 8 (the right to respect for a person's private and family life and home) will not succeed, since the Article cannot be used 'to diminish the contractual and proprietary rights of the mortgagee under the mortgage' (*Harrow LBC* v. *Qazi* [2003] UKHL 43, para. 135, per Lord Scott, and see 1.6 above)).

Although the lender may choose when to sell and does not have to wait for an upturn in the market, when he does sell he is under a duty to the borrower to take reasonable care to get the best price reasonably obtainable 'on the day'.

In a Privy Council case from Hong Kong, *China and South Seas Bank* v. *Tan* [1990] 1 AC 536, there was a mortgage loan of $HK30m on the security of shares. When the repayment became due, the shares were worth enough to repay the debt but by the time the mortgagee decided to exercise his power of sale the shares were worthless. The mortgage's surety argued that the mortgagee owed him a duty of care to sell as soon as possible, but this was rejected:

> If the creditor chose to exercise his power of sale over the mortgaged security he must sell for the current market value but the creditor must decide in his own interest if and when he should sell. The creditor does not become a trustee of the mortgaged securities. (Lord Templeman at p. 545)

In another case from Hong Kong, *Tse Kwong Lam* v. *Wong Chit Sen* [1983] 1 WLR 1349, Tse had granted a mortgage to Wong in 1963 on a large development in Hong Kong. Three years later he was in arrears and the land was sold at auction to the only bidder, a company owned by the lender and his wife and children. This in itself would not necessarily have been relevant, but the lender could not show that:

he protected the interests of the borrower by taking expert advice as to the method of sale, as to the steps which ought reasonably to be taken to make the sale a success and as to the amount of the reserve [minimum price]. (Lord Templeman, p. 1359)

The normal remedy in such a case is for the sale to be set aside, but here the Privy Council did not do so because the borrower had been 'guilty of inexcusable delay'; he had not pursued the matter for many years. He won the alternative remedy of damages, the difference between the price which was obtained and the price which should have been obtained.

An example of where the lender was negligent in exercising its power of sale is *Cuckmere Brick Ltd* v. *Mutual Finance Ltd* [1971] Ch 949. In this case, the lender had failed to advertise to prospective purchasers the full extent of the planning permission which attached to the property, and as a result was liable to the mortgagors for the shortfall.

Once the land is sold, the lender is under a duty to account to the borrower. He must also take care to protect the interests of others. He uses the proceeds of sale to pay his expenses and to pay himself the capital and interest due under the mortgage; he then holds the rest for whomever is entitled (s.105 LPA 1925). This will usually be the borrower but it may be a second or subsequent mortgagee if there is more than one mortgage. Thus, although he is not a trustee of his power of sale, he is a trustee of the proceeds of sale and must act in good faith.

A buyer from a mortgagee must check that a power of sale exists but need not make sure that it has actually arisen. However, if he knows of, or suspects, any 'impropriety' he might not get a good title and for this reason he would be wise to ensure that the mortgagee has taken reasonable care, otherwise he might lose the land and have to try to get the purchase price back from the mortgagee.

Preventing sale

Sometimes, especially when the value of land has been falling, the mortgagee might seek to prevent, rather than to force, a sale of the mortgaged land. Where there is negative equity, the borrower may be keen to have the land sold to repay as much of the debt as possible in order to prevent the interest due on the loan from spiralling upwards, whereas the lender may be as keen to prevent a sale, leasing out the land in the meantime in the hope that it might increase in value at some point in the future.

This situation arose in *Palk* v. *Mortgage Services Funding plc* [1993] 2 WLR 415 where the borrower had found a buyer for the land, but the price was about £50 000 less than the then mortgage debt. The interest on the debt was accumulating at a rate of £43 000 a year and an annual rent – as sought by the mortgagee – would not be more than about £13 000. The mortgagee argued that it could prevent a sale if the price was less than the amount needed to repay the debt in full. Mrs Palk claimed, however, that under s.91 LPA (originally intended to facilitate sales in foreclosure proceedings) the court has a discretion to order a sale of mortgaged property. Here the Court of Appeal held for Mrs Palk: any borrower, even one suffering with a negative equity, can ask the court to order a sale because the court has an 'unfettered discretion' under s.91 to prevent 'manifest unfairness'.

Occasionally, as in *Target Home Loans Ltd* v. *Clothier* [1994] 1 All ER 439, the courts will postpone a possession order to allow the borrower, rather than the lender, to sell the property, since the borrower is much more likely to get a higher price. Following the Court of Appeal decision in *Cheltenham & Gloucester plc* v. *Krausz* [1997] 1 All ER 21, however, it is unlikely that the courts will take this line in cases where there is negative equity, and the borrower will be entitled to possession and sale (see also Kenny [1998] Conv 223).

Appointing a receiver

A lender can appoint a receiver – who manages the land – in the same circumstances in which he has the power of sale (s.101 LPA). This can be very convenient in a commercial mortgage, for example, if the land is let to tenants and the mortgagee wants the rents to pay off interest which is due. The advantage of appointing a receiver rather than going into possession is that a mortgagee in possession is personally liable to the borrower for any loss but, if he appoints a receiver, the receiver must pay for his own mistakes. This is because, by s.109 LPA, the receiver is deemed to be the agent of the mortgagor (the borrower). In *Medforth* v. *Blake* [2000] Ch 86, the Court of Appeal considered that the duties owed by a receiver to a borrower and others interested in the equity of redemption (see 7.4) are not just confined to a duty of good faith but extend to managing the property with due diligence, subject to trying to create a situation whereby the debt can be paid off. However, in the recent case of *Silven Properties* v. *Royal Bank of Scotland* [2003] EWCA Civ 1409, the Court confirmed that the receiver's duty to manage the property does not require him to go so far as to undertake its improvement in order to increase its value, since his primary duty is to effect the repayment of the secured debt.

Foreclosure

This is an equitable order which ends all the borrower's rights to the land and is now extremely rare. Once the legal date of redemption has passed, the order is theoretically available, but it is only granted if the court is clear that the borrower will never be able to repay. In very special circumstances, the foreclosure order can be reopened.

Suing on the personal covenant

If the amount realised on the sale of the mortgaged land is insufficient to cover the amount owed to the lender, the borrower remains personally liable to the lender for the shortfall, and the lender may sue him for the outstanding sum.

The borrower's liability on his personal covenant can have other, potentially very serious, consequences. In *Alliance and Leicester plc* v. *Slayford* (2000) 33 HLR 743, a lender had been unable to get an order for possession against a borrower, whose wife had a very small equitable interest in the house and had successfully claimed that the lender was fixed with her husband's undue influence. The lender decided to sue on the borrower's personal covenant to repay, which would have had the eventual effect of making the borrower bankrupt. The trustee in bankruptcy could then apply for sale of the house under s.14 Trusts of Land and Appointment of Trustees Act 1996 and probably succeed (see 12.8). Although the lender would lose its priority over the bankrupt borrower's unsecured creditors, at least by these means it would get some of its money back. The wife, however, would lose her home, despite the mortgage having earlier been declared void against her. In somewhat forthright language the trial judge stated that the mortgagee's tactic amounted to an abuse of the process of the court. However, the Court of Appeal had little difficulty in finding for the mortgagee: it was not an abuse for it to employ any or all of the legal remedies available to it. (For comment on this case, see Thompson [2002] Conv 53.)

Consolidation

In rare cases, where the mortgagee has lent money on mortgages granted by the same borrower over different pieces of land, he has a right to consolidate them. This means that he may join the various mortgages together; he can refuse to allow the borrower to redeem one of the mortgages without redeeming the other(s). Consolidation can be useful if one piece of land is not sufficient security for the debt. The right arises when the power is contained in the mortgage itself, and is exercisable only when the contractual date for redemption has passed. There are a number of technical rules, very clearly explained in Megarry, 2002, pp. 515–18.

Holding the title documents

The first legal mortgagee of unregistered land is entitled to hold the deeds which are returned to the borrower on redemption. However, if such a mortgage were created after March 1998, this first legal mortgage would have triggered the first registration of the land (see 11.4 below) which would have required the deeds to be sent to the Land Registry.

If the title is registered, it used to be the case that the land certificate would remain in the Land Registry and the mortgagee would hold the charge certificate. The system has recently changed and, from 13 October 2003 when the Land Registration Act 2002 took effect, the land certificate can remain with the borrower, charge certificates are no longer issued and any charge is protected by entry on the register (see Chapter 11).

The equitable lender

Both equitable mortgagees and equitable chargees can sue on the borrower's personal promise to pay but, apart from this, their rights differ.

The equitable mortgagee

If an equitable mortgage is not made by deed then there is no automatic power to sell or appoint a receiver, but the mortgagee can get a court order to do so (s.91 LPA 1925). If there is a deed, the equitable lender generally has the same remedies as a legal lender but he must be careful to draft the document to give him the right to sell the legal estate. It is not clear whether he has an automatic right to go into possession.

The equitable chargee
The rights of 'a mere equitable chargee' are fewer than those of other lenders. This kind of lender only has the remedy of sale or appointment of a receiver, both by order of the court.

7.4 The Position of the Borrower

As well as the rights which arise directly out of the lender's duties – for example to take precautions against undue influence and to obtain a good price on sale – the borrower has special rights to protection against oppression by a mortgagee, especially in relation to the terms of the contract.

The equity of redemption

The equity of redemption is the name given to the whole bundle of rights which equity created to protect borrowers against exploitative money-lenders. This bundle of rights is an equitable interest in land and includes:

1 the equitable right to redeem the mortgage;
2 the right to have oppressive terms removed from the contract;
3 the right to seek relief from an extortionate bargain under the Consumer Credit Act 1974.

Historically, equity looks at the substance of an agreement and not at the name given to it and, if it is actually a loan on the security of land, equity will recognise it as a mortgage and protect the borrower, following the maxim 'once a mortgage always a mortgage'. The rules are summarised in the expression that there must be 'no clogs or fetters on the equity of redemption' and are explained in the following sections. However, it must be noted that some of the older cases reflect a different financial world, and, furthermore, one in which the House of Lords was bound to follow its own earlier decisions. It is becoming evident that modern judges will attempt to find a way around inconvenient precedents by, for example, applying general contractual doctrines such as duress and restraint of trade, rather than considering whether a term amounts, in mortgage law theory, to a clog.

The equitable right to redeem
As mentioned in 7.2 above, mortgage agreements always specify a contractual date of redemption. However, if it was fair to do so, equity would refuse to enforce this contractual date and, in creating an equitable right to redeem, would require the lender to accept the money even after the date had passed.

Equity will make void any promise that prevents a borrower from ever redeeming. For example, *Samuel* v. *Jarrah Timber and Wood Paving Co Ltd* [1904] AC 323 concerned a mortgage of company stock (a debenture). In the mortgage deed the borrower gave the lender an option to purchase; the lender could therefore choose to buy the stock from the borrower, thus preventing the borrower from redeeming the mortgage. The House of Lords declared the option void because it made the equitable right to redeem 'illusory'. The decision was made very reluctantly – in 1904 the House could not reverse its own judgments – as their Lordships felt that this arrangement, made by two large companies, was quite different from the kind of case for which the rule had been established:

> The directors of a trading company in search of financial assistance are certainly in a very different position from that of an impecunious landowner in the toils of a crafty money-lender. (Lord Macnaghten, p. 327)

If the option to purchase is seen as a separate agreement from the mortgage agreement, it will be enforced. In *Reeve* v. *Lisle* [1902] AC 461, a mortgage of a ship was created and, some 12 days later, the mortgagor granted the lender an option to purchase it. This was not seen by the court as a clog, since the later agreement could be separated from the mortgage, and the option was held to be enforceable.

In *Jones* v. *Morgan* [2002] 1 EGLR 125, the Court of Appeal struck out a term in a mortgage agreement that purported to give the lender a right to buy a half share in the mortgaged land. In an ordinary contract, the term would have been valid, but since the term was contained within a mortgage agreement, the doctrine of clogs and fetters applied since, again, the Court found itself bound by precedent. However, the doctrine received considerable criticism in the case:

> the doctrine of a clog on the equity of redemption is, so it seems to me, an appendix to our law which no longer serves a useful purpose and would be better excised. (Lord Phillips MR, para. 86)

On the facts in *Jones* v. *Morgan*, the minority judge held the right to buy the half share to be a separate agreement, and was prepared to uphold it on that basis.

In *Warnborough Ltd* v. *Garmite Ltd* [2003] EWCA Civ 1544, the Court of Appeal had the opportunity of reviewing the law on the extent to which an option to purchase amounts to a clog on the equity of redemption. Jonathan Parker LJ stated:

> that the mere fact that, contemporaneously with the grant of a mortgage over his property, the mortgagor grants the mortgagee an option to purchase the property does no more than raise the question whether the rule against 'clogs' applies: it does not begin to answer that question ... the court has to look at the 'substance' of the transaction in question: in other words, to inquire as to the true nature of the bargain which the parties have made. (para. 73)

He went on to state that where the original seller of the property was also both mortgagee and the grantee of the option, as in *Warnborough*, there would be a strong likelihood that the transaction would be held to be one of sale and purchase rather than one of mortgage, and so the doctrine of clogs would not apply.

An agreement which postpones the equitable right to redeem so that it effectively becomes meaningless is likely to be void. This happened in *Fairclough* v. *Swan Brewery Co Ltd* [1912] AC 565, where Mr Fairclough held a 17-year lease of a hotel. His lessor was the Swan Brewery, which lent him money on the security of his lease. The contractual date of redemption was fixed for a few weeks before the lease was due to expire. As the equitable right to redeem does not arise until the contractual date has passed, the mortgage was effectively irredeemable and the promise was therefore held void. However, in *Knightsbridge Estate's Trust Ltd* v. *Byrne* [1939] Ch 441, a case between two large companies, the contractual date for redemption of the mortgage (for £310 000) was set 40 years in the future. Given the reluctance of the courts to intervene when the parties are of equal bargaining power, and also the fact that the land was freehold, the Court of Appeal held that the term was enforceable. This was:

> a commercial agreement between two important corporations, experienced in such matters, and has none of the features of an oppressive bargain. (Greene MR, p. 455)

Another of equity's concerns was the unfair advantage taken by a lender who sought to restrict the borrower's commercial activities, such as requiring a shopkeeper mortgagor to buy wholesale goods only from the mortgagee. These kinds of agreements are known as solus agreements and are common between oil companies and filling stations, and breweries and publicans. Equity had declared void any terms in a mortgage agreement which would prevent the borrower from freely enjoying his land after he had repaid all the money. An example of this is *Noakes & Co Ltd* v. *Rice* [1902] AC 24, where the owner of a 26-year lease of a pub mortgaged it to a brewery, promising he would buy liquor only from the lender for the whole term of the lease. The House of Lords held that the promise was ineffective: the lender could not prevent him regaining his property free of ties when he repaid the loan. In *Kreglinger* v. *New Patagonia Meat & Cold Storage Co Ltd* [1914] AC 25, however, the House decided that a collateral promise that the borrower would sell his sheepskins to no-one but the lender for five years, regardless of when the loan was repaid, was valid. This was not a clog on the equitable right to redeem. The mortgage agreement was a commercial arrangement on reasonable terms between two companies at arm's length and, after redemption, the mortgagor would be able to enjoy the land in the same state as it had been before the mortgage. Nowadays, the courts tend to apply the contractual doctrine of restraint of trade to this kind of issue – see *Esso Petroleum Co Ltd* v. *Harpers Garage (Stourport) Ltd* [1968] AC 269.

Oppressive terms
Equity developed rules against other clogs on the equity of redemption, and declared void any other 'unconscionable or oppressive terms' in the mortgage. In *Multiservice Bookbinding Ltd* v. *Marden* [1979] Ch 84, the bookbinding company granted a mortgage as security for a loan of £36 000. The interest rate was linked to the Swiss franc, because the pound was very unstable. The fluctuation in the money markets meant that the borrower would have to pay £45 000 in interest. Browne-Wilkinson J held that this may have been unreasonable but it was not oppressive or unconscionable. For a promise to be struck out, it must be shown that the objectionable terms were imposed 'in a morally reprehensible manner ... which affects [the mortgagee's] conscience'. Again, the court showed its reluctance to intervene in a commercial agreement between equals.

Many mortgage agreements permit the lender at its discretion to vary the interest rate payable by the borrower. The Court of Appeal in *Paragon Finance plc* v. *Nash* [2002] 1 WLR 685 protected the borrower against the arbitrary exercise of this discretion by holding that such agreements contain an implied term that the interest rates 'would not be set dishonestly, for an improper purpose, capriciously or arbitrarily' (para. 36).

Extortionate bargains
The Consumer Credit Act 1974 replaced older statutes about money-lenders. It is a very important part of consumer law and is only briefly referred to here. (Details can be found in Gray and Gray, 2001, pp. 1380–3.) Sections 137–140 concern agreements between an individual borrower (including an individual in the course of business) and anyone who lends money. Under s.137 the court can – amongst other powers – 'reopen' the agreement if the payments are 'grossly exorbitant' or 'grossly contravene ordinary principles of fair dealing'. In practice, these loans are often second mortgages, for home improvements, for example, but sometimes they are an act of desperation by a defaulting borrower and it is particularly here that the borrower needs protection. However, the courts seem to have upset few agreements, perhaps because the more needy (and therefore weak) the borrower, the more justified is the lender in imposing a high interest rate because of the risk he is taking. The counter-argument, that if the borrower defaults the lender can realise the security of the land, appears to hold little attraction.

A case in which the County Court *was* prepared to interfere in a mortgage transaction under the Consumer Credit Act was *Falco Finance* v. *Michael Gough*, unreported, 28 October 1998, a case in which the rate of interest paid by the borrower rose by an additional 5 per cent for the remainder of the mortgage term (amounting to some £25 000) if any payment was even a day late. This was held to be an 'extortionate credit bargain' under s.138 and also unfair under the Unfair Terms in Consumer Contracts Regulations 1994 (now Unfair Terms in Consumer Contracts Regulations 1999, SI 1999/2083).

7.5 **Discharge of Mortgages**

A mortgage is ended when the lease, sublease or charge is removed from the title to the property. Normally, in unregistered land, the borrower obtains a signed receipt on the mortgage document; in registered land a form is sent to the Land Registry. In the case of a mortgage by a long lease, repayment of the loan means that the lease becomes a satisfied term.

7.6 **Priority of Mortgages**

The general rules

The rules about priority in mortgages come into play when there are several mortgages of one piece of land. If the borrower defaults and the land is not worth enough to pay back all the debts, then one or more of the lenders may lose money; the priority rules determine which of them is to be unlucky. There have been few cases in the last hundred years on priorities but some land lawyers greatly enjoy creating and solving priority puzzles, especially those concerning three or more mortgages. The basic rules are stated very briefly in the next sections; for further details see, for example, Megarry, 2002, pp. 535–46.

There are also special rules about the situation where several mortgages exist on one piece of land and a mortgagee owns two or more of them; under such circumstances, he may be allowed to 'tack'. This means that where (1) Oliver has borrowed money on a mortgage of his flat from Andy, and then (2) borrowed on a (second) mortgage from Belinda, if (3) Andy lends more money (by a third mortgage) on the security of the flat, Andy may be able to jump over Belinda's second mortgage and tack (or attach) his first and third mortgages (compare consolidation of mortgages, 7.3 above).

Priority of mortgages of a legal interest in unregistered land
The basic rules in unregistered land are the same as those which apply in any conflict between interests, but they are subject to the rules about registration of land charges (Chapter 10). Where a mortgage of a legal interest has to be registered as a land charge because there is no deposit of title deeds, it ranks according to the date of registration, not the date of its creation. Briefly, subject to fraud or negligence, any legal mortgage with deposit of title deeds takes priority over all mortgages except any earlier mortgage which was properly registered. Any mortgage without deposit of title deeds is subject to (a) any earlier mortgage with deposit of deeds, and (b) any other mortgage which was properly registered.

Mortgages of a legal interest in registered land
In registered land the general rule is that, once a mortgage or charge has been protected on the Register, it will defeat all later mortgages as well as earlier mortgages which have not been so protected. Thus the first mortgage

entered on the Register ranks first and the remainder rank according to the date of their registration (s.48 Land Registration Act 2002).

Mortgages of an equitable interest in any land
Where there are competing equitable mortgages, the general rule is that they will rank in the order in which they were created. In registered land, though, an equitable mortgage which has been protected by entry on the Register will take priority over all later interests. In the rare case where the interest mortgaged is an equitable interest under a trust, the mortgages rank according to the order in which notice of the mortgage was received by the trustees, whether the title is registered (s.5 Land Registration Act 1986) or unregistered (s.137 LPA 1925).

7.7 Comment

The law of mortgages illustrates very clearly the difference between legal rules and what really happens: in every part of this area of law, theory and practice diverge. In 1991 the Law Commission (No. 204) recommended that the complex theoretical foundations and the miscellaneous protections offered by a random combination of common law, equitable and statutory rules should be completely replaced by new interests in land, called 'formal' and 'informal land mortgages'. The only function of these new interests would be to provide security for the loan, and some of the terms would be laid down in legislation. At the same time, the jurisdiction to set aside unfair terms would be codified.

The existing law, however, shows how, behind the façade of unchanging concepts and rules, it is possible to provide a flexible response to social and economic change. Although the courts may occasionally be finding difficulty with the traditional equitable doctrine of clogs and fetters, cases such as *Palk* indicate how judges can generally readjust the balance between borrowers and lenders according to changes in lending practice and in the marketplace.

The case of *Etridge* is an example of how the courts have decided where to draw the line between commercial expediency and the need to protect the vulnerable. Institutional lenders will be alerted more frequently than before to the possibility that undue influence may have taken place, but it will not be difficult for them to discharge their obligations. The use of the mortgage of family property remains such an important source of capital for small businesses, and any shift in the balance towards the further protection of the wife would tend to limit that source of financial provision. Equally, if the restrictions on lenders are eased too much, the consequences will be unacceptable for vulnerable and emotionally involved occupiers who have been persuaded by their partners in financial difficulties to agree to a risky mortgage loan. This real tension in land law will be addressed again, in a slightly different context, in Chapter 11.

Summary

7.1   Legal mortgages are made by deed; in unregistered land they may be created by demise (or subdemise) or legal charge, but in registered land by legal charge only.

7.2   Equitable mortgages may be of a legal or equitable interest. Legal interests may be mortgaged equitably by a contract to grant a legal mortgage or by equitable charge. Equitable interests can also be mortgaged by conveyance and reconveyance.

7.3   The lender must take care to avoid being fixed with the undue influence of a mortgagee over a surety where there is a non-commercial relationship between the two.

7.4   The legal lender has the right to take possession of property but usually only does so when the borrower defaults; mortgagors of residential premises are given limited protection by statute.

7.5   In a legal mortgage, the power of sale (or to appoint a receiver) normally arises once the legal date of redemption has passed, and becomes exercisable if s.103 is satisfied: the lender is then a trustee of the proceeds, not the power, of sale.

7.6   Equitable mortgagees and chargees may have fewer rights than legal lenders.

7.7   The borrower's rights (the equity of redemption) include the rights (reinforced by statute) not to have the equitable right to redeem restricted, or to suffer unconscionable or oppressive terms; cases now often depend on whether the lender has taken an unfair advantage.

7.8   Where there is a succession of mortgages, priority rules decide in what order the lenders should have their money repaid.

Exercises

7.1   Why are there both legal and equitable rights to redeem a mortgage?

7.2   When does a mortgagee have a power of sale?

7.3   How may a legal lease be mortgaged?

7.4   Can there be a term in a mortgage which continues after the mortgage has been redeemed?

7.5   To what extent is a mortgagee a trustee?

7.6   What protection does a wife have when her husband is pressuring her to agree to mortgage the family home in order to support his ailing business?

7.7   Clayton owns a freehold shop with a flat above, where he lives with Emily who has an equitable share in the land. For some years he has run a business selling computer games from the shop. In 2002, a rival company set up nearby and took away most of Clayton's trade. In 2003, in order to clear his previous mortgage and his other debts and to provide a financial restructuring of the business, he borrowed £150 000 on mortgage from Sharks Ltd who gave him documents for Emily to sign; she did so without reading them when he told her that they were 'just something about my will'. The interest rate was set at 5 per cent above the bank rate.

   The restructuring has not worked out, and in the last six months Clayton has been unable to make any repayment. There is little or no equity in the property. Advise Emily.

Further Reading

Andrews, 'Undue Influence – Where's the Disadvantage' [2002] Conv 456

Cousins and Clarke, *Law of Mortgages*, 2nd edn (London: Sweet and Maxwell, 2001)

Dixon, 'Combating the Mortgagee's Right to possession: New Hope for the Mortgagor in Chains?' [1998] Legal Studies 279

Fisher and Lightwood, *Law of Mortgage*, 11th edn (London: Butterworth,1999); Supplement 2003

Haley, 'Mortgage Default: Possession, Relief and Judicial Discretion' [1997] Legal Studies 483

Kenny A., 'No Postponement of Evil Day' [1998] Conv 223

Kenny P., 'Etridge – A Practical Guide to taking a (Spouse's) Surety for Mortgage' [2002] Conv 91

Robinson, 'In the Chancery Adventure Playground' (1997) 113 LQR 533

Rook, *Property Law and Human Rights* (London: Blackstone, 2001)

Thompson, 'The Cumulative Range of a Mortgagee's Remedies' [2002] Conv 53

Whitehouse,'The Homeowner: Citizen or Consumer' in Bright and Dewar (eds), *Land Law Themes and Perspectives* (Oxford: OUP, 1998)

8   Easements and Profits

8.1 Introduction

Easements and profits (*profits à prendre*) are property interests over someone else's land. In medieval times, profits – rights to take something from another's land – were very nearly as important as the fee simple; the rules were settled centuries ago and have changed little. Easements – rights to do something on another's land – are also ancient but they only achieved their present form within the last hundred years or so, after the enclosures of commonly held rural land and the rapid growth of towns and cities. Easements are now much more important than profits, which are rarely created these days, having largely been replaced by contractual licences. Both profits and easements are generally liable to be affected by decisions in the law of tort, and this chapter illustrates some of the interrelationships of contract, tort and land law.

The nature of land means that its value can often be increased by a right over neighbouring land; an extreme example is the right to drive across a neighbour's field in order to reach land which is otherwise accessible only by helicopter. More common instances are the running of gas and water pipes, drains and electric cables from one house or flat to the next.

The essential problem for the judges in this area of land law – which is hardly touched by the 1925 legislation – is that they have to balance at least two conflicting demands. They would like to increase the value of land, for example by allowing a right to walk through a neighbour's garden as a short cut to a garage, because this will make that land 'a better and more convenient property'. This will, however, decrease the value of the other land by reducing privacy and restricting what may be done there, including its future development. As in the old rules about the running of leasehold covenants, the judges seek to ensure that the market in land is not depressed, either by making agreed rights unduly insecure, or by unduly burdening land and preventing the exercise of other valuable rights. As well as these tensions between the interests of private landowners, and between them and the general public interest in the market in land, there is also the tension between private landownership and public access to land, although this latter question is not usually addressed in this country through the law of easements.

The general rule is that landowners cannot simply create easements as they will: '[i]ncidents of a novel kind cannot be devised and attached to property at the fancy or caprice of any owner' (Lord Brougham LC in 1834). At the same time, '[t]he category of ... easements must alter and expand with the changes that take place in the circumstances of mankind' (Lord St Leonards LC in 1852). If a new right is, in the judges' view, not capable of being an easement, it will be only a licence. The significance of this is that, while an easement is a property right, attached to the land and passing automatically with it on assignment, a licence is seen as a personal right rarely binding third parties and thus probably neither passing to a new owner of the land nor burdening a successor of the licensor (see Chapter 14).

Easements and profits have the vocabulary appropriate to their great age: 'dominant tenement' and 'servient tenement' are most important. In the law of easements (and sometimes in profits), the claimed right to use the land of another must benefit ('accommodate') one piece of land, known as the dominant tenement; the land which provides the benefit and is therefore burdened by the easement or profit is known as the servient tenement.

In problem questions, there are usually just two issues:

---

1 Is the right claimed capable of being an easement (or profit)?

2 If so, has it been acquired here?

These problems are usually straightforward to answer, providing the two issues are tackled separately and in order, although in many decided cases the two issues merge.

8.2 Easements

The nature of easements

It is easy to give examples of easements, but more difficult to find an adequate generic definition. In order for a right to be classified as an easement, it must comply with the four traditional requirements listed by Dr Cheshire in his *Modern Real Property* in 1925, and reviewed by Lord Evershed MR in one of the leading cases on easements, *Re Ellenborough Park* [1956] Ch 131:

1 There must be a dominant and a servient tenement.
2 The easement must accommodate the dominant tenement.
3 The dominant and servient tenements must be owned or occupied by different people.
4 The easement must be capable of being the subject of a grant.

In *Ellenborough Park*, owners of houses near the park (in a square near the sea at Weston-Super-Mare) had been granted the right to use it 'as a leisure garden', but during the Second World War it had been taken over by the government. By statute, individual landowners were entitled to compensation if they had been deprived of a legal right, and the only possible such right was an easement. They were eventually successful in persuading the Court of Appeal that the right to enjoy the park could amount to an easement.

Dominant and servient tenements

Clearly in *Ellenborough Park*, there was a servient tenement (the park) and there were dominant tenements (the houses). Sometimes, however, this is not so obvious. In *Miller* v. *Emcer Products Ltd* [1956] Ch 304, a tenant had an easement to use the landlord's lavatory, and here the dominant and servient tenements were not two plots of land, but two estates in land, the freehold and the leasehold; the tenant had the dominant tenement and the landlord, the servient.

In *London and Blenheim Estates Ltd* v. *Ladbroke Retail Parks Ltd* [1993] 4 All ER 157, the Court of Appeal held that there can be no easement if, at the time the easement is purported to have been created, the dominant land is not in the possession of the grantee and if the grantor does not at the same time own the servient land. In this case, an option was claimed for an easement to park cars on land owned by the grantor. At the time the option was granted, the plaintiff did not own the land which was to benefit from it. When he eventually acquired this land and attempted to exercise the option, the land to be burdened had been sold by the grantor to someone else who was able to argue that the claim to an easement could not succeed.

The requirement that there must be a dominant tenement seems to have been adopted during the nineteenth century under the influence of Roman law, and Sturley ((1980) 96 LQR 557) argues that the authority is very weak. He claims that allowing easements to exist in gross (that is, easements which are not attached to benefiting land), such as the right to land a helicopter on distant land, would not now unduly burden titles but could encourage maximum utilisation of land. However, it would also mean that the next requirement in Dr Cheshire's list, that the easement must relate to the land, would now be unnecessary, leading to the further burdening of land with new rights, contrary to some of the policy issues discussed earlier.

Accommodating the dominant tenement

Just as in the pre-1996 law of leases where the covenant must 'touch and concern' the land (see 6.4 above), the test is whether the claimed easement benefits the land itself and not merely the landowner. In *Ellenborough Park*, the Court of Appeal found it difficult to decide whether the easement touched and concerned (or 'accommodated' or benefited) the dominant tenement. Earlier cases had been divided on whether the right to use a garden could accommodate land, but Lord Evershed MR concluded that it is 'primarily a question of fact'. In this case, the dominant tenements did benefit from the garden use; it might have been different if they had not been family homes. In the recent case of *Mulvaney* v. *Gough* [2003] 1 WLR 360, the right to tend a communal garden was 'clearly' held to benefit the dominant tenement.

In *Hill* v. *Tupper* (1863) 2 H & C 121, the claim to an easement failed because it did not accommodate the dominant tenement. The owners of the Basingstoke Canal leased part of the canal bank to Hill and granted him the sole right to hire out pleasure boats. A local publican then also rented out boats and Hill tried to stop him, arguing that the publican was interfering with his easement. The court found that the exclusive right to hire out boats benefited Hill's business rather than his land, was thus a personal right only and therefore could not be an easement. By contrast, in *Moody* v. *Steggles* (1879) 12 Ch D 261, the right to hang a pub sign on neighbouring land was held to be an easement. Although it benefited the business, it also benefited the land; given the way in which the land was used and had been used for many years, it was not possible to distinguish between the land and the use to which it was put.

Different ownership or occupation

People cannot have rights against themselves. If both tenements come into the hands of one person, the easement is ended ('extinguished by unity of seisin'). If what was formerly an easement continues to be used by the owner of both tenements, for example to cross one field to get into the next, this still looks like an easement (but is not because of unity of seisin); it is known as a quasi-easement and might one day come back to life (see 8.5 below).

Capable of being the subject of a grant

The requirement that the easement must be capable of being the subject of a grant is not altogether clear. In theory it means that the right claimed must be capable of being conveyed in a deed, and this in turn means that the nature and extent of the right must be capable of sufficiently accurate definition. *Aldred's Case* (1610) 9 Co Rep 57b confirms that the right to a good view cannot amount to an easement since such a thing is too imprecise to describe (although the law on freehold covenants might help here – see Chapter 9).

There must also be a capable grantor and a capable grantee – both parties must be the owners of the land which are to become the dominant and servient tenements (see *London and Blenheim Estates Ltd* v. *Ladbroke Retail Parks Ltd*, above) and both must be legal persons.

Common easements

A right of way over a neighbour's land is an obvious and well-known easement. Another is the right to light, normally restricted to enough light coming through a specific window for the 'comfortable' use of the premises. There are also easements for the use of naturally running water and for the support of a building (for example, terraced and semi-detached houses have mutual easements of support). A more detailed list of easements can be found in Megarry and Wade, 2000, pp. 1161-2.

Restrictions on new easements

No exclusive use

The right claimed as an easement must not amount to a claim to the whole of the servient tenement so that an owner is actually excluded from her own land. The tenant in *Miller* v. *Emcer Products Ltd* (above) succeeded because he would only have been using the lavatory some of the time. Similarly, the right to store goods can be an easement, as in *Wright* v. *Macadam* [1949] 2 KB 744, providing the servient owner is not excluded and the right is clearly defined. In *Copeland* v. *Greenhalf* [1952] Ch 488, on the other hand, the defendant, a wheelwright who for many years had used a strip of the plaintiff's land alongside a road for storing and mending vehicles, claimed an easement acquired by long use. He failed, because his claim amounted to a claim over the whole of the land; an argument based on adverse possession would have been more appropriate. It should be remembered, though, that an adverse possession claim where title to the land is registered is now much less likely to succeed than formerly (Chapter 3).

It is possible that car parking is capable of being an easement, since this can accommodate the dominant tenement, but it depends on the precise nature of the claim and whether the servient owner still has reasonable use of her land; such a claim succeeded in *Hair* v. *Gillman* (2000) 48 EG 117, where the defendant had been given permission to park her car anywhere 'on a forecourt that was capable of taking two or three other cars'. In *Central Midlands Estates Ltd* v. *Leicester Dyers* [2003] 2 P & CR D1, however, a claim to park an unlimited number of vehicles anywhere on the neighbour's land could not be an easement. It would have prevented the neighbour from using his land, except occasionally, and would have made his ownership of the land illusory. A claim for adverse possession also failed, on the facts.

Negative easements

The courts are 'very chary' of creating new kinds of negative easements. In *Phipps* v. *Pears* [1965] 1 QB 76, a neighbour demolished a house which was built very close to that of the plaintiff, who claimed he had an easement of 'protection from the weather' with which the neighbour had interfered. This would have been a negative easement, preventing the neighbour from developing his land. In this case, Lord Denning MR defined the difference between positive and negative easements:

> positive easements, such as a right of way, which give the owner of land a right himself to do something on or to his neighbour's land: and negative easements, such as a right of light, which gives him a right to stop his neighbour doing something on his (his neighbour's) own land. (p. 82)

(Servient owners, of course, may not do things on their land which interfere with the exercise of any easement.) It is understandable that such negative rights, with the exception of the rights to light and support, should not be capable of being easements, not just because of the policy reasons discussed above, but also because a servient owner might not know that the easement was being acquired (for example by prescription – use over a long period of time – see 8.5) and would therefore be unable to prevent acquisition. The right claimed as an easement in *Phipps* was held not to be an easement of support and, indeed, was not an easement at all because it would 'unduly restrict the enjoyment' of the servient land and prevent its development.

Restrictive covenants may offer more appropriate solutions in situations like this, but the answer might also be found in the law of tort. In *Bradburn* v. *Lindsay* [1983] 2 All ER 408, Mr Bradburn, owner of one of a pair of semi-detached houses, was concerned that the dry rot in his neighbour's derelict house would spread to his own property. The house had to be demolished by the council and Mr Bradburn claimed damages from his neighbour for loss of support and exposure of the side of his house to dry rot and decay. There was clearly an easement of support, but Mrs Lindsay was under no obligation to maintain it by keeping the wall in repair. Mr Bradburn therefore successfully relied on the torts of negligence and nuisance.

No expenditure by the servient owner
All the easements referred to thus far have been capable of being enjoyed without the owner of the servient tenement having to take any positive action or spend money, and in general this will be the case. There is, however, an exception to this: the 'spurious easement of fencing' which requires the servient owner to keep in repair her boundary fence if it is used as part of an enclosure to contain livestock on the dominant land.

In *Liverpool City Council* v. *Irwin* [1977] AC 239, the House of Lords dealt with the issue of whether a landlord had to maintain easements of access to the flats in a tower block. The tenants had stopped paying rent because the common parts of the block were in such a bad condition. They had no written tenancy agreement, only a list of rules. Easements to use the passages, lifts and rubbish chutes were implied into the tenancies by the judges, along with an obligation to maintain and repair them:

> there appears to be no technical difficulty in making an express grant of an easement coupled with an undertaking by the servient owner to maintain it. That being so, there seems to be no reason why the easement arising in the present case should not by implication carry with it a similar burden on the grantor. (Lord Edmund-Davies, p. 268)

This, though, is probably exceptional, since in attempting to achieve a balance between the competing demands of landowners and aware of the need to maintain a healthy property market (see above), the courts do not want to see servient land further burdened.

8.3 Profits

The rules on profits are fairly similar to those on easements, but profits can be either 'appurtenant' (benefiting a dominant tenement) or exist 'in gross' (without a dominant tenement). Thus, a person can own a profit to graze a goat on someone else's meadow, even though she owns no land which can benefit.

Where a profit is attached to land, it must accommodate the dominant tenement, just like an easement. In *Bailey* v. *Stephens* (1862) 12 CB (NS) 91, the owner of a field claimed a profit appurtenant to take wood from a neighbouring copse. It was held that this was not valid because it did not benefit the field. (It might have been different if the alleged dominant tenement were a house and the wood used as firewood.)

A profit may be 'sole' where only one person can take the thing and the owner of the servient tenement is excluded from it. Alternatively, it can be shared with the servient owner and is then known as a profit 'in common'.

There are profits of piscary (fish), turbary (turf), estovers (wood for firewood or other purposes) and pasture (the right to graze as many animals as can be supported through the winter months); some of them are still economically very important to their owners.

8.4 Legal and Equitable Easements and Profits

Easements and profits can be both legal and equitable.

A legal easement or profit must be:

- for the proper length of time, and
- created by deed (or by implication or by long use).

An easement or profit can be legal provided it is to last for ever, like a fee simple, or for a period of time with a fixed beginning and end, like a lease (s.1(2)(a) LPA). If the easement is for an indefinite but limited time, such as 'until I sell my house' or 'for your life', it cannot be legal (see 5.3 above). However, even if the easement or profit is 'for ever', or 'for two years, starting next Monday', it may still be equitable if it has not been created with the proper formalities (except for those easements or profits created by implication or by long use – see 8.5 below), or if the grantor owns only an equitable estate in the land.

As usual, it is important to know whether an easement or profit is legal or equitable, since this has a fundamental bearing on whether a successor of the owner of the dominant tenement will be able to enforce it and, equally, whether it will be binding on a successor of the servient owner. In unregistered land, a legal interest binds the world; for the detail of the rather complicated rules in registered land, see 11.5 below. All equitable easements should be protected by registration (for unregistered land, see 10.3 below; for registered land, see 11.6 below).

8.5 Acquisition of Easements and Profits

There are a number of ways of acquiring a legal easement or profit. The obvious way is to create one in a deed, but other methods of creation are

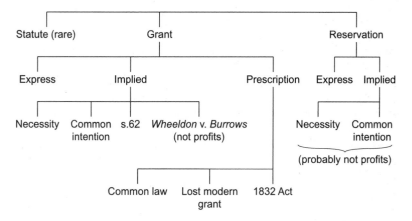

Figure 8.1 Acquisition of easements and profits

based on behaving as if such a right already existed, together with a – usually mythical – deed. Legal easements and profits can also be directly created by long usage (compare adverse possession in 3.1 above).

Easements

Figure 8.1 shows the various ways in which an easement can be acquired. A *grant* of an easement is where the seller gives a right over a part of her land to a person buying another part of it. *Reservation* is where she reserves for herself a right over a part of her land which she is selling. The distinction between the two is important, especially when considering easements which have been acquired by implication.

There is a considerable body of law on the acquisition of easements. Judges tend not to use categories consistently, so in practice they overlap (especially easements of necessity and intended easements). Additionally, some of the cases could just as easily be explained by reference to the old principle of non-derogation from grant (see 6.2 above) and it is suggested that much of the law on easements created by implication is based on that principle. *Wong* v. *Beaumont Property Trust Ltd* [1965] 1 QB 173 is a good example of this and of the relationship between easements of necessity and common intention. A basement was let for use as a restaurant, but could not be used as such without a ventilation duct over the land retained by the landlord. It was therefore necessary to imply such an easement into the lease; alternatively, it must have been the common intention of the parties that there should be such an easement, since without it the basement could not be used as a restaurant.

Only the bare outlines of the rules are given here. The main thing is to understand the variety of ways in which these interests can be created and acquired, so that you can recognise the circumstances in which one might arise, either to take advantage of it or to avoid it.

Express grant
If Imran, the owner of a block of flats, sells a fourth-floor flat to Paula, he will probably expressly grant her an easement over the hall and staircase.

Grant implied by necessity
Where land is (at the time of the sale) completely unusable without an easement, the courts may imply one into the conveyance, although this will not be the case if the conveyance expressly excludes the grant of an easement (see *Nickerson* v. *Barraclough* [1981] Ch 426). In the example given above, Paula's lease would be useless without a right also to use the stairs so, if no such easement had been expressly created, then one would be implied, by necessity, into the lease, just as in *Liverpool City Council* v. *Irwin* (see above).

Grant implied by common intention
If the buyer and seller of land share an intention that the land should be used in a particular way, the courts may find an implied easement, provided that this is necessary for the intention to be fulfilled. In *Cory* v. *Davies* [1923] 2 Ch 95, terraced houses had been built along a private drive which gave out on to public roads at either end. There had been an intention that all the houses should have easements along all parts of the drive and on to the public roads, but such easements had never been expressly granted. The owner of the house at one end of the terrace obstructed his end of the drive, forcing everyone to go the other way. Given the common intention of the parties, the court found little difficulty in implying the necessary easements and requiring the blocked drive to be reopened.

Easements implied by s.62 LPA
S.62 LPA is a 'wordsaving provision' which, on conveyance, transfers with the land all benefits which are attached to it (see 2.7 above); it can be (and frequently is) expressly excluded by the parties.

   Wright v. *Macadam* (8.2 above) illustrates the potential of s.62. Here, with her landlord's permission, a tenant was storing coal in a shed; then, when a new lease was granted to her (the 'conveyance'), her licence was converted into an easement: it was an 'advantage ... appertaining to the land' and, when s.62 implied it into the deed, it grew into a legal easement and could not be revoked by the landlord. (In any problem about a person who lives on land owned by another and has permission to do something extra, and who then receives a grant, the answer will probably involve s.62.)

   Wright v. *Macadam* was recently followed in *Hair* v. *Gillman* (8.2 above), a case in which a licence to park a car was given to the tenant of land used as a nursery school and later 'crystallised' into an easement under s.62 when she was granted the freehold. Chadwick LJ felt it to be a matter of regret that a property right binding the servient land could be created unintentionally, and repeated the comments of Tucker LJ in

Wright, that such decisions 'may tend to discourage landlords from acts of kindness to their tenants. But there it is: that is the law' (p. 755).

It has been argued that the section should only operate where the dominant and servient tenements are already in separate ownership or occupation. This was stated by a minority in the House of Lords in *Sovmots Investments Ltd* v. *Secretary of State for the Environment* [1979] AC 144, a case concerning a controversial compulsory purchase order made by a London borough. The order would have been invalid unless s.62 applied to create an easement of way along hallways in the building. It was held that s.62 did not apply to a compulsory purchase order and, further, the section could not be invoked because the building was wholly owned and occupied by Sovmots at the time of the 'conveyance'. The order was therefore invalid. This decision has been subject to criticism (see Smith [1978] Conv 449) and does not take into account the possibility that s.62 may operate even where there is common ownership if the use of the quasi-easement (see above, 8.2) has been continuous and apparent. In *P & S Platt Ltd* v. *Crouch* [2003] EWCA Civ 1110, the owner of a hotel by a river also owned an island in the river on which he had moorings which could be used by the hotel guests. The hotel was sold. The sale did not include the moorings, but the new owners argued that they had an easement to use them. Peter Gibson LJ stated that:

> the rights in question did appertain to ... and were enjoyed with the hotel, being part of the hotel business and advertised as such and enjoyed by the hotel guests. The rights were continuous and apparent, and so it matters not that prior to the sale of the hotel there was no prior diversity of occupation of the dominant and servient tenancies. (para. 42)

Grant implied under the rule in Wheeldon v. Burrows (1878) 12 Ch D 31
Thesiger LJ stated the rule in this case twice, but unfortunately not consistently. The basic principle is this: where a person sells part of her land which has the benefit of a quasi-easement, the buyer will gain the benefit of the quasi-easement if, at the time of the grant:

1. the seller was using the quasi-easement for the benefit of the land she was selling;
2. the use of the quasi-easement was 'continuous and apparent' (such as an obvious track, or a drain which could have been discovered on inspection) and/or
3. was necessary for the reasonable enjoyment of the land sold.

It is not known whether Thesiger LJ meant conditions 2 and 3 to be alternatives; in many cases, of course, if the quasi-easement (for example a right of way) satisfies one test, it will also satisfy the other. The third condition does not mean 'essential' (as in easements implied by necessity), but that there can be no reasonable enjoyment of the land without the easement.

In *Millman* v. *Ellis* [1996] 71 P & CR 158, the Court of Appeal held that Millman had successfully proved an easement under the rule. He had bought a large house from Ellis and also part of Ellis' remaining land; he claimed the right to use the driveway which Ellis had always used to get to the house and which was safer than using the main road. In *Wheeler* v. *J.J. Saunders Ltd* [1995] 2 All ER 697, however, Wheeler had bought part of a farm and claimed an easement to allow him to pass through a gap in a wall southwards to get to a road. It was held that this access was not 'necessary for the reasonable enjoyment of the house' because there was another equally suitable access in the east.

The requirement that the easement should be necessary for the reasonable enjoyment of the land has been described by Thompson, 2003, p. 458 as 'hopelessly imprecise'. He suggests that any continuous and apparent easements should pass on conveyance under the second limb of s.62, as there is no requirement for necessity, and that the use of *Wheeldon* v. *Burrows* should be confined to transactions where there has been no conveyance.

It is important to be aware that although easements can be granted by implication under the rule in *Wheeldon* v. *Burrows*, implied reservation for the benefit of the retained land is not possible under the rule, confirmed recently by the Court of Appeal in *Chaffe* v. *Kingsley* [2000] 10 EG 173.

Reservation
When a seller reserves an easement for herself in a conveyance, the courts will interpret it in as limited a way as they can (the *contra proferentem* rule), since the seller generally has control of the terms of the agreement and because of the rule against derogation from grant (see above). It is possible impliedly to reserve an easement by necessity or common intention, although this is very difficult to establish. In *Manjang* v. *Drammeh* (1991) 61 P & CR 194, a person owned land situated between a river and a road. He sold that part of his land by the road but failed to reserve for himself an easement to cross it in order to reach the rest of his land on the bank of the river. The Privy Council refused to imply an easement across the land he had sold, since it was possible for him to get to his retained land by boat, and occasionally in the past he had done so.

Prescription
The use for many years of a right which is capable of being an easement can create a legal easement by 'prescription'; the rules are extraordinarily obscure. Prescription may arise if an easement has been used openly, as of right, without permission and continuously, by one fee simple owner against another. There are three forms, common law, 'lost modern grant' and statutory, under the Prescription Act 1832. The periods of use required vary according to the method of prescription claimed and the type of easement (see Megarry and Wade, 2000, pp. 1124–41). In 1966, the Law Reform Committee recommended the simplification of prescription law (14th Report, Cmnd 3100), but no new statute was ever forthcoming. The Law Commission and the Land Registry proposed (in their 1998

Consultation Paper 'Land Registration for the Twenty-First Century', Law Com No 254, paras 10.79 *et seq.*) that the sole method of acquiring an easement by prescription in registered land should be by the Prescription Act 1832.

Profits

Profits can be acquired in most of the same ways as easements. However, because a profit cannot be 'continuous and apparent', *Wheeldon* v. *Burrows* probably cannot apply. In addition, under the Prescription Act the periods are longer for profits than for easements.

8.6 Remedies for Infringement of Easements and Profits

The remedies available to the aggrieved owner of an easement or profit are through the self-help remedy of abatement and by means of an action in the courts.

Abatement means that the owner of the easement or profit can go on to the servient tenement and, for example, break a padlock on a gate if this is necessary. However, the courts are wary of abatement and the dominant owner must choose the least mischievous method and refrain from causing unnecessary damage.

The owner of the easement or profit may claim an injunction and/or damages and/or a declaration against the owner of the servient land. She can also take action against third parties who interfere with her right, so the owner of a profit of piscary could win damages from a factory upstream which polluted the river and killed the fish.

8.7 The Ending of Easements and Profits

Easements and profits may be ended by statute or through an act of the parties, either by release, through abandonment or through unity of seisin.

Statute

The punitive Acts of Enclosure often extinguished such rights, especially profits in common. Today they can also be ended under the Commons Registration Act 1965; the right to keep a pig on common land, and to collect firewood is no longer a matter of life and death for most people, and the Act seems to be less concerned with registering such interests than with allowing owners of common land to destroy them.

There is no provision equivalent to s.84 LPA which allows the Lands Tribunal to discharge or modify a restrictive covenant (see 9.4 below), but under the Town and Country Planning Act 1971, local authorities, in the course of development, may end easements and profits.

Act of the parties

Release
An easement or profit can be released explicitly by deed. An agreement to release – without a deed – may be enforceable in equity.

Abandonment
If the owner of the easement or profit abandons the right, she cannot later resurrect it. However, there must be a clear intention to abandon, and this is very difficult for the servient owner to establish. It can be implied from the circumstances, but rarely is. In *Benn* v. *Hardinge* (1992) 66 P & CR 246 the Court of Appeal held that 175 years of non-use did not, in itself, indicate the necessary intention to abandon. *Moore* v. *Rawson* (1824) 3 B & C 332 held that, even where the windows which benefit from an easement of light are blocked up for years, this only amounts to abandonment if there is no intention to open them up again (and see Davis [1995] Conv 291).

The Law Commission has recommended ((1998) Law Com No 254, para. 5.24) that, in registered land, an easement created by implication or prescription should be deemed to have been abandoned if the dominant owner cannot show it has been used within the previous 20 years.

Unity of seisin
As stated in 8.2 above, a person cannot have an easement or profit against herself, so an easement ends if one person owns both tenements; of course, as indicated earlier, it might be resuscitated under s.62 LPA or under the rule in *Wheeldon* v. *Burrows*.

8.8 Other Rights over Another's Land

Listed below are a number of other interests in land which appear similar to easements or profits, but which are classified differently by lawyers.

Public rights

These are rights which can be used by anyone, such as the right to fish between high- and low-water marks. The most familiar are rights of way, which include roads as well as footpaths, but the 'right' to use a road is now more like a licence, since it can be denied at the discretion of a police officer (see Public Order Act 1986).

The Countryside and Rights of Way Act 2000 provides a limited statutory right of public access to open countryside (the 'right to roam') and is intended to bring about the modernisation of the public rights of way network.

Natural rights

These rights exist automatically and arise out of the nature of land. There is a right to water flowing naturally in a definite channel, but not to water which percolates through the land. All land has a natural right of support from neighbouring land, so you may not dig a large hole in your garden if your neighbour's land consequently collapses. The question has recently arisen as to whether an action lies against a landowner for failing to prevent the natural subsidence of her neighbour's land. In *Holbeck Hall Hotel* v. *Scarborough BC* [2000] 2 All ER 705, the council owned land between the sea cliffs and the hotel. Coastal erosion caused part of the hotel to disappear into the sea and the rest of it had to be demolished. Its owners sued the council in the tort of nuisance. The Court of Appeal stated that a landowner could be liable for not acting to prevent the hazard, but only if she could reasonably be expected to know about it. In this case, the danger could not reasonably have been foreseen by the council and it was therefore not just and reasonable to impose a liability on it. Even where the damage is reasonably foreseeable, if the cost of remedial work would be disproportionate, as here, the duty might be limited to sharing the information with the neighbour.

There are no automatic rights to light and air, so if such rights are to exist they must amount to easements, unless the tort of nuisance can provide a remedy. The quick-growing bush Cupressus leylandii has deprived many landowners of natural light for their gardens and homes (see for example *Stanton* v. *Jones*, unreported, 6 October 1994). The Anti-social Behaviour Act 2003, Part 8, although not in force at the time of writing, contains measures designed to provide local authorities with powers to intervene in such neighbourly disputes and to issue remedial notices if they are satisfied that a hedge over 2 metres high is adversely affecting a neighbour's reasonable enjoyment of her property.

Customary rights

Sometimes a group of people – for example, the residents of a particular village – have a right which looks like an easement, but it is not because 'the inhabitants of a village' are not a legal person.

Licences

See Chapter 14.

Access to Neighbouring Land Act 1992

A particular difficulty can arise for a landowner whose premises are built right up to the boundary with the neighbouring land. In the past, if she did not have an easement to go onto her neighbour's land to repair or maintain her own property and the neighbour refused to give her permission to do so, there was little she could do except watch her wall crumble away. Now, however, under the Access to Neighbouring Land Act 1992, in cases where it is reasonably necessary to carry out work to preserve her land and this work can really only be carried out from her neighbour's land to which she cannot otherwise gain access, a landowner may apply to the court for an order to allow her access to carry out the work. The court will not automatically make the order and may impose conditions on the applicant.

Party Walls Act 1996

Extensive rights are given under the Party Walls Act to landowners who wish to go onto the neighbouring property in order to carry out repairs to the party wall, so landowners should use this Act rather than the more restrictive Access to Neighbouring Land Act if it is appropriate to do so. The adjoining owner must first be served with a notice in prescribed form; the person carrying out the works has the right to enter any land (and may break open doors to do so, if necessary, so long as a police officer is present); weatherproofing may need to be provided to protect the neighbouring property and there may be a requirement to pay compensation for loss or damage caused to the adjoining owner. This Act would have been very helpful to Mr Bradburn in *Bradburn* v. *Lindsay* (8.3 above) and exists to prevent exactly that kind of mischief.

8.9 **Comment**

This chapter has indicated the wide variety of interests which can exist within the categories of easements and profits, and has attempted to show how land law attempts to adapt to changing land use, such as the development of tower blocks of flats and the increasing need for car parking facilities. Although there have been two statutory reforms in recent years, the Access to Neighbouring Land Act and the Party Walls Act, modern requirements need further reform of the law of easements. As long ago as 1971, the Law Commission in its Working Paper No. 36, 'Transfer of Land: Appurtenant Rights', recommended that certain important easements, such as the right to support, should automatically be statutory rights, and the need to reform the law on the acquisition of easements by prescription has already been discussed.

The law of contract (in relation to profits) and tort (especially nuisance), together with statute law, have to provide for other situations where the law of easements cannot satisfactorily resolve conflicts between neighbours.

Summary

8.1   To be an easement, a claim over another person's land must fulfil the four requirements: there must be dominant and servient tenements, accommodation of the dominant tenement, different ownership or occupation, and it must be capable of being the subject of a grant.

8.2   Easements include a wide variety of rights but, in order for a new one to be recognised, it must fit the general character of easements.

8.3 Profits are rights to take something from another person's land; they may or may not be appurtenant, and may be in common or sole.

8.4 A legal profit or easement must be equivalent to an interest in fee simple or to a lease, and must be created expressly by deed or impliedly or by long use; all other profits and easements are equitable.

8.5 Easements and profits may be acquired expressly or impliedly, by grant or reservation or by court order. They may also be acquired by prescription.

8.6 Remedies for infringement of an easement or profit are abatement or action.

8.7 Easements and profits may be ended by statute, release, abandonment or unity of seisin.

8.8 Easements and profits must be distinguished from other claims, such as natural, customary or public rights, from statutory rights and from licences.

Exercises

8.1 What is an easement? In what ways is it different from a profit?

8.2 What is the importance of dominant and servient tenements in the law of easements and profits?

8.3 Is there an easement to provide protection against the weather? Should there be?

8.4 What is necessary in order for an easement or a profit to be held to have been abandoned?

8.5 In 1985 Megan sold half her farm to Jeff, but she continued to keep her tractors in a barn on the land she sold to him. In 1995 she leased one of her remaining fields to Jeff, by deed, for 20 years, giving him permission to use a short cut to the field across her land 'for as long as he needs to'; he had in fact already been using the field and short cut for several weeks. Last year Jeff agreed in writing with Megan that the children attending her nursery school could play on his smallest field.

Megan has just died and her heir, Sam, wants to know if any of these arrangements will affect him.

Further Reading

Davis, 'Abandonment of an Easement: Is it a Question of Intention Only?' [1995] Conv 291.

Gale, *Easements*, 17th edn (London: Sweet and Maxwell, 2002)

Harpum, 'The Acquisition of Easements' [1992] CLJ 220

Smith P., 'Centre Point: Faulty Towers with Shaky Foundations' [1978] Conv 449

Sturley, 'Easements in Gross' (1980) 96 LQR 557

Tang Hang Wu, 'The Rights of Lateral Support of Buildings from Adjoining Land' [2002] Conv 237

Tee, 'Metamorphoses and s.62 of the Law of Property Act 1925' [1998] Conv 115

9   Covenants in Freehold Land

9.1 **Introduction**

This chapter is about promises made between freeholders in relation to the use of their land. While the law of easements relates to one landowner's use of another's land, this chapter is concerned with one landowner's direct control over what another does with his land. Unlike nuisance law, it deals with contractual relationships, but – unlike leasehold covenants – here there is no privity of estate.

It had long been possible for the *benefit* of any promise to be transferred with the land without a leasehold relationship, but in the mid-nineteenth century the courts of equity for the first time allowed the *burden* of certain covenants to be attached to land so that they affected anyone who owned the land. Eventually, the only burdens which equity enforced were those of covenants which were 'restrictive': that is, which prevented the owner from doing something. Even today, restrictive covenants can only be equitable interests; they therefore suffer limitations because they must be protected and any remedies for breach are discretionary. These new equitable rules were derived from the law of leases and easements, for the courts inevitably adopted the established policy test of 'touch and concern'/ 'accommodate': in all these areas of land law the courts are concerned with finding a balance between protecting third-party interests in land and encouraging land development.

Tulk v. *Moxhay* (1848) 2 Ph. 774 is the first case in which a court enforced a covenant on freehold land against a successor to the original covenantor. Tulk sold freehold land in Leicester Square in London and the buyer promised, on behalf of himself and his successors in title, to:

> keep and maintain the said parcel of ground and square garden, and the iron railing around the same in its [present] form and in sufficient and proper repair, as a square garden and pleasure ground, in an open state, uncovered with any buildings, in a neat and ornamental order. (p. 775)

The land changed hands several times and a later owner decided to build on the garden, although he had known about the covenant before he had bought the land and had paid less because of it. In a dramatic decision by the Court of Chancery, Tulk, the original covenantee (that is, the person to whom the promise had been made) successfully enforced the covenant against the later owner. The decision was based on the doctrine of notice and the inequitable consequences that would follow if:

> the original purchaser should be able to sell the property the next day for a greater price, in consideration of the assignee being allowed to escape from the liability which he had himself undertaken. (Lord Cottenham, p. 778)

In succeeding decisions, equity came to provide a cheap and effective planning law a hundred years before the state seriously took on the control of land use, and many urban areas have their present shape and character because of covenants imposed by careful developers. Nowadays the public restrictions on the use of land (for example planning law and building regulations) are normally of greater significance, but covenants are still imposed and enforced because they allow for a more detailed and individual control than public planning law is able to provide.

Under certain circumstances, statute permits covenants to be discharged or modified, since public policy requires that, for example, a covenant rendered obsolete because of a change in the character of a neighbourhood should no longer be enforceable. This jurisdiction is briefly reviewed at the end of the chapter, but first it is necessary to explain the rules about covenants 'running with the land'.

The basic pattern is simple: there are two sets of rules, legal and equitable, and each set is divided into rules for the benefit and for the burden. The legal and equitable rules in regard to the benefit are similar but not identical; the sets of rules for the burden are quite different. These sets of rules are the result of case law and are therefore open to argument – and are expressed differently in each textbook. The present statement is as simple and accurate as possible, and there is a summary at the end of the chapter for reference – see Table 9.1).

The first thing to do when approaching a problem in this area of land law is to identify who might have the benefit of a covenant and who might have the burden, that is, who might be able to enforce it and who might be bound by it. The easiest way to do this is by using diagrams and a technique explained in 9.2 below.

9.2 The Running of Covenants

The use of diagrams

To take a typical story in this area of land law: Eve was the fee simple owner of Paradise House and in 1980 she sold a part of her garden to Adosh who promised her that he would not build on the land. Eve moved to the seaside for her health and sold her remaining land to Mike. Adosh took early retirement and sold his land to Claire who has obtained planning permission for a block of flats on the land. Advise Mike.

In order to find an answer, it is necessary to establish the relationships of the plaintiff and the defendant to the promise which has been or may be broken. The promise is usually represented by a vertical line with the benefiting person (the covenantee, Eve in this case) at the top and the burdened person (covenantor, Adosh) at the bottom. As with leases, sales of the land are usually shown by horizontal lines as in Figure 9.1.

Claire is clearly planning to breach the promise made by Adosh, her predecessor. The question is, 'Can Mike prevent Claire building the flats?' For lawyers this becomes two questions, 'Has the burden of the covenant

Figure 9.1

passed to Claire? Has the benefit passed to Mike?' In order to find the answers, some of the rules below must be applied. (An answer is given in 'Applying the rules' later in this section.)

The legal rules

The running of the burden at law
As indicated earlier, the common law did not allow the burden of a freehold covenant to be attached to land so as to bind buyers: in *Austerberry* v. *Corporation of Oldham* (1885) 29 Ch D 750, the Court of Appeal applied the contractual doctrine that only a party to an agreement can be burdened by it. The decision in *Austerberry* was confirmed by the House of Lords in *Rhone* v. *Stephens* [1994] 2 All ER 65 (below). (There are, however, several ways in which the strictness of the rule can be avoided at law – see 9.5 below.)

The running of the benefit at law
In answering the question, 'Can the plaintiff sue at law?' ('Has the benefit passed to the plaintiff at law?'), two separate rules must be examined: the first provides for the express transfer of the benefit of a contract, and the second for the automatic running (implied transfer) of a benefit when the land is sold.

First, anyone can expressly transfer the benefit of any contract to which he is a party except one which is purely personal: thus, under s.136 LPA, the benefit of a promise relating to the use of land can be sold. The benefit will be enforceable at law by the buyer, provided that the assignment is in writing and express notice in writing has been given to the covenantor.

Second, if there has been no express assignment of the benefit of a covenant, the law provides rules allowing its automatic implied assignment if (a) it benefits the land; and (b) the covenantee had a legal estate in the land when the promise was made; and (c) the plaintiff now has a legal estate in that land; and (d) the benefit was intended to pass. For the covenant to benefit the land, it must be shown that the promise affects the land itself rather than its owner (see *P & A Swift Investments* v. *Combined English Stores Group plc* [1989] AC 632 (6.4 above)). By s.78 LPA the benefit of a promise which 'relates to' (that is, touches and concerns) land is deemed to be made not only with the covenantee but also with all his successors in title. The section means that since 1926 anyone who owns a legal estate in land automatically has the benefit of any covenant which touches and concerns it.

The basic rule can be traced back to medieval times, but the modern statement is found in *Smith and Snipes Hall Farm* v. *River Douglas Catchment Board* [1949] 2 KB 500. In 1938 the Board promised Ellen Smith that it would maintain the banks of the Eller Brook adjoining her land in Lancashire. She sold the land to John Smith (the first plaintiff) and he leased it to Snipes Hall Farm. When the river flooded the fields because of the Board's failure to carry out proper maintenance, John Smith and the farm tried to recover their losses from the Board on the ground that the benefit of the promise had automatically passed to them when they bought the land. It was held that (1) the covenant did benefit their land; (2) it had been made with a legal owner of the land; (3) the present plaintiffs were both legal owners; and (4) the covenant had been intended to run by s.78. Both plaintiffs could therefore claim damages for the Board's breach of covenant. The tenant farmer succeeded only because of s.78 LPA (above) which enables any legal owner – freeholder or leaseholder – to enjoy the benefit of a covenant relating to land.

The equitable rules

The running of the burden in equity
Since the burden of a covenant cannot bind a successor at law, it is necessary to examine the position in equity. *Tulk* v. *Moxhay* (9.1 above) appeared to be a straightforward decision; if the court had failed to enforce the promise, Lord Cottenham believed that 'it would [have been] impossible for an owner of land to sell part of it without incurring the risk of rendering what he retains worthless'. This is true, although one way in which a landowner can maintain control over a part of his land after he had sold it is to create a long lease with the appropriate covenants, and these leasehold covenants would be enforceable against subsequent assignees of the lease.

Later in the nineteenth century, the judges seem to have thought that the depressed land market required minimal restrictions on land use in order to encourage purchasers. They therefore introduced increasingly complex and technical requirements limiting the effect of *Tulk* v. *Moxhay* (which had allowed the burden of positive covenants to run with the land in equity and which could equally have been used to allow other kinds of non-property obligations to bind successors, based as the case was, on the doctrine of notice). Today the burden of a covenant runs in equity if (1) it is restrictive, and (2) it benefits land once owned by the covenantee and now owned by the plaintiff (or is part of a building scheme – see below), and (3) it was intended to run. Further, because this is merely an equitable interest, (4) the notice or registration rules must be complied with, and (5) the plaintiff must have clean hands. (The doctrine of notice and the registration rules are set out in Chapters 10 and 11.) In more detail:

1 *The covenant must be restrictive.* Whether a covenant is 'restrictive', or negative, is a question of its substance, not its form; what matters is the real meaning of the covenant rather than what it appears to mean. For

example, a covenant to maintain the land uncovered with buildings, although positive in form, is negative in substance because the covenantor can comply by doing nothing (that is, without spending money). In reality, it simply requires the covenantor not to build on it.

The rule that equity will enforce the burden of only those covenants that are restrictive was restated by the House of Lords in *Rhone* v. *Stephens* (above, and see Snape [1994] Conv 477). The case concerned a promise to maintain a roof in good condition – the whole roof belonged to the main house, but part of it protected an adjoining cottage owned by the claimant. The original owners of the house had promised the original buyers of the cottage that they would maintain the roof, but a subsequent owner of the cottage found that the covenant could not be enforced against a new owner of the house because it was positive: the burden could not pass.

Lord Templeman reviewed all the authorities and concluded that the rule of restrictive covenants is a rule of property: an owner of land cannot exercise a right which has never been transferred to him. Equity follows the law, and:

> Equity cannot compel an owner to comply with a positive covenant entered into by his predecessors in title without flatly contradicting the common law rule that a person cannot be made liable upon a contract unless he was a party to it. Enforcement of a positive covenant lies in contract; a positive covenant compels an owner to exercise his rights. Enforcement of a negative covenant lies in property; a negative covenant deprives the owner of a right over property. (at p. 69)

Further, he stated that any judicial alteration of the rule now would cause chaos for landowners.

2 *The covenant must benefit the plaintiff's land once owned by the covenantee (or be part of a scheme of development – see below).* The plaintiff's land must be 'benefited' ('accommodated') by the covenant and it must be identifiable. The point here is that equity will enforce a restrictive covenant if its purpose is to protect the value and amenity of the covenantee's neighbouring land. The person trying to enforce the covenant need not own a legal estate and need not have bought the whole of the covenantee's land, so long as the part he owns is capable of benefiting from the promise. In *London County Council* v. *Allen* [1914] 3 KB 642, Mr Allen promised the Council that he would not build on a strip of land needed for the continuation of a road. The land was conveyed to Mrs Allen and she proceeded to build on it. It was held, with great regret, that the claimant authority could not enforce the covenant because it had sold the benefiting land. (Statutes now provide that local authorities and certain other bodies, such as the National Trust, are exempt from this rule.)

In *Dano Ltd* v. *Earl Cadogan* [2003] All ER (D) 240, the sixth Earl Cadogan had conveyed some land in 1929 to a local authority which covenanted with him on behalf of itself and its successors that the land would be used for no other purpose than the housing of the working classes 'so long as such adjoining or neighbouring property or any part thereof forms part of the Cadogan Settled Estate in Chelsea but not further or otherwise'.

In the 1960s the Cadogan family rearranged its affairs and the Settled Estate was ended. Later, Dano Ltd acquired the land from the local authority, received planning permission to build private houses on some of the land and sought a declaration that the covenant was unenforceable. Although the neighbouring land was still in the Cadogan family, it no longer formed part of the 'Cadogan Settled Estate in Chelsea', and on that basis the Court of Appeal held that there was no longer any land capable of benefiting from the covenant, which was therefore unenforceable, despite its philanthropic objectives.

3 *The parties must intend the covenant to run.*   This intention will usually be expressed, but if not, it may be implied by s.79 LPA. The operation of s.79 can be excluded, generally by clear words in the agreement, although the courts can construe the document as a whole in order to determine the intention of the parties – see *Morrells of Oxford Ltd* v. *Oxford United F.C. Ltd* [2001] Ch 459.

The running of the benefit in equity

Equity also developed its own rules about the running of the benefit, based on the legal rules but slightly more complicated. They were radically simplified by the decision of the Court of Appeal in *Federated Homes Ltd* v. *Mill Lodge Properties Ltd* (1980) 1 WLR 594 (and see Todd [1985] Conv 177). The facts of the case were relatively simple. M Ltd owned a large estate which was divided into three plots, blue, green and red. They sold the blue land to Mill Lodge Properties who promised, for the benefit of the green and red land, that they would not build more than 300 houses on it. Both the green and the red land then came into the hands of Federated Homes. There was an unbroken chain of express assignments of the benefit of Mill Lodge's promise with the green land, but not with the red (see Figure 9.2).

Federated Homes successfully claimed an injunction for breach of the covenant when Mill Lodge began building 32 houses more than was permitted under the covenant. The defendant's arguments centred on

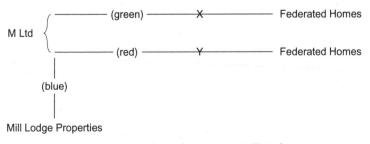

Figure 9.2   *Federated Homes* v. *Mill Lodge*

technical details of the planning permission, but this was decided in the claimant's favour. It then became clear that, as owners of the *green* land with an unbroken chain of express assignments, Federated Homes had the benefit of the covenant and could enforce it against Mill Lodge. However, the judge at first instance went further and said that, under s.62 LPA (by which a conveyance of land transfers all rights which benefit it, see 2.7 and 8.5 above), Federated Homes could also enforce the covenant as owners of the *red* land.

The Court of Appeal agreed with the judge on the planning issue and the green land, but took a different view on the red land. Rather than s.62 they chose to use s.78 LPA to pass the benefit of the covenant to the plaintiff. Until then, it had been thought that the section was merely a 'wordsaving' provision but Brightman LJ rejected this interpretation as it seemed to him to 'fly in the face of the wording'.

The widest interpretation of *Federated Homes* is that the benefit of any covenant made since 1925 automatically runs in equity if it touches and concerns the land, but this represents the radical obliteration of a century of case law about the annexation or assignment of freehold covenants. Annexation and assignment cases (briefly outlined at the end of this section) had been lovingly analysed by generations of academics and the Court of Appeal's decision surprised many commentators. However, the decision has not been challenged. In a recent case, *Stocks* v. *Whitgift Homes* [2001] EWCA Civ 1732, the Court of Appeal stated that the effect of *Federated Homes* is to annex the benefit of covenants to the land, even in cases where the covenant does not expressly specify the land to be benefited, providing there is sufficient extrinsic evidence by which it may be identified.

One difficulty with s.78 is that, unlike the other wordsaving provisions in s.62 and s.79, it does not allow the original contracting parties to express a contrary intention. In *Roake* v. *Chadha* [1984] 3 WLR 40 there was a 50-year-old covenant not to build more than one house per plot on land in a London suburb, and a further clause in the conveyance that the benefit of the covenant would not pass unless it was expressly assigned. All the land changed hands, and a later owner of the burdened land wanted to build another house in his garden. The then owner of the benefiting land sued for an injunction; he argued that, although there was no express assignment of the benefit, this was unnecessary because of s.78 and *Federated Homes*.

Judge Paul Baker QC found himself in a difficult position, for the Court of Appeal in *Federated Homes* had not considered the possibility of a contrary intention. He held that the *Federated Homes* decision on s.78 was binding on him, but he interpreted it so as to give effect to the intention of the original covenantor and covenantee in this case:

> The true position as I see it is that even where a covenant is deemed to be made with successors in title as s.78 requires, one still has to construe the covenant as a whole to see whether the benefit of the covenant is annexed. (p. 46)

Thus, despite *Federated Homes*, the benefit of the covenant had not passed to the plaintiff.

There are a number of additional complications with *Federated Homes'* simplification of the law. For example, the operation of s.78 is probably limited to covenants made since 1925. In addition, because of the wording of the section, it may only apply to the running of the benefit of restrictive covenants.

In cases where the statute will not apply, therefore, it may be necessary to fall back on the old concepts of annexation and assignment created in nineteenth-century cases. Annexation – the attaching of the benefit of a covenant to the land – can be illustrated by *Rogers* v. *Hosegood* [1900] 2 Ch 388. In 1869, the Duke of Bedford had bought a plot of land in Kensington and had promised not to build more than one house on it. The deed stated that this was:

> with intent that the covenants might so far as possible bind the premises ... and might enure to the benefit of the [sellers] ... their heirs and assigns and others claiming under them to all or any of their land adjoining or near to the said premises. (p. 389)

The Duke's land passed to Hosegood who decided to build a large block of flats on it, but Rogers, an owner of adjoining land, wanted to prevent the development. The burden of the covenant had clearly passed to Hosegood, so the question was whether the benefit had passed to Rogers. It was held that the benefit had been annexed to his land by the words of the deed, so anyone who subsequently owned that land could enforce the covenant.

Whether or not the benefit has been expressly annexed in this way depends solely on whether the kind of wording in the covenant in *Rogers* v. *Hosegood* can be found in the original conveyance. If it cannot, the successor to the covenantee may attempt to show that annexation of the covenant can be implied by considering all the surrounding circumstances – see *Marten* v. *Flight Refuelling Ltd* [1962] Ch 115.

If there is no annexation, the only alternative is to find a chain of assignments such as existed for the benefit of the green land in *Federated Homes*. If there is no complete express chain, it may be that there could yet be an implied assignment of the benefit. For this to happen, the covenant must have been intended to benefit the land of the original covenantee, and the successor who is attempting to enforce the covenant must have had the benefit expressly assigned to him. In *Newton Abbot Cooperative Society* v. *Williamson and Treadgold Ltd* [1952] Ch 286, a covenant preventing the use of a shop as an ironmongery was not expressed to be for the benefit of the land belonging to the covenantee. The judge, however, was able to look at the surrounding circumstances, and found that the covenantee (who herself ran an ironmongery and understandably did not want competition):

> took the covenant restrictive of the user of the defendants' premises for the benefit of her own business of ironmonger and of her property ... where at all material times she was carrying on that business ... (p. 297)

When the covenantee died, her heir received the land and the benefit of the covenant, which he could then assign expressly to his successor who could enforce it.

If the covenant does not touch and concern the land, or if s.78, annexation and assignment all fail, then the benefit of the covenant does not run to the claimant and he cannot enforce it.

Schemes of development

A third method by which successors in title of the original covenantee might enforce covenants is through what is known as a scheme of development. A scheme of development (or 'building scheme') is another creation of equity and provides a useful method for the modern developer to create and preserve new estates. If the conditions for a scheme are fulfilled, then the burdens (provided the covenants have been protected by registration) and the benefits of restrictive covenants which touch and concern the land run automatically to all owners in the area, thus greatly simplifying the question of whether one owner can stop another breaching a covenant.

There is a scheme of development if there is a defined area of land and all the original purchasers of plots within the area knew that the covenants imposed on them all were intended to be mutually enforceable. As Stamp J said in 1970, '[it is a kind of] local law involving reciprocal rights and obligations' (*Re Dolphin's Conveyance* [1970] Ch 654).

The first known scheme was created in 1767 and upheld in 1866. A large number were created in the nineteenth century and upheld by the courts but, after 1889, the number of successful schemes began to fall. Strict rules were laid down in the judgment in *Elliston* v. *Reacher* [1908] 2 Ch 374, which later judges treated as if it were part of a statute. Four conditions had to be satisfied: there had to be (1) one seller, (2) the plots laid out in advance, (3) mutual restrictions established for mutual benefit, and (4) knowledge by the purchasers of the intended mutual enforceability.

Between 1908 and the 1960s only two schemes were successfully enforced in reported cases but then the climate appears to have changed. In *Re Dolphin's Conveyance* there was neither a common vendor nor were the plots laid out in advance, but the local authority in Birmingham was nevertheless prevented from developing the site because it was held that a building scheme had been created and that the development would have been in breach of covenant. The judge said that *Elliston* v. *Reacher* was only part of a wider rule; here, a scheme arose because of the existence of 'the common interest and the common intention actually expressed in the conveyances themselves' – an intention to create a 'local law' with mutually binding covenants applying within a clearly defined and commonly understood area. In every case it is a question of fact as to what the intentions of the original seller and buyers actually were.

There are often problems in the older cases in finding sufficient numbers of the original documents, and often the original owners are beyond recall as well. Where, as in *Emile Elias & Co Ltd* v. *Pine Groves Ltd* [1993] 1 WLR 305, common interest and intention cannot be shown from the covenants, the courts will apply the rules in *Elliston* v. *Reacher*. In this case the Privy Council emphasised the necessity for a 'common code of covenants'.

In *Stocks* v. *Whitgift Homes* (above), a large residential estate of some 440 acres had been developed in the 1920s and 1930s. Some of the estate was clearly intended to be within a building scheme, but there was a good deal of uncertainty about the rest. In finding that no building scheme existed, even between owners of the properties situated within the area originally intended to be part of the scheme, the Court of Appeal stated that:

> the authorities show that [a] number of characteristics must be established. Among them is certainty: otherwise, in relation to each plot of land said to fall within the scheme, the question will continually arise: does it or does it not so fall? More precisely, is it, or is it not subject to mutually enforceable benefits and obligations, and, if enforceable, by and against the owners of which plots? This essential requirement of certainty makes obvious practical sense. (Judge LJ at para. 110)

Applying the rules

A return to the story of Claire and Mike told earlier in this chapter (see 'The use of diagrams') may make the application of all these rules clearer. The question was whether Mike had the benefit and Claire the burden of the promise made by Adosh to Eve that there should be no building on the land. (There is no building scheme here, of course.)

A glance at the summary of the rules relating to the benefit and the burden (Table 9.1 in the Summary) shows that the strictest requirement relates to the running of the burden. This is therefore always the place to start in a problem of this kind, since otherwise you may go to all the trouble of tracing the benefit and then find that the burden does not run anyway.

To decide whether the *burden* has passed with the land from Adosh to Claire, it is necessary to apply the equitable rules in *Tulk* v. *Moxhay* since the burden cannot run at law: (a) the covenant is negative in substance, (b) it does benefit the land of the original convenantee (Eve) now owned by Mike, and (c) by s.79, it is deemed to have been intended to run (there is no evidence of a contrary intention). As Mike appears to have behaved properly, so that an equitable remedy will not be denied, the final answer regarding the burden depends on whether the covenant was properly protected by registration (see 10.3 and 11.6 below).

The next stage is to test whether the *benefit* has passed with the land from Eve to Mike. Here a fundamental principle emerges. It is not permitted to mix legal and equitable rules: *burden and benefit must run in the 'same medium'*. (In practice this means that if the burdened land has changed hands, and thus equitable principles must be applied, then the equitable rules must also be used for the benefit.) The covenant here does touch and concern the land, so by *Federated Homes* the benefit probably passes in equity. Therefore – subject to registration – Mike will probably be able to prevent Claire building her block of flats.

Note that the original covenantor – Adosh, in this case – will always be liable in contract law (unless a contrary intention is expressed in the contract), but the remedy against him can only be damages if he no longer owns the burdened land.

9.3 The Use of s.56 LPA

Section 56 LPA 1925 may be relevant whenever the person claiming the benefit (or his predecessor in title) owned land nearby at the time the covenant was made. In a sense, it is a legal extension of privity of contract and provides that:

> A person may take ... the benefit of any ... covenant ... over or respecting land ... although he may not be named as a party to the conveyance or other instrument.

It is a way of giving the benefit of a covenant to someone other than those who are named in the deed, providing the covenant purports to be made with him. The section applies if the person alleged to have the benefit of the covenant was identifiable in the covenant agreement, and was in existence at the date of the covenant. The reason for these rules is that it would be unfair if the covenantor were effectively making his promise to everyone in the neighbourhood; he needs to be able to identify, on the day he made the promise, the land-owner(s) who might be able to take action against him.

The rules were established in *Re Ecclesiastical Commissioners for England's Conveyance* [1936] Ch 430. In that case, the court had to decide (in an application under s.84(2) LPA) whether a large house by Hampstead Heath in London was subject to a restrictive covenant. The issue was whether neighbouring landowners had the right to enforce it, and this depended on whether the original landowners who had owned the neighbouring land at the time of the covenant could enforce it through s.56. It was held that a clause in the conveyance which stated that the original covenantor made the promise:

> also as a separate covenant with ... owners for the time being of land adjoining or adjacent to the said land hereby conveyed

was enough for s.56. The neighbours were identifiable from the agreement and were in existence at its date. Their successors in title were able to claim the benefit from them by the usual rules for the running of the benefit, and thus were able to enforce the covenant.

For covenants made after 11 May 2000, the Contracts (Rights of Third Parties) Act 1999 can also be used in this situation. Under s.1 of the Act, a person who is not a party to the contract may enforce it if it purports to confer or expressly confers a benefit on him, so long as the contract identifies him by name, as a member of a class or as answering a particular description, even though he was not in existence when the contract was entered into (see also 6.4). From its wording, it therefore seems that operation of the Act is wider than s.56, since it will allow a landowner to enforce the benefit of a covenant even though it is not purported to be made with him and even though he might not have been identifiable when the covenant was created.

9.4 Discharge and Modification

Covenants are automatically ended ('discharged') in two ways: by the common law, and by statute. Statute also allows covenants to be modified.

Common law

First, if the burdened and benefiting lands are owned by the same person, the covenant cannot be enforced: a person does not have rights against himself. However, if the covenant is part of a building scheme, life after death is possible: the covenants revive if the plots come into separate ownership again later.

Second, if the covenant has been abandoned the courts will not enforce it. This was argued in *Chatsworth Estates* v. *Fewell* [1931] 1 Ch 224. In this case, there was a covenant on a house in a seaside resort restricting its use to that of a private dwelling only. Thirty years later, the then owner started taking paying guests. The claimants warned him of the breach and asked whether he wished to apply to have the covenant modified or discharged under s.84 LPA (below) but he did nothing. When taken to court for the breach, he argued that the claimants had waived breaches by others in the neighbourhood and had therefore abandoned the benefit. The claimants won their injunction to end the breach. Abandonment is a question of fact in every case; here the essential residential character of the area still remained, and the claimants could not be expected to have to 'conduct inquisitorial examinations into their neighbours' lives' in order to see how they were using the land.

In *Shaw* v. *Applegate* [1977] 1 WLR 970 a café owner in another resort was allowed to keep his amusement arcade, contrary to the covenant, because of the claimant's delay in enforcing it. On the facts, the delay had not meant that the claimants had acquiesced in the breach, which would have made the covenant unenforceable, but an injunction – an equitable remedy – was refused on the grounds that the café owner had been lulled into a false sense of security because of the delay, and damages were awarded instead.

Statute

Several statutes authorise the discharge of a covenant; a well-known example is s.127 Town and Country Planning Act 1971 which allows a local authority to carry out a development against a covenant, providing they pay compensation. The most important provision, however, is s.84 LPA, as amended by s.28 LPA 1969. The power to discharge or modify covenants is important because the very existence of the power encourages people to agree to waive covenants. In many cases which do not go to litigation, it is merely a question of the developer 'buying off' the covenants.

A statutory power to end freehold covenants was deemed necessary in 1925 because restrictions on land use could 'enclose individual premises and often whole streets and neighbourhoods in a legal straitjacket' (Polden (1986) 49 MLR 195). There was no discussion of s.84 in Parliament, although it allows the state to destroy private property (the right to enforce the covenant), sometimes without compensation, and the question is whether this is in breach of Article 1, Protocol 1 of the European Convention on Human Rights. This issue has been tested before the European Commission of Human Rights in *S* v. *UK* (Application No. 10741/84). The applicant lost her case there, on the particular facts, but it seems unlikely that any other application, even on different facts, would succeed because of the doctrine of proportionality and the public interest element: 'ensuring the most efficient use of the land for the benefit of the community' (see Dawson [1986] Conv 124 at p. 126).

Applications under the section are made to the Lands Tribunal, a body which spends much of its time determining land valuations for the purposes of rating and compulsory purchase. Appeal on a point of law can be made to the Court of Appeal. Under s.84 the Tribunal has power to modify or discharge any restrictive covenant and some covenants in long leases. There is provision for compensation to be paid in certain cases.

Under s.84, a covenant may be discharged or modified if:

- it should be deemed obsolete due to changes in the character of the property or neighbourhood; or

- it impedes some reasonable use of the land, provided money is sufficient compensation and either (a) 'it provides no practical benefits of substantial value or advantage' or (b) it is contrary to the public interest; or

- the parties agree, expressly or impliedly 'by their acts or omissions'; or

- it will not injure anyone entitled to the benefit.

The Tribunal must have regard to any planning permissions or local plans but these are not decisive. There are innumerable cases on s.84 and each turns on its own facts; two examples are briefly considered here.

Re Bass Ltd's Application (1973) 26 P & CR 156 concerned an application to use land, restricted to housing, as a lorry park; the owner of the burdened land already had planning permission, and the objectors to the covenant's discharge (the owners of the benefit) already suffered from serious traffic noise. The adjudicator found, from a visit to the site, that, although living close to heavy lorries was far from pleasant, the restrictive covenant still conferred a substantial advantage on the objectors in preventing any increase in the number of lorries, and the application therefore failed. (This case is useful in that it lists the questions which must be asked in an application under s.84.)

In *Re University of Westminster* [1998] 3 All ER 1014, the university applied to have discharged or modified covenants restricting the use of one of its properties to particular educational purposes. The Court of Appeal upheld the Lands Tribunal's determination that the covenants could be modified to permit the use of the property for the wider educational purposes the university proposed, but that the covenants could not be discharged entirely. Although the parties who had the benefit of the covenants had not objected to the proposal for discharge, the Lands Tribunal was not satisfied that they realised their possible effect – that the university, or any subsequent owner for that matter, would be able to use the property for any purpose – and that they had not therefore agreed to the discharge of the covenants, as required by s.84(1)(b); nor was the Lands Tribunal convinced that some reasonable use of the property would be impeded by a failure to allow discharge.

It can be seen, even from this brief review, that the Lands Tribunal has a challenging role. Many different interests are involved in these cases: developers, nearby landowners intent on preserving the status quo, 'expert' planners, the general policy that contracts be respected, the wider public interest in land use, and the views of particular political parties (such as the Conservative government's policy of reducing planning restrictions during the 1980s and 1990s). These difficult issues are part of the background of all planning law, private and public.

9.5 Comment

Restrictive covenants are part of the private law of planning, but are just one of several legal strategies to control use of land by others. Alternative ways are: long leases, which may be enlarged to a freehold with the covenants remaining enforceable; conditional fees simple subject to a right of re-entry (see 4.2); and the 'pure principle of benefit and burden' as in *Halsall* v. *Brizell* [1957] Ch 169: a person will not be allowed to escape from positive obligations under a covenant if he wishes to enjoy a related benefit. All these methods can also provide the means to avoid the rule that the burden of positive covenants cannot pass, as will the new commonhold interest (see 6.6 above). However, such arrangements require careful planning: *Rhone* v. *Stephens* illustrates the problems which may arise if the buyer of land fails to consider fully the implications of the non-enforceability of a positive covenant.

Reform of covenants in freehold land has been considered several times in the past. The Law Commission Report No 127 (1984) proposed a new and simple law to govern the running of benefit and burden at law of both restrictive and positive covenants through the creation of new legal interests in land, 'Neighbour Obligations', and a new kind of building scheme in 'Development Obligations'. This proposal was supplemented by a Report in 1991 (Law Com No 201) which recommended that a restrictive covenant should cease to be enforceable after 80 years unless the owner of the benefit could show it was not obsolete.

These proposals have not been taken up, and eventual implementation is uncertain. However, even if the current rules with all their complexities and uncertainties are replaced by a more coherent scheme, the difficult decisions about land use will remain, often providing evidence of the usually concealed political and economic forces affecting land law.

Summary

9.1   There are separate sets of rules to pass the benefit of a covenant at law, and to pass both the benefit and the burden of a covenant in equity. Equity also provides for building schemes which create a mutually enforceable local law (see Table 9.1).

Table 9.1   Summary of the rules relating to the running of freehold covenants

	At Law	*In Equity*
Does the benefit run?	Expressly (s.136 LPA), or Impliedly if: 1. it benefits the land; 2. the covenantee had a legal estate in the benefiting land; 3. the claimant has a legal estate in the benefiting land; 4. it was intended to run.	1. It benefits the land, and 2. Either: i) s.78 applies, or ii) annexation or assignment.
Does the burden run?	Generally not possible.	Under the rule in *Tulk* v. *Moxhay*, if: 1. it is restrictive; 2. it benefited land owned by the covenantee and now owned by the claimant; 3. it was intended to run (s.79); 4. it is protected by registration; 5. the claimant will not be denied an equitable remedy.

Note also building schemes

9.2 Section 56 LPA allows a person not named in a deed to be a party to it if he was referred to in the deed and identifiable at that time. The Contracts (Rights of Third Party) Act 1999 is wider and potentially more helpful.

9.3 Covenants (except those in building schemes) may be ended at common law if the benefiting and burdened land come into the same hands or if the benefit is abandoned.

9.4 Section 84 LPA provides a machinery for the discharge or modification of restrictive covenants which have outlived their useful life; each case is decided on its own facts.

Exercises

9.1 To what extent does equity supplement the legal rules about covenants in freehold land?

9.2 Did the decision *Federated Homes* improve the law?

9.3 What are the advantages of proving a building scheme in an action for enforcing a restrictive covenant?

9.4 What are the limitations of s.56 LPA? What is the effect of the Contracts (Rights of Third Parties) Act 1999?

9.5 In 1930 Karen sold part of her large garden in the Chequers Estate to Barry who built 'The Palace' on it. In 1945 she sold another part of her garden to Phil who promised her that he would not build more than one house on the land and that he would erect and maintain a fence around the land. The promise was stated to be made 'also with owners for the time being of adjoining land, formerly part of the Chequers Estate'.

In 1990 a council estate was built in the fields neighbouring the estate. Karen died and her executors sold her remaining land to Yehudi. Rita has bought Phil's land and plans to build a block of flats with an open, unfenced garden.

Who can enforce the covenants, and who is bound by them? What remedies are available to the parties?

Further Reading

Davis, 'The Principle of Benefit and Burden' 57 CLJ 522

Dawson, 'Restrictive Covenants and Human Rights' [1986] Conv 124

Gravells, 'Enforcement of Positive Covenants Affecting Freehold Land' (1994) 110 LQR 346

Harte, *Landscape, Land Use and the Law* (London: Spon, 1984)

Martin, 'Remedies for Breach of Restrictive Covenants' [1996] Conv 329

Polden, 'Private Estate Planning and the Public Interest' (1986) 49 MLR 195

Preston and Newsom, *Restrictive Covenants Affecting Freehold Lands*, 9th edn (London: Sweet and Maxwell, 1998)

Snape 'The Burden of Positive Covenants' [1994] Conv 477

Todd, 'Annexation After *Federated Homes*' [1985] Conv 177

Part III

Transferring Land

10 Conflicting Interests in Unregistered Land

10.1 **Introduction**

This chapter describes what happens to interests when land is sold which is not yet registered. Chapter 2 was concerned with the normal methods of buying and selling land, but here the issue is not how to transfer an interest; rather, the question is what happens when there is a conflict between the new owner of land and a person who owns another, pre-existing interest in the land, such as a lease or an easement. Although all land must now be registered on transfer or when it is subject to a first legal mortgage, it is still necessary to understand the rules about unregistered land: about 20 per cent of titles remain unregistered and, although the Land Registry is committed to universal registration of title, whether this will ever be achieved is uncertain. It is important to recognise that the systems of unregistered and registered title are fundamentally separate and different. Registered title is dealt with in the next chapter (see 11.1 for a comparison between the two systems).

As in other areas of land law, the rules on unregistered title are easier to grasp if they are seen as answers to real questions. For example, suppose that Mr and Mrs B are about to complete their purchase of a house and have just found out about Jean who lives in the attic and has paid the mortgage instalments for the past five years. Further, their new neighbour, Lloyd, tells them that they cannot alter the outside of their house. They want to know whether they can get rid of Jean, and whether they can install a bay window at the front of the house. Their question is, 'Do Jean and Lloyd own interests which will affect us?' At the same time, Jean and Lloyd (who claims to own the benefit of the restrictive covenant) would each ask: 'Will Mr and Mrs B be able to defeat my interest?' (The same questions arise in relation to a buyer of any interest in land, such as a mortgagee or a lessee: see 2.1 above.)

In order to answer such questions, it is necessary to be able (1) to identify all the interests which can exist in land, and (2) to decide whether they are legal or equitable; a glance at the summaries of the preceding chapters may therefore be useful from time to time.

When the land is unregistered there are three sets of rules to be applied in turn: the rules relating to the register of land charges, the rules on overreaching and the doctrine of notice:

> *The register of land charges* (10.3 below) is a list of burdens on unregistered land.
>
> *Overreaching* (10.4 below) simplifies the buying of land which is subject to a trust, so that a buyer need not worry about beneficiaries: if the buyer pays the purchase price to two trustees, any beneficial interests under the trust are automatically detached from the land and attached to the money.
>
> *The doctrine of notice* was explained in 1.5 above (and see 10.5 below).

10.2 The General Framework

The basic picture

Before the great flood of the 1925 legislation, the basic rules were (briefly) as set out in the box below. (The most important words to concentrate on are *legal* and *equitable*.) Understanding these old rules is essential to grasping the present law because the 1925 changes were a refinement, not a replacement. Briefly:

Pre-1925 Rules

A buyer of a legal interest was bound by all pre-existing legal and equitable interests except:

- trust interests which were overreached, and
- equitable interests of which the buyer for value did not have notice, provided she acted in good faith.

A buyer of an equitable interest was bound by all pre-existing legal and equitable interests.

Legal interests would normally be discovered during the enquiries made before purchase but if, for example, a buyer later found a legal mortgage she would be bound by it. (Of course, the seller would be liable in damages if she failed to deliver the unburdened land she had promised.)

In practice, a buyer of the legal estate normally would have notice of an equitable interest either from an inspection of the land itself or from the deeds: a restrictive covenant might be found in an earlier conveyance of the land, for example, and it was common practice for someone who gained an equitable interest in another person's land to protect that interest by having a note of the details written on the title deeds of the burdened land. Buyers had to act with caution because the courts would hold that they had constructive notice of anything a prudent buyer would have discovered.

The basic picture in unregistered land after 1925

Post-1925 Rules

A buyer in good faith and for value of a legal interest is bound by:

- any pre-existing legal interest, except an unregistered puisne mortgage (see below), and
- any interest which must be registered under the Land Charges Act 1972, and is properly registered, and
- any other interest which has not been overreached, and of which the buyer has notice, actual, imputed or constructive.

(The rules relating to a buyer of an equitable interest remain unchanged.)

After 1925, therefore, the basic scheme in unregistered land was changed by the establishment of a set of registers. Registering interests is intended to protect both the buyer, who is no longer subject to the uncertainties of the doctrine of notice, and the holder of the interest. Thus, registering an interest in the appropriate register is deemed to be 'actual notice' of the charge, so that it binds the buyer, while failure to register usually means that the charge is void, and so does not bind her. Of the five separate registers kept by the Land Charges Department under the Land Charges Act 1972 (LCA) (which replaced the Land Charges Act 1925), the most important is the Land Charges Register (see 10.3 below). Land charges are burdens on land; there are 11 altogether, divided into 'classes' A to F. The interests which can be registered there are, in theory, those which are otherwise difficult for the buyer of land to discover; equally, it would be hard to protect them by notice. These registrable interests are mostly equitable and are often described as 'commercial' rather than 'family' interests. ('Family' (trust) interests are dealt with since 1925 by overreaching.)

Alongside the five charges registers and overreaching (10.4 below), the doctrine of notice resolves any remaining conflicts (10.5 below).

The Land Charges Register should not be confused with the register of local land charges held by each local authority under the Local Land Charges Act 1975, which records those burdens on land, either financial, perhaps resulting from non-payment of council tax, or restricting the use or development of the land, such as a tree preservation order.

10.3 The Land Charges Register

The registrable charges

Under s.2 LCA, the following interests are registrable in the Land Charges Register held by the Chief Land Registrar:

Class A	charges created by a person applying under a statute.
Class B	charges created by a statute, not by a person's application: for example a charge on land created under the Legal Aid Act 1988.
Class C(i)	a puisne mortgage: this is a legal mortgage where the borrower did not deposit the title deeds with the lender; it is therefore frequently not a first mortgage.
C(ii)	a limited owner's charge: this arises where an owner's interest is limited by a trust: if she pays a tax bill herself instead of mortgaging the land to pay it, she owns this equitable interest.
C(iii)	a general equitable charge: this seems to cover, for example, an equitable mortgage of a legal estate without deposit of title deeds, and certain annuities.
C(iv)	an estate contract: a contract to transfer a legal interest in land (see below).
Class D(i)	an Inland Revenue Charge: a charge on land arises automatically if the tax due on an estate at death is not paid.
D(ii)	a restrictive covenant created since 1925, excluding leasehold covenants.
D(iii)	an equitable easement created since 1925 (see below).
Class E	annuities: now obsolete.
Class F	a spouse's right of occupation in the matrimonial home (see below).

Further details of difficult classes

Estate contract

> An estate contract is a contract by an estate owner ... to have a legal estate conveyed to him to convey or create a legal estate, including ... a valid option of purchase, a right of pre-emption or any other like right. (s.2(4)(iv) LCA)

As shown in 2.3, a buyer of land (whether of a fee simple or a lease or some other interest) is normally recognised as having some equitable interest in the land as soon as there is a contract: this right is an estate contract. Most solicitors do not bother to register estate contracts because the contracts are nearly always successfully completed. If, however, completion is delayed, or if the buyer is suspicious of the seller, then the charge should be registered.

An option to purchase arises, for example, where Maria agrees that Jason can buy her land at a certain price, if he decides he wants to. A right of pre-emption (or a right of first refusal), on the other hand, is where Maria agrees with Jason that if she decides to sell her land she will offer it first to him. Both are estate contracts; however, although the option to purchase will bind a purchaser only if protected by registration, as one would expect, it appears that the right of pre-emption needs to be registered only when it can be exercised, that is, when Maria decides to sell (see *Pritchard* v. *Briggs* [1980] Ch 338). The decision in *Pritchard*, that no interest can arise until the decision to sell is made, has been heavily criticised and was recently distinguished in *Dear* v. *Reeves* [2002] Ch 1 (although this case was not about the LCA).

An equitable lease is also an estate contract and ought to have been registered as such in *Hollington Bros Ltd* v. *Rhodes* [1951] 2 All ER 578. Here the owner of the equitable lease failed to protect it by registration and it was therefore held void against the buyer of the freehold reversion – even though he had known about it from the start and had paid less in consequence.

A tenant's option to renew a lease, or to buy the freehold, is a registrable interest within this class; this is so even if it is contained within a legal lease and was known about by all parties (*Phillips* v. *Mobil Oil Co Ltd* [1989] 1 WLR 888).

Equitable easement
This is:

> an easement, right or privilege over or affecting land ... being merely an equitable interest. (s.2(4)(iii) LCA)

Unfortunately, this definition is not as simple as it appears. An equitable easement is the sort of informal, neighbourly arrangement which no one would think of seeing a solicitor about, so it is unlikely to be protected by registration. In *Ives (ER) Investment Ltd* v. *High* [1967] 2 QB 379, a block of flats was being built on a bomb-site and it was discovered that the foundations trespassed on the neighbouring plot. The owner of that plot agreed, unfortunately not by deed, that he would allow the foundations to remain there if he could use a drive over the developer's land. This arrangement was clearly an equitable easement but it was never protected by registration as a Class D(iii) land charge.

Both plots of land changed hands and the new owners of the flats decided they wanted to stop their neighbour's use of their drive. They argued that the equitable easement was void for non-registration. The Court of Appeal decided that the LCA 'was not the end of the matter' since there were rights arising from the mutuality principle and from estoppel (see 13.5) which were not affected by the failure to register. Mutuality is an ancient principle: a person cannot reject a burden, the neighbour using the drive, so long as she wants to enjoy a related benefit, the trespass of the foundations (see also 9.5). The neighbour was therefore allowed to continue to use the drive so long as the foundations of the flats remained on his land. (See also 14.5.)

Ives v. *High* represents one of the very few examples of courts finding a way around the LCA in order to arrive at a just result. In most cases, the principle may be expressed as 'Register or be damned!'.

Spouse's right of occupation
Section 30 of the Family Law Act 1996 gives a married person, as long as she is not a co-owner, a statutory right to occupy the matrimonial home owned by the other spouse. This right of occupation, available to either spouse, was originally created under the Matrimonial Homes Act 1967 in an attempt to solve some of the problems which can arise when one spouse (typically, the husband) is the sole legal owner of the home. Under the pre-1967 law he could sell it and run off whenever he liked, and the deserted spouse could not protect herself and their children in advance – see *National Provincial Bank Ltd* v. *Ainsworth* [1965] AC 1175. In theory, the Class F charge is a simple, cheap and efficient solution – except that many wives do not discover the possibility until it is too late. It is also of no use to people living together who are not married. Although the right of occupation is binding on a purchaser if it has been protected by registration, the court has a discretion to terminate the spouse's rights against a purchaser where it is just and reasonable to do so (s.34(2) FLA), placing on a statutory footing the decision in *Kashmir Kaur* v. *Gill* [1988] 2 All ER 288.

The mechanics of the register

Registering a charge
Registering an interest is a simple matter. Its owner fills in a short form giving her own details, the nature of the charge and the name of the owner of the land which is subject to the charge (the estate owner). All charges are registered against the name of the landowner and not against the land itself, although a name-based register like this causes all kinds of problems, not least because people who fill in forms make typing errors; apparently the register contains charges registered against people with first names like Nacny, Brain and Farnk.

If the wrong name is given on the charge registration form, the registration may well be ineffective. In an extraordinary case where both the registration and the search were against (different) incorrect names, the attempt at registration was held to be valid against a mortgagee, who had taken two years from his discovery of the mistake to take action (*Oak Cooperative Building Society* v. *Blackburn* [1968] Ch 730).

It is of course possible to register ineffective charges on the register, because registration alone does not make the charge valid; for example, a prospective purchaser may need to ensure that the benefit and burden of a registered restrictive covenant have run with the land. The Registrar has the power to remove invalid charges (to 'vacate the register'). In fact, many charges in the register are a waste of space, such as all the estate contracts which have been completed and the puisne mortgages which have been redeemed. The Registrar thus tends to increase rather than reduce the apparent burdens on title.

Searching for a charge

To search for a charge it is simply necessary to fill in a form giving the names of the people who have owned the land. Anyone can search the Register but it is usual – and safer – to have an official search. The staff at the Registry search against the estate owners' names as requested and send back a form giving details of any charges they discover. In practice, these are often already known to the buyer from the investigations before exchange of contracts (see 2.2 above).

The official certificate of search is conclusive (s.10 LCA); if it fails to give details of a charge, the charge (although registered) is void. However, the owner of the charge will receive compensation for the negligence of the Registry. The official certificate also gives the person who required the search 15 working days' protection from having any further charges registered (s.11 LCA). Thus, once the official search has been made, the buyer is safe provided the sale is completed within the 15 days.

It is of course possible that a charge was registered, say in 1930, against the name of the then estate owner, but today's buyer of the land may never discover her name because it is hidden 'behind the root of the title' (the document establishing the seller's title over a minimum of the last 15 years: see 3.2 above). The buyer is deemed to have notice of the registered charge and to be bound by it although no amount of prudence could have uncovered it. In these circumstances, the buyer can claim compensation (s.25 LPA 1969).

As time passes, more and more charges lie behind the root of title. Wade described this problem as a 'Frankenstein's monster' which grows more dangerous and harder to kill as the years pass (Wade [1956] CLJ 216).

The effect of registering a charge

Section 198 LPA states that:

> The registration of any instrument or matter under the provisions of the Land Charges Act ... shall be deemed to constitute actual notice ... to all persons and for all purposes connected with the land affected.

The system thus creates a new way of giving notice of an interest to a buyer of land: registration of a charge binds everyone because registration is 'actual notice'. There is, however, a change from the pre-1925 rule that a prudent buyer could protect herself, because now the buyer has actual notice of the charge, whether or not she could ever have found it in the Register. The only exception to the rule that registration is actual notice is where the official search certificate omits to mention a charge (see 'The mechanics of the register', above). It is therefore effectively the official certificate of search which counts as notice, not the Register.

The effect of failing to register a charge

As shown in *Hollington Bros Ltd* v. *Rhodes* (10.3 above), an unregistered estate contract did not bind the buyer: it was void. However, the rules of voidness are in fact more detailed:

Unregistered Land Charges: s.4 LCA

- Classes A, B, C(i), C(ii), C(iii), F are void against anyone who gives 'value' for any interest.
- Classes C(iv), D(i), D(ii), D(iii) are void against anyone who gives 'money or money's worth' for a legal interest.

Charges in the first group are therefore void for non-registration against anyone who buys any interest in the land, legal or equitable. 'Value' means money, money's worth or an agreement to convey land in consideration of marriage.

The second group of charges is only void for non-registration against a person who buys a *legal* interest and who has paid *money or money's worth for it*; 'money's worth' means exactly what it says, that is anything which is worth money, such as other land or company shares. Where someone is buying only an equitable interest, or is getting married as consideration, an unregistered charge in this group is not void as far as she is concerned. Whether or not she is bound depends not on the LCA but on the pre-1925 law (10.2 above). It is interesting to note that in *registered* land, marriage has ceased to be valuable consideration. The Law Commission ((1998) Law Com No 254) was of the view that:

> marriage consideration is an anachronism and should cease to be regarded as valuable consideration in relation to dealings with registered land. A transfer of land in consideration of marriage is in substance in most cases a wedding gift. (para. 3.43)

It is only when the burdened land changes hands that a charge becomes void for non-registration. Between the original parties, the charge is, of course, enforceable and damages for breach of contract may still be available even if a charge is void against a later buyer of the land. Anyone who gains land through adverse possession or as a gift will also be bound by all interests in the land, whether or not protected by registration, because she is not a buyer.

Section 4 LCA is given even more force by s.199 LPA which provides that an unregistered charge is void even if the buyer did actually know about it:

> A purchaser shall not be prejudicially affected by notice of ... any instrument or matter capable of registration under the provisions of the LCA ... which is void or not enforceable against him under that Act ... by reason of non-registration thereof.

This section has been ruthlessly interpreted by some judges, as in the *Hollington Bros* case (above), where express notice in writing of an unregistered estate contract (an option to renew a lease) was held to be irrelevant. This was taken even further in *Midland Bank Trust Co Ltd* v. *Green* [1981] AC 513. A father granted his son a 10-year option to purchase his farm, which the son was managing and occupying with his family. This was an estate contract, registrable as a Class C(iv) land charge, but which the son never registered. Later the father changed his mind about the option and discovered that, if he sold the legal estate in the land to 'a purchaser for money or money's worth', the son's estate contract would be void. He did just that; the purchaser was his wife, mother of the owner of the unregistered charge, and she knew about the father's scheme and paid far less than the market value of the land. One after another, those concerned in the conflict died and the executors had to sort out who had owned what, and who was now entitled to it.

The House of Lords (reversing the Court of Appeal) held that the unregistered charge was void against the mother. She was the purchaser of the legal estate for money and that was all that was needed:

> The case is plain: the Act is clear and definite. Intended as it was to provide a simple and understandable system for the protection of title to land, it should not be read down or glossed; to do so would destroy the usefulness of the Act. (Lord Wilberforce at p. 528)

The result is not what the creators of the 1925 legislation intended and it conflicts with the position in registered land (see 11.5 below). They wanted to ensure that a the owner of a charge who was living on the land should not lose her interest if she failed to register it, thus retaining, in this respect at least, the principle of constructive notice. This rule is contained in s.14 in Part I of the LPA but unfortunately it was wrongly placed there; it should have been moved to the LCA when that Act was carved out of the original 1922 Act (see 1.2 above). As the effect of s.14 is limited to 'this part of the Act', it cannot affect either s.199 LPA or the LCA.

In *Lloyds Bank plc* v. *Carrick* [1996] 4 All ER 630, an estate contract to buy a long lease of a maisonette was void for non-registration against a later mortgagee. Mrs Carrick had paid the full price to the seller, her brother-in-law, and had moved in – acts sufficient for part performance of the (pre-1989) contract. The parties did not complete the contract and so the legal title was never transferred. The brother-in-law then secretly mortgaged the property to the bank which, when he defaulted on the repayments, sought possession. Mrs Carrick argued that her brother-in-law either held the property on a bare trust for her (as any seller does between exchange of contracts and completion) or under a constructive trust (see 13.3 below) or through estoppel. If the trust arguments had found favour with the Court of Appeal, then Mrs Carrick's rights against the bank would have depended on the doctrine of notice – since she was in occupation, the bank would have had constructive notice of her interest. However, the Court held that her rights arose as a consequence of the contract, and her failure to protect it by registration as a land charge meant that it was void against the bank.

The harsh simplicity of these cases, where the buyer either knew or could easily have discovered the interest of the occupier of land, is the sort of thing that makes people cynical about lawyers and their justice. Just as in *Midland Bank Trust* v. *Green*, the opposite result would have been reached in *Carrick*, as Morritt LJ pointed out, if the rules of registered land (which offer protection to occupiers who have rights in the land – see 11.5 below) had applied: the farmer's son would have been able to exercise his option and Mrs Carrick would have kept her home.

10.4 Overreaching

In order to simplify the process of buying and selling land subject to a trust, it was intended by the framers of the 1925 scheme that trust interests should all be capable of being overreached. Section 2 LPA states:

> A conveyance to a purchaser of a legal estate in land shall overreach any equitable interest or power affecting that estate, whether or not he has notice thereof.

Providing the buyer of any interest in land pays the purchase price to at least two trustees or a trust corporation such as a bank, beneficial interests under a trust are kept behind the 'curtain' of overreaching, a curtain which the buyer need not lift. On overreaching, the rights of the beneficiaries are automatically detached from the land and attached to the purchase price in the hands of the trustees (see Chapter 12 for the roles of trustees and beneficiaries in the new 'trusts of land').

Overreaching applies to any interest under a trust of land, and to a sale by a mortgagee or a personal representative or under a court order. None of the LCA interests, such as equitable charges, restrictive covenants and estate contracts, can be overreached. As Robert Walker LJ pointed out in *Birmingham Midshires Mortgage Services Ltd* v. *Sabherwal* (2000) 80 P & CR 256:

> The essential distinction is ... between commercial and family interests. [A commercial interest] cannot sensibly shift from the land affected by it to the proceeds of sale. [A family interest] can do so ... since the proceeds of sale can be used to acquire another home. (p. 263)

Overreaching beneficiaries' interests simply by paying two trustees is very convenient for buyers; in theory, the beneficiaries are happy too because they are entitled to their share of the proceeds in the safe hands of their trustees (certainly safer than in the hands of a single trustee who might be tempted to run off with the cash). However, it is only convenient for beneficiaries if they agree that the money is as good as the land. The Law Commission has recommended (Law Com No 188) that the consent of beneficiaries in occupation should be obtained before overreaching can take place (as is common practice where there is only one trustee), but this recommendation has not been taken up.

A recent development, although making sound commercial sense, further prejudices the position of beneficiaries: in the registered land case of *State Bank of India* v. *Sood* [1997] Ch 276, in breach of trust two trustees mortgaged a house which they held on trust for themselves and five other beneficiaries, in order to secure past indebtedness and future borrowing – no capital money was paid to the trustees. In a somewhat strained interpretation of s.2 LPA, the Court of Appeal held that this was a transaction which enabled the bank to overreach the equitable rights of the beneficiaries despite the fact that no money was paid to the two trustees: the overreaching took effect on the execution of the charge and at that time the interests of the beneficiaries became attached to the equity of redemption. This decision is consistent with the 1925 policy of encouraging free alienability of land and conforms with lending practice, but removes protection for beneficiaries which is normally in the capital money paid to the trustees. Peter Gibson LJ stated:

> Much though I value the principle of overreaching as having aided the simplification of conveyancing, I cannot pretend that I regard the resulting position in the present case as entirely satisfactory. The safeguard for beneficiaries under the existing legislation is largely limited to having two trustees or a trust corporation where capital money falls to be received. But that is no safeguard at all, as this case has shown, when no capital money is received on and contemporaneously with the conveyance. (p. 290)

10.5 The Doctrine of Notice

If an interest cannot be registered because it does not fit into the categories set out in the LCA, the next step is to decide whether the interest can be overreached. If it cannot be (or if it has not been) overreached, then any conflict between the interests of buyers and owners of pre-existing interests must be resolved by the pre-1925 rules (see 10.2 above). The same is true for a buyer of land who is not the kind of buyer against whom an unregistered charge is void under the LCA (see 10.3 above).

In these situations, conflict between the buyer of a *legal* interest in land and the owner of some pre-existing *equitable* interest in it must be resolved by the doctrine of notice. A buyer in good faith of a legal estate for value ('equity's darling') is only bound by equitable interests of which she had notice, actual, imputed or constructive (see 1.5 above). Constructive notice means that a buyer is deemed to have notice of the rights of anyone living there (or receiving rent from the person living there). Therefore, in addition to checking the deeds, all buyers must carefully inspect the land to discover who is there and what rights they may have.

In *Kingsnorth Finance Co Ltd* v. *Tizard* [1986] 1 WLR 783, a husband was the sole legal owner but his wife shared the equitable interest in their home. The marriage deteriorated and Mrs Tizard spent most of her nights away from home, unless her husband was away on business, but she looked after the house, cooked the children's meals and kept most of her belongings there. He then mortgaged the house without telling her and went to America with the money, leaving Mrs Tizard and the finance company to fight it out. Judge Finlay QC held that the mortgagee had constructive notice of her rights because she was, on the facts, 'in occupation'. The bank's agent knew that the legal owner, the husband, was married, although he had described himself as single on the mortgage application form, and so the agent ought to have made more enquiries about the wife:

> the plaintiffs had, or are to be taken to have had [through their agent], information which should have alerted them to the fact that the full facts were not in their possession and that they should make further inspections or inquiries; they did not do so and in these circumstances I find that they are fixed with notice of the equitable interest of Mrs Tizard. (p. 794)

What a prudent buyer ought to do depends on the facts of each case. There is no need to open drawers and wardrobes to see what clothes are there, but in suspicious circumstances an unannounced visit should probably be made. In this case, there should have been further enquiries and Mrs Tizard should have been interviewed.

The generous view taken of occupation in this case applies to all cases of constructive notice. In the *Tizard* case it was probably the right decision, although the wife's occupation there was borderline. Of course, if the finance company had paid two trustees, Mrs Tizard's interest would have been overreached and she would have had to leave the house.

Table 10.1 shows some of the important cases where the doctrine has been applied, but it must be stressed that, since any interest in unregistered land which is not governed by the rules of land charge registration and has not been overreached is subject to the doctrine of notice, this is a residual

Table 10.1   Doctrine of notice in unregistered land

Case	Type of interest	Result
Kingsnorth Finance v. *Tizard* (above)	Equitable interest behind a trust	Notice; wife won
Ives v. *High* (above)	Equitable easement, mutual rights, estoppel	Notice; drive-user won
Binions v. *Evans* [1972] Ch 359	Contractual licence	Notice; widow won
Shiloh Spinners Ltd v. *Harding* [1973] AC 691	Equitable lessor's right of re-entry	Notice; lessor won

but open-ended category. Note also that all pre-1926 restrictive covenants and equitable easements are subject to the doctrine of notice, as well as Class C(iv) and Class D charges against a purchaser for marriage.

10.6 **Comment**

Interests in unregistered land are governed by an assortment of rules. The Land Charges Act represents a small part of the system but its complexity usually absorbs more time than its importance deserves. The major problem must be the way in which, contrary to the aim of the 1925 draftsmen, buyers can destroy the unregistered interests of occupiers even though they knew, or ought to have known, about them before buying the land. It is also unjust and unjustifiable since it is relatively easy for a buyer to inspect land and discover an occupant: to enforce a rule protecting occupiers would not necessarily lead to injustice through uncertainty – indeed, this is what happens in registered land.

Other problems with the LCA are the narrow definitions of the registrable interests, the illogical difference between the provisions for voidness, the nature of the name-based register and the way in which the system tends to clog titles rather than to clear them. These have led to much criticism. Various reforms have been suggested; but the final answer seems to be that of the 1956 Report on Land Charges (Cmnd 9825). The Committee confessed that 'to rectify the machinery is a task beyond the wit of man' (Wade [1956] CLJ 216). However, the importance of the actual custom and practice of conveyancers is shown by the fact that, 'fortunately, none of these deficiencies seem to matter in real life' (Wade, p. 234).

The difficulties are such that lawyers have given up, in the expectation that, if all the land in the country ever becomes registered, the Land Charges Register can be given a quick and efficient burial, preferably in an unmarked pauper's grave. However, you may consider over-optimistic the hope that the move towards universal registration of title will solve all the problems of buyers and sellers of land. The next chapter continues the story of tensions between the rights of beneficiaries and others in occupation and those of buyers of the land (often a bank or building society lending money on the security of a mortgage) where title to land is registered.

Summary

10.1 A buyer of any interest in unregistered land is automatically bound by (nearly) all existing legal interests in the land.

10.2 Eleven 'commercial' interests must be registered in the Land Charges Registry if they are to bind a buyer of the burdened land.

10.3 If interests which are registrable under the Land Charges Act have not been properly registered against the correct name of the estate owner, or do not appear on the official search certificate, they do not bind the buyer even if she actually knew about them.

10.4 Much of land charges registration law is complex, illogical and unfair, but probably impossible to reform.

10.5 'Family' (trust) interests are not registrable but can be overreached by a buyer who pays two trustees.

10.6 If an equitable interest is not registrable and has not been overreached, the rights of a buyer of a legal interest in the land depend on the doctrine of notice; the buyer of an equitable interest is probably bound by any existing equitable interests.

Exercises

10.1 When does equity's darling appear on the scene in unregistered land?

10.2 Against whom is an unregistered land charge void?

10.3 Did the House of Lords come to the right decision in *Midland Bank Trust Co v. Green*?

10.4 Hilary is the sole legal owner of a four-storey house, title to which is unregistered, and which is subject to a restrictive covenant that it should be used as a private dwelling house only. She lives on the first floor and her aged mother, Lucy (who contributed a quarter of the cost of the house when it was bought), occupies the ground floor.

Hilary is a compulsive gambler on the Stock Exchange and recently lost a good deal of money. She met Emma at the hairdresser's and in the course of a chat they agreed that Emma should rent the basement of Hilary's house for three years. Emma moved in and has paid rent regularly. Hilary then accepted £2000 from Clive, a colleague, as a deposit on a ten-year lease of the top floor of her house. Nothing was put in writing for tax reasons.

Six weeks later Hilary decided to emigrate. Clive has discovered that she has made an agreement in writing to sell the whole house to Dee.

Clive, Lucy and Emma seek your advice.

Further Reading

Harpum, 'Purchasers with Notice of Unregistered Land Charges' [1981] CLJ 213

Offer, *Property and Politics 1870-1914* (Cambridge: Cambridge University Press, 1981)

Thompson, 'The Purchaser As Private Detective' [1986] Conv 283

Wade, 'Land Charge Registration Reviewed' [1956] CLJ 216

Yates, 'The Protection of Equitable Interests under the 1925 legislation' (1974) 37 MLR 87

11 Registered Title

11.1 Introduction

The idea of a register of landownership was promoted in the nineteenth century by a non-lawyer, Robert Torrens. Working in a deeds registry in South Australia, he was dismayed by the complexity of traditional unregistered conveyancing. His scheme, which worked efficiently in Australia, spread through the common law world, although it was never widely accepted in the United States. After two earlier attempts in the nineteenth century to introduce a system of voluntary land registration in England, some success was achieved when the Land Transfer Act 1897 made registration compulsory in London.

A more effective scheme was introduced by the Land Registration Act 1925, eventually extending the system of registration across England and Wales, district by district. The move towards complete registration of all land has accelerated in recent years. In 1990, all districts of England and Wales became areas of compulsory land registration, in which freehold land and leases over 21 years were required to be registered on sale (and, in the case of such leases, on creation). In 1998, previously unregistered freehold land and legal leases over 21 years were required to be registered, not just on sale, but whenever transferred or subject to a first legal mortgage. The Land Registration Act 2002 has now extended compulsory registration to leases with more than seven years to run in order to include the increasing number of shorter commercial leases.

A strategic objective of the Land Registry is to complete the Land Register by 2012. There are currently about 18 million titles on the Register, accounting for over 80 per cent of the estimated potential titles. Some five million titles remain unregistered, and the Land Registry is taking positive steps to persuade these landowners, predominantly the Crown Estate, public bodies and the owners of large private estates, of the advantages of land registration.

The historical complexity and lack of clarity in the registered land system had long been recognised and over the years a number of amendments to the 1925 Act were introduced. In 1998, the Law Commission and Land Registry together published their consultative document 'Land Registration for the Twenty-First Century', Law Com No 254, which contained a summary and criticism of the operation of the law along with initial proposals for a radical reform of registered conveyancing through electronic conveyancing. They published a draft

Bill in Law Com No 271 in 2001 which was enacted as the Land Registration Act 2002 and came into force on 13 October 2003, abolishing the LRA 1925. The operation of the 2002 Act is supported by a new regulatory framework contained in the Land Registration Rules 2003.

The 2002 Act has brought about major changes to the system of title registration. Perhaps the most important will be a progressive introduction of voluntary electronic conveyancing from 2006 which will allow the instantaneous creation and transfer of estates and interests in land. The Electronic Communications Act 2000 has implemented the legal changes necessary for the future reforms to take place, and the move towards electronic conveyancing has already started with a trial of registering the discharge of mortgages by electronic means.

Registered and unregistered systems compared

Unregistered conveyancing is a private system of transferring interests in land, whereas the Register acts as a public record of land ownership. A fundamental distinction between the systems of unregistered and registered land is that in the former the basis of title is possession, established by producing the title deeds, whereas in the latter it is the registration of ownership at the Land Registry which counts.

In the unregistered system, as we have already seen, estates and interests can be legal or equitable. In registered land, interests cannot be legal unless they are entered on the Register (with the notable exception of certain interests which have what is known as 'overriding' status (see below, 11.5)).

For a purchaser of unregistered land, third-party interests are discovered by examining the deeds or the Land Charges Register or through inspection (and the doctrine of notice). (The difficulties associated with unregistered conveyancing, especially the Land Charges Register and the residual use of the doctrine of notice, have been examined in the previous chapter.) A person who buys land which is already registered will only be bound by those third-party interests which appear on the Register or are interests which override registration (although, admittedly, these latter interests do also require inspection and enquiry).

Traditionally, there are three essential elements or principles of title registration, known as 'Mirror', 'Curtain' and 'Guarantee'. The Register is supposed to *mirror* the actual structure of title and third-party rights in the land, so that, in theory at any rate, a potential buyer (or anyone else, for that matter) simply has to read the entry in order to discover who owns the land and who else has an interest in it – the uncertainties of the doctrine of notice should have no place in a system of registered title. The *curtain* principle refers to overreaching, the mechanism by which land subject to beneficial trust interests can safely be bought (see 10.4 above). Finally, since it is fundamental that there should be confidence in the system, the state *guarantees* the accuracy of the titles on the Register and will indemnify anyone who suffers loss as a result of any mistake on it.

11.2 The Register

The divisions of the Register

The Register, the mirror of the title to the land, is held on computerised record at one of 24 District Land Registries. It is now an open record and, for the payment of a small fee, anyone can easily get a copy of an individual Register, either by completing a form and sending it to the appropriate District Land Registry, or instantaneously on line through the Land Registry website.

Each individual Register is divided into three sections:

Divisions of the Register
- Property Register
- Proprietorship Register
- Charges Register

The Property Register

This part of the Register describes the title to the land (freehold or leasehold) and any benefits attached to it (such as the benefit of an easement). One plot of land may have several registered titles – for example the freehold and one or more long leases; each has its own title number and entry in the Register. The address is given and reference is made to a plan on which the plot of land is outlined in red. Thus, unlike the Land Charges Register, the Land Register is a 'land-based', not a 'name-based' register.

The Proprietorship Register

This gives the nature of the title under the registration system; there are several kinds (see 11.4 below). The Proprietorship Register states the name and address of the owner, who is called 'the registered proprietor'. (In problem questions therefore, any reference to 'fee simple owner' suggests the land is not yet registered, while a 'registered proprietor' means that it is registered.) The Proprietorship Register also contains any restrictions to which the land is subject, protecting some third-party interests by limiting the power of the registered proprietor to deal with the land (see 11.6 below).

The Charges Register

This part of the Register contains details of burdens on the land, such as the interests which, in unregistered land, would appear in the Land Charges Register.

11.3 Interests in Registered Land

The basic rule in a conflict between a buyer and the owner of a third-party interest in the land is that a buyer is bound by any interest which is on the Register, and by any interests which override either first registration or subsequent dispositions by the registered proprietor.

The normal range of interests – freeholds, leases, easements and all the rest – still exists in registered land, but its original proponents were prepared to pay the price of legal complexity in the hope of functional simplicity by superimposing a new set of categories on the traditional structure:

Categories of interests in registered land

Title interests

These are the most important interests and must be substantively registered (11.4 below).

Interests which override either first registration or subsequent dispositions by the registered proprietor

This category of interests, although binding on everyone who gains a later interest in the land, is not protected by entry on the Register and can only be discovered by means of inspection and enquiry. These interests are listed in LRA 2002, Schedules 1 and 3 (11.5 below).

Other interests which are subject to entry on the Register

These were formerly known as 'minor interests' and comprise those third-party interests which burden the title but which are not listed in Schedules 1 and 3. Unless the owner of the particular interest is also in occupation of the land, these interests bind a purchaser only if entered on the Register (11.6 below).

11.4 Title Interests

These are the interests which, on sale, transfer or first legal mortgage (and also, in the case of leases, on creation), must be substantively registered with independent title and will therefore have their own title number. Essentially, this means freeholds, and leases granted for more than seven years (although, by s.118 LRA 2002, this period of seven years can be, and probably will be, reduced in the future by the Lord Chancellor). In addition, certain other short leases must be registered, the most important of which are reversionary leases (see 5.3 above) granted for less than seven years which take effect in possession after three months from the date of the grant (an example might be student tenancies granted in May or June but not taking effect until the new academic year in September or October).

Classes of title

In unregistered land, some titles are in practice not as secure as others, such as a title obtained by adverse possession, since there are no title deeds to prove it. In registered land the Register reflects the actual state of the title to the land, so it is necessary to classify the titles to show how strong they are. There is provision for second-rate titles to be upgraded (s.62 LRA 2002). A registered title may be any of the following (ss 9, 10 LRA 2002):

- absolute
- possessory
- qualified

'Absolute' freehold or leasehold title is the strongest: the registered proprietor with absolute title has a better right than anyone else to the land (although there are still circumstances where the title might be open to alteration by courts or the Registrar (see 11.8 below)). Absolute title is subject only to third-party interests protected on the Register and by interests which have overriding status (11.3 above); if the registered proprietor is a trustee, his rights are also subject to the trust or, if a lessee, to the covenants in the lease.

'Possessory' titles are rare; they are granted by the Registrar when the alleged owner's title is based only on possession, not on title deeds. The Registrar guarantees the title only as far as dealings after first registration are concerned; no promises are made concerning the right of the first registered proprietor to the land.

'Qualified' titles are almost unheard of; they are granted only if the Registrar has some specific reservation about the title.

For leases, there is an additional class of title: 'good leasehold'. Good leasehold title is as valuable as absolute leasehold title except that, because the freehold has not yet been registered, the Registrar does not guarantee the right of the freeholder to have granted the lease.

11.5 Interests which override registration

There are certain third-party interests which are not required to be protected by entry on the Register but which override the buyer's interests, whether or not he knew, ought to have known, or even could have known, about them. Since they do not appear on the Register, the greater the number of interests which are given overriding status, the less the Register acts as an accurate reflection of the title. The traditional explanation given for the existence of overriding interests is that people who have the benefit of these particular rights cannot reasonably be expected to protect them through registration. By their very nature, some of the overriding interests (the list of these was formerly contained in s.70(1) LRA 1925) did not lend themselves to protection by entry on the Register, such as easements created through prescription or by implication and, where there is actual occupation, rights arising under a constructive trust or through estoppel. That argument, however, did not apply to others (for example expressly created legal easements and legal leases for 21 years or less) and it was the objective of the Law Commission and the Land Registry to limit these as far as possible ((2001) Law Com No 271, para. 2.25). The 2002 Act has reduced the number and scope of these interests, and others will require formal protection on the Register in due course.

Since a buyer of unregistered land will already be bound by third-party interests under the rules of unregistered conveyancing, the 2002 Act makes certain distinctions beween those interests which will override first registration (listed in Schedule 1) and those which will override subsequent, registered dispositions of the land (listed in Schedule 3).

Short leases (Schedule 1, para. 1; Schedule 3, para. 1)

Leases granted for more than seven years are substantively registrable (11.4 above). Leases granted for seven years or less override on first and subsequent registration and a purchaser will be bound by them. Note that, as discussed above, those reversionary leases taking effect more than three months after the date of the grant must be substantively registered and therefore cannot have overriding status, even if they do not exceed seven years.

Rights of occupiers (Schedule 1, para. 2; Schedule 3, para. 2)

The 1925 Act recognised the need to protect the third-party interests of people who were in actual occupation of land but who had not protected their rights in the land by registration, perhaps because the right had arisen informally or because they thought that the mere fact of their occupation was enough protection against a purchaser (see (2001) Law Com No 254, para. 5.61).

By s.70(1)(g) LRA 1925, perhaps the most contentious and certainly the most litigated of the overriding interests under the 1925 Act, the interests of a purchaser or mortgagee would be defeated if the person claiming the interest could prove three things:

1. that he had a right 'subsisting in reference to land', and
2. that he was in 'actual occupation' (or in receipt of rents and profits), and
3. that no enquiry was made of him.

With certain modifications, the 2002 Act maintains the protection offered to occupiers who have interests in the land they are occupying. Much of the s.70(1)(g) case law remains relevant.

In order to override, both Schedules provide that the interest must be '[a]n interest belonging to a person in actual occupation, so far as relating to the land of which he is in actual occupation'. In addition, Schedule 3 contains certain exceptions which prevent the interest of an occupier from overriding subsequent registered dispositions of the land. These are considered below, but it is first necessary to examine the meanings of 'interest' and 'actual occupation'.

Interest

The interest must be a proprietary interest in the land, for example possessory rights arising out of a period of adverse possession, or an estate contract (a contract to buy land). A beneficial interest under a trust of land is sufficient (see *Williams & Glyn's Bank Ltd* v. *Boland* [1981] AC 487, below) and a right arising out of an estoppel (s.116 LRA 2002). Most licences to occupy land are not seen as property interests: in *Ashburn Anstalt* v. *Arnold* [1989] Ch 1 a 'mere contractual licence would not be binding on a purchaser of land even though he had notice of the licence'. However, if such a licence affected the conscience of the buyer, then a constructive trust might be imposed (see 13.3, 14.4 below) and this would be sufficient to override. Some rights are excluded by statute: a spouse's right of occupation under the Family Law Act 1996; rights under the Access to Neighbouring Land Act 1992; an original tenant's right to an overriding lease under the Landlord and Tenant (Covenants) Act 1995.

Contrasting examples of s.70(1)(g) in action will serve to show the necessity of being able to establish an interest in the land. (It must be stressed that occupation, of itself, is insufficient to override the interests of a purchaser.) In *Williams & Glyn's Bank Ltd* v. *Boland* (above), Mrs Boland had a beneficial interest in the family home but had failed to protect it on the Register. Her husband, the sole registered proprietor, mortgaged the house to the bank. He was unable to repay the loan and the bank wanted to sell the house. The House of Lords decided that Mrs Boland's beneficial interest included the right to occupy and was sufficient to amount to an interest in the land. Coupled with her actual occupation (and the fact that the bank had made no enquiry of whether she had an interest in the land), this amounted to an overriding interest which would defeat the mortgage.

However, in *City of London Building Society* v. *Flegg* [1988] AC 54, Mr and Mrs Flegg had an unprotected beneficial interest under a trust in a house with two registered proprietors, their daughter and son-in-law, who failed to repay the mortgage loan. The Fleggs were in actual occupation and no enquiry had been made of them, and yet the building society was able to defeat their interest. The parents had argued (successfully in the Court of Appeal, following *Boland*) that they had a right 'subsisting in reference to land' for the purposes of s.70(1)(g) when the mortgage was registered, and that they therefore had an overriding interest which should defeat the bank. The basis of their claim under s.70(1)(g) was their right to occupy the land under the trust. The House of Lords held that, from the moment that the lender overreached the beneficial interests by paying the mortgage money to two trustees, the beneficiaries no longer had a right to occupy the land but merely a right (under the rules of the old trust for sale) to share in the proceeds of sale. Lord Templeman said:

> The right of the [beneficiaries] to be and remain in actual occupation of Bleak House ceased when [their] interests were overreached by the legal charge ... There must be a combination of an interest which justifies continuing occupation plus actual occupation to constitute an over-riding interest. Actual occupation is not an interest in itself. (pp. 73, 74)

Flegg was applied in *State Bank of India* v. *Sood* [1997] Ch 276 where the interests of the five beneficiaries were overreached on execution of the charge to the bank, even though no capital money was payable (see 10.4 above).

The moral for beneficiaries is that they must protect themselves by entering their interest on the Register. However, if there is only one legal owner, the beneficiary is safe for as long as he remains in actual occupation (unless, of course, a second trustee is appointed). Conversely, a buyer of registered land paying two trustees is safe from any beneficial owners, but, if he pays only one, his rights are subject to what Lord Templeman referred to in *Flegg* as 'the waywardness of actual occupation'.

Actual occupation

Under s.70(1)(g), an overriding interest arose when there was a right in land coupled either with actual occupation, or where the owner of the right was 'in receipt of rents and profits'. The 2002 Act has removed the protection afforded to the owner who was in receipt of rents and profits (except where the protection already existed under s.70(1)(g) before 13 October 2003), who must now protect any lease through registration, unless of course it has overriding status in its own right as a legal lease for seven years or less.

Whether or not a person is 'in actual occupation' can sometimes be problematic. It used to be the case, for example, that where a husband was the sole registered proprietor, his wife, even though she may have contributed to the purchase price and therefore have had a beneficial interest in the land, would not, due to the perceived unity of husband and wife, be seen as being in actual occupation. This idea of the wife's occupation as 'nothing but a shadow of her husband's' was considered to be obsolete by Lord Wilberforce in *Boland* (above), who held that occupation in every case was a question of fact.

A person may be deemed to be in actual occupation even though he is elsewhere, provided that there remains sufficient physical presence to put the purchaser on notice that there is someone in occupation (see *Malory Enterprises Ltd* v. *Cheshire* [2002] Ch 216). If such physical presence is lacking, under the 2002 Act the interest will not be overriding unless the purchaser had actual knowledge of it (Schedule 3, para. 2(c) – see below). In *Abbey National Building Society* v. *Cann* [1991] 1 AC 56, the House of

Lords held that a mother whose belongings were moved into her new house some 35 minutes before completion of the purchase was not sufficiently in occupation at the time, Lord Oliver stating that actual occupation 'involves some degree of permanence and continuity'.

A related question is the stage at which the person must be in actual occupation. It was established in *Cann* that, for s.70(1)(g), both the right and the occupation must have existed at the moment the transfer was executed, rather than at the time of registration, as the statute seemed to indicate. This pragmatic interpretation is now supported by Schedule 3, para 2, which expressly states that the interest and the occupation must exist 'at the time of the disposition'.

It is also necessary to consider the position where a person has a right over land but is occupying only part of it. In *Ferrishurst* v. *Wallcite* [1999] 1 All ER 977, Ferrishurst took a sublease of some offices, along with an option to purchase from its landlord the lease of the whole premises which also included a garage. It failed to protect the option by registration but, when the landlord sold the lease to Wallcite, it argued successfully in the Court of Appeal that it had an overriding interest over both offices and garage. The 2002 Act has reversed this decision, and any interest protected by occupation is restricted to the land which is actually occupied.

When the interest of a person in actual occupation will not be overriding
Under Schedule 3, the interest of a person in actual occupation does not override a registered disposition in three situations. Firstly, there is no protection where the occupier does not disclose his right when asked about it, when he could reasonably have been expected to do so (para. 2(b)). Secondly, there is no protection where the person's occupation is not obvious on a reasonably careful inspection of the land and where the purchaser does not have actual knowledge of the interest (para. 2(c)). The third exception (para. 2(d)) concerns those reversionary leases of less than seven years which take effect in possession after three months from the date of the grant and should have been substantively registered (above). Where possession under the lease has not yet taken place, any occupation by the prospective tenant of the lease will be under some other right, and the lease cannot be used to override the transfer to the purchaser. It is unlikely that this third exception will occur very often.

Comment
Paragraph 2 protects those occupiers who have an otherwise unprotected interest in the land. In the future, when electronic conveyancing becomes compulsory, many of the equitable interests which are now protected if there is actual occupation will no longer be so protected. Such interests will not exist at all until they are entered on the Register, and so there will be nothing for the occupation to protect. Paragraph 2 will be restricted to protecting those occupiers' interests which have arisen informally, through resulting or constructive trusts or through estoppel. Given the policy behind the 2002 Act, this makes sense but, as has been seen, certain anomolies and injustices remain – *Boland* represented the high point of

protection for beneficial owner-occupiers in registered land, but decisions since 1981 such as *Flegg* and *Cann* have shown a gradual withdrawal from it.

The effect of *Boland* was that institutional lenders began, properly, to ensure that there were no resident beneficiaries with rights. Anyone who was going to live in the house was required to agree that the mortgage would take priority over their interest, if any, and this meant that occupying beneficiaries would not be caught out by a secret mortgage or sale by their trustee. It was also the case that beneficiaries who were aware of their rights in the land began to insist on their names being placed on the legal title, so that their co-owners could not mortgage the land without their agreement and, as in the case of *Flegg*, destroy their property rights. This is certainly a contributing factor to the considerable increase in the number of cases of undue influence in recent years which itself, as we have seen, has led the courts to develop principles which must be followed by mortgage lenders in order to prevent their commercial interests being defeated (see *Royal Bank of Scotland* v. *Etridge* [2002] 2 AC 773 and 7.3 above).

Easements and profits (Schedule 1, para. 3; Schedule 3, para. 3)

Under s.70(1)(a) LRA 1925 and following the controversial case of *Celsteel Ltd* v. *Alton House Holdings Ltd* [1985] 1 WLR 204, both legal and equitable easements were overriding interests. In line with the policy of reducing the number of interests which are binding yet do not appear on the Register, the 2002 Act has restricted the overriding effect of easements and profits. Only legal easements and profits now override first registration, (Schedule, 1 para. 3). By s.27(2)(d) and Schedule 3, para. 3, the types of legal easement and profit which can override subsequent dispositions of the land are substantially limited. Those which have been expressly created must be registered and cannot override a registered disposition. An easement or profit which has arisen informally, either impliedly or through prescription (see 8.5 above) is capable of overriding, unless the new proprietor did not actually know about it and its existence was not apparent on a reasonably careful inspection of the land. However, an informally created legal easement which amounts to what Law Com No 271 terms an 'invisible' easement (para. 8.70), such as a right of drainage, could now easily be defeated, and so an exception is made of those easements and profits which can be shown to have been exercised in the year preceding the disposition of the land to the purchaser. This provision encourages owners of easements which are used only intermittently to protect them by registration rather than rely on them being disclosed to the prospective purchaser during pre-contract enquiries (which provides actual notice of the interest). This reform is an attempt to find a balance between the two competing objectives of protecting important third-party rights in land and the need not to burden land with rights which a new owner could not have discovered.

Transitional provisions

Clearly, many easements and profits which would have had overriding status under the 1925 Act are excluded from protection under Schedule 3. In order that the benefit of these pre-existing rights is not lost, Schedule 12, para. 9 provides that easements and profits which existed as overriding interests under s.70(1)(a) before 13 October 2003 will continue to have overriding status. In addition, an easement or profit created impliedly or by prescription within a period of three years from that date will have overriding status, even if the new registered proprietor did not have actual knowledge of it, it was not obvious on a reasonable inspection and it had not been used for a year before the disposition.

Squatters' rights

The new law on adverse possession of registered land has been covered in Chapter 3. However, a further question arises as to whether a new registered proprietor will be bound by the existing rights of an adverse possessor of the land. Under s.70(1)(f) LRA 1925, the rights of an adverse possessor amounted to an overriding interest. This led on occasion to the situation where the title of the new registered owner could be defeated by the possessory rights of a person who had successfully adversely possessed land for 12 years but who perhaps was no longer in possession, even though there might be no way for the new owner to know about the squatter.

With two exceptions, under the 2002 Act the rights of a squatter do not override first registration, so a new owner will be comparatively safe. The first exception is that the first registered proprietor will take the land subject to any rights under the Limitation Act 1980 of which he has notice (s.11(4)(c) LRA 2002); in other words a squatter who has successfully adversely possessed the (unregistered) land for 12 years, although no longer in possession, will be able to have the Register altered in his favour, providing the new owner had notice of the adverse possession. The second exception is a transitional provision: until 13 October 2006, the new owner will be bound by any such rights whether he has notice of them or not (this second exception also applies where the land is already registered).

These reforms, along with the new regime of adverse possession in registered land which is much more favourable to the paper owner than formerly, are an enticement to land owners with unregistered title to apply voluntarily for first registration, an important part of the strategy of the Land Registry in moving towards complete registration of titles.

Other rights which override registration

For the sake of completeness it is necessary consider other rights which override. Perhaps the most important of these is the local land charge. Although not appearing on the Register, anyone contemplating the purchase of land will automatically check at the local authority's Local Land Charges Registry for any local land charges affecting the property.

Other rights which will bind a purchaser on first registration and subsequent transfers of the land are: customary rights; public rights; an interest in coal or a coal mine; and certain rights to mines and minerals.

There is a further category of old s.70(1) overriding interests which had their origin in feudal tenure and currently retain overriding status. These interests, such as manorial rights, have been described as 'relics from past times' ((2001) Law Com 271, para. 8.88) and will be phased out ten years from the introduction of the Act, on 13 October 2013. They will not necessarily disappear altogether (since if they had, the state would perhaps be in breach of ECHR Article 1, Protocol 1), because their owners have 10 years to protect them by registration or, if the land is not yet registered, by a caution against first registration.

11.6 The Protection of Third-party Interests which do not Override

This section refers to the class of interests which, under the 1925 scheme were known as 'minor interests' and consisted of those interests which were not capable of substantive registration with their own title number, nor amounted to overriding interests within the list in s.70(1). These minor interests had to be protected by entry on the Register, and a failure to do so meant that the purchaser would not be bound unless the interest was also coupled with occupation and therefore amounted to an overriding interest under s.70(1)(g). Similarly, under the 2002 Act such interests must be protected by registration, although they are no longer known as minor interests.

There used to be four methods of registering a minor interest, depending on the kind of interest which was to be protected: by notice on the Charges Register, and by restriction, caution or inhibition on the Proprietorship Register. The Law Commission believed ((1998) Law Com No 254, paras 6.43 *et seq.*) that these four methods of protecting minor interests were unnecessarily complicated, particularly since only the entry by notice automatically bound a purchaser and, consequently, the 2002 Act has now simplified the rules.

Restriction

A restriction prevents dealings with a property unless certain conditions are met. It is usually entered (in the Proprietorship Register) by the registered proprietor or the Registrar and is frequently used to protect beneficiaries under a trust by requiring payment to two trustees in event of sale or other disposition. When used in this manner, the restriction gives effect to the 'curtain' principle in registered land.

Inhibition

Under the 1925 Act, an inhibition could be placed on the Proprietorship Register by order of the court or the Registrar forbidding any dealing with the land. Although quite rare, it was used in cases of bankruptcy or suspected fraud. No new inhibitions can be created after 13 October 2003. Instead a form of restriction is used.

Caution

There were two kinds of caution under the 1925 Act: firstly, a *caution against first registration*, which, on first registration, allowed the cautioner an opportunity to argue his claim to a third-party interest in the land; and secondly, a *caution against dealing*, which prevented any disposition of the land unless the cautioner had been informed and had been given the opportunity to object and, again, argue his case for an interest in the land. There can be no new cautions against dealing from 13 October 2003, although cautions against first registration continue to be used, and the Registrar maintains an index and register of these cautions.

Notice

A notice registered before 13 October 2003 was an effective way of protecting an interest, since it was binding on any new proprietor, providing the interest itself was valid. It required the agreement of the registered proprietor (except for the registration of a spouse's right of occupation). The 2002 Act, in abolishing new inhibitions and cautions against dealing, has expanded the scope of the notice. All registrable interests (except for those arising under a trust) are now protected either by an 'agreed notice', supported by the registered proprietor, or by a hostile 'unilateral notice' which replaces the caution against dealings and can be challenged by the registered proprietor.

Priorities

If a registered estate is sold for valuable consideration (which, by s.132(1) LRA 2002, does not include marriage or merely nominal money consideration), the new owner is bound only by those third-party interests protected by entry on the Register and by those which override registration, even if he has notice of any unprotected interest (s.29 LRA 2002). As a corollary to this, therefore, someone who receives land as a gift, either *inter vivos* or by will, takes it subject to any unprotected third-party interests.

Where there is a conflict between third-party interests, they are ranked in order of their creation (not in order of registration). Therefore, an unprotected third-party interest will have priority over one which, even though created later, has been protected on the Register.

Notice in registered land

A main objective of the scheme of registration is to do away with the difficulties caused by the doctrine of notice. Law Com No 271 stated that the doctrine 'as a general principle ... has no application whatever in determining the priority of interests in registered land' (para. 5.16). The report recognised, however, that on first registration, the new proprietor would take the land subject to any rights under the Limitation Act 1980 of which he had notice (see 11.5 above). It also recognised that notice is relevant in two further categories of interests that have overiding status: the interests of those in actual occupation and certain legal easements (11.5 above). The report was at pains to point out, though, that notice in these circumstances is not the same as the old doctrine of notice in unregistered land, but comes from a conveyancing rule which requires a seller to disclose to the buyer any burdens on the land which would not be obvious on a reasonable inspection and which the buyer does not know about.

A case under the LRA 1925 seemed to have undermined the general principle that the doctrine of notice plays no part in registered land. In *Lyus* v. *Prowsa Developments Ltd* [1982] 1 WLR 1044, Lyus had an estate contract – an option to purchase a plot of land in a housing development. The developer went bankrupt, and the mortgagee sold the land to Prowsa. This first sale was expressly subject to the option, although it did not have to be because the estate contract was not an overriding interest (Lyus was not 'in actual occupation') and it had not been protected by entry on the Register. Prowsa sold the land on, again expressly subject to the estate contract 'so far as, if at all, it might be enforceable'. Dillon J found the question of whether the buyer was bound one 'of considerable difficulty' but imposed a constructive trust on the buyer because it would be a fraud if he were able to ignore the term in the transfer. Despite the provisions of the 1925 Act, Lyus was able to enforce his unprotected interest: the buyer was bound, effectively because to ignore the special terms of the agreement would be a fraud, and a statute may not be used as an instrument of fraud.

It is interesting to compare *Lyus* with decisions in unregistered land such as *Midland Bank Trust Co Ltd* v. *Green* [1981] AC 513 (see 10.3 above). Although many people would say that justice was done in *Lyus*, the case creates another blank spot on the magic mirror of the Register. The Law Commission's view is that cases such as *Lyus* should be disregarded and that a buyer need not be in good faith since notice is irrelevant.

11.7 The Mechanics of Registered Land

Registration of title

We have examined some of the technicalities of the system of registered title in England and Wales. This section deals with the operation of the scheme in practice.

Procedure at the Land Registry

Title is first registered, and later dealings are recorded, by filling in the appropriate form and sending it with the fee to the District Land Registry.

On first registration, the Registrar checks the title as if he were buying it and decides whether the title is good enough for 'absolute title' (see 11.4 above), or only something less. Any benefits he discovers will be entered on the Register, as will any burdens, such as restrictive covenants found in the Land Charges Register. Once the land has been registered, however, anything in the Land Charges Register becomes irrelevant. Any other details, such as the title number of the freehold reversion of a lease, will also be noted in order to ensure that the Register really does mirror the title to the land. If a mistake is made by Registry staff, there are provisions for compensation: the state indemnity (see 11.8 below).

It used to be the case under the 1925 scheme that, on registration, a land certificate containing a copy of the Register would be issued to a new proprietor by the Registry, and would have to be produced when registering a notice or a restriction, or disposing of the land. The Law Commission and the Land Registry now consider them unnecessary, and incompatible with electronic conveyancing and, in line with the Registry's policy of 'dematerialisation' (that is, as little paper-based process as possible), the intention is that it should fall into disuse. However, after consultation and in order to reassure those who are not convinced by this policy, the Registry proposes to issue 'title information documents' to the registered proprietor whenever the Register is changed.

Sanctions for failure to register

As we have seen, those unregistered interests which are capable of substantive registration with their own title numbers – legal freeholds and legal leases over seven years – must be registered when there is a transaction which affects the legal title: either a conveyance or a first legal mortgage (s.4 LRA 2002). Where this first registration is a consequence of the *transfer* of the legal freehold or legal lease over seven years and no application has been made to the Registrar to register the title within two months of the conveyance, the legal title, which has already been vested in the new owner under the traditional unregistered procedure, will revert to the former owner who will hold it on a bare trust for the new owner (ss 6, 7 LRA 2002). If the first registration concerns the *creation* of a new lease, such failure to register will merely take effect as a contract for valuable consideration (s.7 LRA 2002). In other words, if the first registration rules are not complied with, only equitable titles ultimately pass.

If title to the land is already registered, the legal title will only pass to the new owner if the disposition goes through the Register (s.27 LRA 2002). Until that time, all the purchaser will own is the equitable title.

Mortgages in registered land

Section 23(1)(a) LRA 2002 has abolished the creation of mortgages by lease and sublease in registered land (see 7.2 above). The view of the Law Commission is that, when compared to the charge by way of legal mortgage, they are long-winded and complex and do not lend themselves easily to electronic conveyancing.

Where there is more than one registered charge, priority between them is determined according to the date of registration, unless the chargees agree otherwise (which they may do without the chargor's consent).

The old charge certificate, the document received by the lender on the creation of the charge, is seen as no longer serving any useful purpose, especially now that it is already possible to discharge mortgages electronically. It has been abolished under the 2002 Act.

11.8 **Alteration of the Register and Indemnity**

The Land Registry is concerned to ensure that the Register accurately reflects the title interests and third-party interests in the land, since prospective new owners have no choice but to rely on it. Even so, however careful the Registrar may have been at first registration, and however carefully a buyer may have checked the Register, a registered proprietor might find he has in fact bought nothing since, under certain circumstances, the Register can be altered.

Alteration

The provisions on alteration of the Register are found in Schedule 4 of the 2002 Act. This Schedule provides that the court may order alteration (para. 2) and the Registrar may alter the Register (para. 5) in order to correct a mistake on the Register, bring it up to date or to give effect to any estate, right or interest excepted from the effect of registration. The Registrar is also able to remove superfluous entries.

There is a certain kind of alteration known as a 'rectification' (which should not be confused with the same term used in the 1925 Act and which had a much wider meaning). Rectification is defined in Schedule 4, para. 1 as the correction of a mistake in circumstances where the correction prejudicially affects the title of the registered proprietor. No rectification may take place against the title of a registered proprietor in possession without his consent unless he substantially contributed to the mistake through fraud or carelessness, or unless it would be unjust for any other reason (para. 6).

The distinction between an alteration which amounts to rectification and one which does not can be seen in the case of *Chowood Ltd* v. *Lyall* [1930] 2 Ch 156. Mrs Lyall was unsuccessfully sued for trespass by Chowood, the first registered proprietor of the land. Having adversely possessed the disputed land for many years, she established that she had an overriding interest (under the equivalent of s.70(1)(f) LRA 1925) which was binding on Chowood, and the court ordered the Register to be corrected to give effect to the overriding interest. Using the terminology of the 2002 Act, this would have amounted to an alteration and not a rectification since, when Chowood bought the land, it was already subject to the overriding interest and the change to the Register merely reflected the existing position at the time of registration. Chowood, therefore, had suffered no prejudice and no loss and was not entitled to an indemnity (below).

Indemnity

Schedule 8 provides for state compensation to be paid for loss caused by rectification or failure to rectify. Anyone hoping for an indemnity must take care, since para. 5 provides that there will be no compensation if the loser caused the loss by fraud or lack of proper care, and his compensation will be reduced if his negligence contributed to his loss.

11.9 **Comment**

Important and far-reaching changes are taking place in land law. The 2002 Act will eventually fundamentally alter the way lawyers think about and deal with land. It has reformed the 1925 regime in order to facilitate the inevitable introduction of compulsory electronic conveyancing which, providing concerns over the security of the process are overcome, will require conveyancers to communicate directly with the Register by means of a secure computer network. Except for interests arising informally, the creation or transfer of interests will only be achievable through the act of registration, thus eliminating the problems of the 'registration gap' which currently exists between disposition and registration, and removing the need for a formal written contract and a deed. The distinction, as we currently understand it, between equitable and legal interests in land will disappear, since many interests will not exist at all until they are registered. This may well mean that the role of estoppel (see Chapter 13) will grow in importance.

The Land Registry's aim of completing the Register within the next decade or so means that it must find ways of bringing unregistered titles on to the Register as a matter of urgency, since there will be reluctance on the part of many landowners to have their titles open to public inspection, not to mention 'the old romantic who loves his deeds and walks his boundaries every morning' (Cooke, 2002). There is provision within the 2002 Act for voluntary registration of freeholds and leases over seven years (s.3) with reduced Registry fees payable. The Registry is currently developing 'strategic programmes of registration' in order to carry out their aim, and will reassess its progress after five years. The Act itself encourages landowners to register their titles. We have already seen how the new rules on adverse possession may stimulate voluntary registration (11.5 above). In addition, s.79 makes specific provision for the Queen to grant herself freehold title out of her demesne land, which she must then register. Demesne land is land which the Crown holds for itself as the 'ultimate feudal overlord' and which is not therefore held on a fee simple or term of years – the only estates which can be registered. The Law

Commission believes that this could lead to the disappearance of feudal tenure in England and Wales – see (2001) Law Com No 271, para. 2.37).

The Law Commission is no longer concerned about the different results which can occur from time to time depending on whether the land is registered or unregistered, and accepts that:

> it is now highly desirable that land registration in England and Wales should develop according to principles that reflect both the nature and the potential of land registration ... there seems little point in inhibiting the rational development of the principles of property law by reference to a system that is rapidly disappearing, and in relationship to which there is a diminishing expertise amongst the legal profession ... both the computerisation of the register and the move to electronic conveyancing make possible many improvements in the law that cannot be achieved with an unregistered system. ((1998) Law Com No 254, para. 1.6)

Although some may regret the passing of unregistered conveyancing (Cooke, *op cit*), registration of title to land is generally considered 'A Good Thing'. Nonetheless, it is valuable to consider its failings and limitations. Only then is it possible to decide whether, as is usually assumed, registration of title really is of benefit to all buyers and sellers of land. For example, it is clear that title registration does not, of itself, solve the conflicts of interests seen in this and the preceding chapter, especially the extent to which occupiers should be protected. Land can be enjoyed in different ways, and people have different needs in relation to it.

At least some of the difficulties are caused by the fact that the Land Register was originally introduced simply to replace repetitive examinations of the title deeds, but this limited aim has now been overshadowed by the need to make the Register as far as possible a perfect mirror of title in preparation for the electronic revolution to come. The danger is that simplification of the conveyancing process becomes the rationale of all land law, at the expense of another, equally important, land law principle, security of occupation.

Summary

11.1 Registration of title to land is designed to provide a simple and efficient form of conveyancing, by providing a guaranteed mirror of most rights in the land and promising state compensation for loss.

11.2 The LRA 2002 abolished the LRA 1925 in order to simplify the law on registered title and to prepare the way for electroninc conveyancing.

11.3 The Register is divided into three sections: property, proprietorship and charges. Each part of the Register contains specific information about the land, the title and the burdens on the land.

11.4 Interests in registered land are also divided into three groups: title interests, interests which override registration, and other interests and charges which are registrable.

11.5 Legal freeholds and leases over seven years are substantively registrable; title to them may be absolute, possessory or qualified, or good leasehold.

11.6 Interests which override registration are listed in Schedules 1 and 3 (depending on whether it is a first registration or a subsequent registered deposition), and include interests such as easements, leases and the interests of people in actual occupation of land. Overriding interests override any buyer of an interest in registered land. Certain transitional provisions apply.

11.7 Other registrable interests are 'everything else'; they are (normally) only binding on a purchaser for valuable consideration if they are entered on the Register by the appropriate method – notice or restriction.

11.8 The Register may be altered, even against a registered proprietor in possession (rectification). The state may provides compensation where anyone suffers loss by reason of rectification, but this does not include a proprietor who has effectively bought nothing because of a pre-existing interest which overrides registration.

Exercises

11.1 What goes where on the Land Register?

11.2 Which interests can be substantively registered with their own title number?

11.3 Which interests which override registration, and what is their importance?

11.4 When are registrable interests, other than title interests, binding?

11.5 Why do the provisions for alteration and indemnity detract from the basic principles of title registration?

11.6 Jake was the registered proprietor with absolute title of Albatross Cottage. He agreed by deed to sell it to Agnes, aged 80, for £140 000. Agnes paid Jake the price and moved in, but failed to register the transaction at the Land Registry because she did not believe in lawyers. Soon afterwards, Jake brought Maria to see the cottage. Maria met Agnes briefly in the kitchen, and asked her what she was doing there. Agnes replied that she was just having a cup of tea. Maria liked the cottage so much that she offered Jake £160 000 for it. Jake agreed to sell it to her.

Maria paid Jake the price and registered the transfer. Jake gave her the keys and she moved in when Agnes was in Majorca for a month. Agnes has now returned and seeks alteration of the Register against Maria.

Who will win?

Would your answer be different if Jake and his sister Josephine were joint registered proprietors?

Further Reading

Cooke, 'The Land Registration Bill 2001' [2002] Conv 11

Dixon, 'The Reform of Property Law and the Land Registration Act 2002: A Risk Assessment' [2003] Conv 136

Hayton, 'Torrens in the United States' (Book Review) [1980] CLJ 220

Kenny, P., 'Vanishing Easements in Registered Land' [2003] Conv 304

Law Commission Consultative Document: *Land Registration for the Twenty-First Century*, (1998) Law Com No 254

Law Commission Report: *Land Registration for the Twenty-First Century: A Conveyancing Revolution*, (2001) Law Com No 271

Wilkinson, 'Land Registration in England and Wales Before 1925' [1972] Conv 390

Part IV

Trusts of Land
Proprietary Estoppel

12   Trusts of Land

12.1 Introduction

Much of this book has been concerned with dividing up or sharing the enjoyment of land: for example between a tenant (entitled to possession) and a landlady (entitled to the rent), or between an owner of land and her neighbour who is allowed to use a path over it. This chapter and the next examine how the ownership of land can be shared.

The general policy of the law, as has been discussed in previous chapters, is to ensure as far as possible that land should be easily alienable: capable of being bought and sold without undue delay or expense. At the same time it is important that land can be shared by more than one owner, either successively or concurrently, with some measure of security, in order to satisfy the needs and ambitions of landowners. The mechanism by which the law attempts to balance these apparently competing objectives is the trust, some aspects of which will by now be familiar from cases such as *Boland* and *Flegg* (see 11.5 above).

The basic principle of the trust is a division between the legal and equitable (or 'beneficial') ownership of the land; in its simplest form, a trustee holds the legal title for the benefit of the beneficiary. However, in trusts of land trustees are often also beneficiaries at the same time, commonly where a couple are the legal owners of family property, holding it on trust for themselves as beneficial co-owners.

Modern developments in this area of law are largely the result of the growth in landownership by ordinary families (including families where the adults concerned are not married). If a family breaks up, those involved will need to resolve the ownership of the family property; the effects of this can be far-reaching since, as well as providing the family

Table 12.1   Examples of legal and equitable ownership

	Legal ownership	Beneficial ownership
Williams & Glyn's Bank Ltd v. *Boland* [1981] AC 487	Husband	Husband and wife
City of London Building Society v. *Flegg* [1988] AC 54	Mr and Mrs Maxwell-Brown	Mr and Mrs Maxwell-Brown and Mr and Mrs Flegg

home, which is perhaps the real and symbolic focus of family life, the land may be the most valuable financial asset owned by any family member.

The courts often have to analyse open-textured and informal family arrangements within the formal structure of trust law; as a result, some of the case law is interesting but not straightforward. The topic is made more challenging because the basic rules are part of wider equitable principles. Further, because many cases lie on the boundary between land law and family law, there can be unseen conflicts of values; crudely, land law is concerned with 'justice through certainty', while family law is more interested in 'justice in the individual case'. Where the demands of certainty and individual justice diverge, there is bound to be some confusion.

There used to be two kinds of trusts of land: the strict settlement and the trust for sale. The device of the strict settlement was used by the great landowning families to hold on to the land they owned, while the trust for sale developed as a means of holding land as a temporary investment. The Trusts of Land and Appointment of Trustees Act 1996 (TLATA) replaced both kinds of trust with the simple 'trust of land'. While this new law provides a radical and simple conceptual basis for trusts of land, much of the old law of trusts remains in place – including the rules on the creation of trusts and on co-ownership. The rules about overreaching are also little directly changed.

12.2 The Old Law on Trusts of Land

The strict settlement

The traditional family arrangements of the aristocracy were aimed at preventing the fragmentation of their great estates. Settlements involving complicated inheritance rules were created within the family, and these sometimes restricted improvements of the land and prevented sale over many generations. Successive reforms were made over centuries to prevent long-lasting settlements (the 'rules against perpetuities') and to free the land from too many restrictions. In 1925, the Settled Land Act provided an elaborate and expensive legal mechanism to govern these trusts; under this Act the 'tenant for life' (the current beneficial owner of the land) became a trustee of the settlement and could deal fairly freely with the land.

Section 2 TLATA states that (with very limited exceptions) strict settlements may no longer be created. Such trusts were already virtually obsolete because of punitive tax laws, but a strict settlement could still be created by accident, for example in a home-made will, or when a child inherited land, and so the whole regime had become largely an expensive trap for the uninformed, or for careless solicitors. (For further details of the old cumbersome and technical rules of strict settlements see Cheshire, 2000, Chapter 9.)

The trust for sale

Until 1997, a trust was a strict settlement if there were *consecutive* beneficial interests, unless it expressly called itself a trust for sale. Any trust with *concurrent* beneficial interests had to be a trust for sale, so this kind of trust included not only family land (for example, where cohabitees were the co-owners) but also land which was held commercially (for example, by a partnership of solicitors).

The trust for sale was imposed on many family arrangements by the LPA 1925, but this kind of trust was never really appropriate, and it was for this reason that the TLATA replaced it with the 'trust of land'. The essence of the problem was that, under a trust for sale, the land was deemed to have been bought mainly as an investment (which, a century ago, was often true), so there was an 'immediate and binding duty' to sell it, with a power to postpone sale in order to receive the rental income. The changing pattern of landownership during the twentieth century meant that land was, with increasing frequency, bought for owner-occupation and, in the minds of home-owners, sale was merely a possibility at some time in the future. However, the trustees' duty of sale meant that if one trustee wanted a sale, the land had to be sold. Section 30 LPA gave the courts a discretion about ordering sale, and a long line of case law resulted from the tension between the duty to sell – when one family member wanted to turn the land into money – and the need of the rest of the family to stay in their home. Such conflicts will, of course, still arise and the provisions of the TLATA now provide a statutory replacement for the old law (see 12.8 below).

A further problem with the duty to sell arose when, as a result of the equitable principle that 'equity looks on that as done which ought to be done', the courts pretended that the land was converted into money so the beneficiaries behind a trust for sale did not have an interest in land, but merely in money (the 'proceeds of sale'). This is the 'doctrine of conversion'. However, a number of cases showed that, although the beneficiaries in theory were only interested in the proceeds of sale, in practice they might still be recognised as having some interest in the land itself. In the well-known case of *Bull* v. *Bull* [1955] 1 QB 234 a son, the sole trustee of the trust for sale and a joint beneficiary under it, wanted to evict his mother (the other beneficiary) but the court held that her interest in the land included a right to occupy it. Cases such as *Williams & Glyn's Bank* v. *Boland* [1981] AC 487 and *City of London Building Society* v. *Flegg* [1988] AC 54 (see 11.5 above) were also concerned with the actual nature of the beneficiary's interest under s.70(1)(g) LRA and their right to occupy the trust land.

In the end, because the machinery of the trust for sale and its accompanying doctrine of conversion were simply inappropriate to the reality of family landowning, there could be no solution to the problem. Now the TLATA has replaced the old trust for sale with the new 'trust of land', and s.3 has abolished the doctrine of conversion for all trusts, except for a trust for sale created by a will where the testator died before the Act came into effect.

12.3 **The Current Law on Trusts of Land**

The TLATA 1996 (and see Hopkins [1996] Conv 411) was the result of the Law Commission's proposals ((1989) Law Com No 181,):

> We consider that the present dual system of trusts for sale and strict settlements is unnecessarily complex, ill-suited to the conditions of modern property ownership, and liable to give rise to unforeseen conveyancing complications. (p. iv)

Having swept away old statute and case law, Part I of the Act imposed on all trusts of land a new, simpler system. A trust of land is defined in s.1 as 'any trust of property which consists of or includes land'. Section 2 prevents the creation of any new strict settlements, or the addition of land to an existing strict settlement. New trusts for sale can be created expressly, but since the trustees can now postpone sale indefinitely, there is little point in doing so unless, perhaps, the purpose of the trust is that the land should be sold, as in *Barclay* v. *Barclay* [1970] 2 QB 677. Section 5 (with Schedule 2) amended existing rules in ss 34–6 LPA which imposed the trust for sale onto concurrently shared trust land. The Act replaced certain sections of the LPA (including s.26, on consulting beneficiaries, and s.30, on disputes between owners of trust land) and also made transitional provisions for existing trusts: most former trusts for sale are subject to most aspects of the new regime.

As will be seen, the trustees of a 'trust of land' have no duty to sell the land, but have a power either to sell or to retain it; in addition, some beneficiaries now have a statutory right to occupy the trust land (see below, 12.6). The relationship between beneficiaries and trustees has been somewhat altered too, for example in respect of consultation, and some beneficiaries have gained limited powers over the appointment of trustees. In order to make dealing with the land simple, buyers of trust land continue to be given special protection (see below, 12.7).

12.4 **Creation of Trusts of Land**

A trust of land may be created expressly or impliedly. An express trust must be evidenced in writing (s.53(1)(b) LPA) in order to be enforceable by the beneficiaries, and should declare the nature of the beneficial ownership and the terms of the trust.

If there is no express declaration of trust, a statutory trust of land will be imposed when land is conveyed or transferred to two or more people (ss 34, 36 LPA).

It is also possible for a person to gain a beneficial share in land in circumstances in which there is no express or statutory trust but where, as a result of the parties' conduct, equity will find that the land is co-owned. These trusts are known as resulting and constructive trusts, and are dealt with in the next chapter, along with proprietary estoppel, a doctrine discussed earlier (in Chapter 2, above) and which has many similarities with constructive trusts.

12.5 Concurrent Co-ownership of Land

Before 1925, there were four methods of co-owning land, and any of them could exist either at law or in equity. Since then, only two survive: 'joint tenancy' and 'tenancy in common'. A joint tenancy can be legal or equitable but, since 1925, a tenancy in common can only exist in equity.

Joint tenancy

The basic principle of joint tenancy is that the owners – as far as outsiders are concerned – are regarded as one person; there is a 'thorough and intimate union', as Blackstone put it. They are united in every way possible, through the four 'unities'.

The Four Unities

- Possession
- Interest
- Title
- Time

(easily remembered by the acronym: PITT)

All the joint tenants are entitled to possess the whole of the land. They each hold an identical interest – fee simple or life interest and so on – obtained by the same document (title), and vested in them at the same time. In *A. G. Securities* v. *Vaughan* [1990] 1 AC 417 (see 5.4 above), for example, a claim that there was a joint tenancy of a legal lease failed because the claimants had arrived at different times; indeed, on the facts of the case Lord Oliver found that none of the unities was present, not even that of possession.

The fact that joint tenants are seen as one person is the reason why joint tenancy is the only kind of co-ownership which is possible at law (ss 1(6), 34(1), 36(2) LPA). If legal tenancies in common were permitted, rather than merely investigating one title, a purchaser would have to investigate the individual titles of each tenant in common, adding considerably to the time and expense of conveyancing. In addition, at law, there can be no more than four joint tenants (s.34(2) Trustee Act 1925). If title to land is conveyed to more than four people, the first four named on the deed, if they are capable and willing, will be the legal joint tenants – the trustees – and the remainder will be beneficial owners only.

The basis of joint tenancy is that the joint tenants do not have shares in the land: each owns the whole of it. As a consequence, and most importantly, joint tenants enjoy the 'right of survivorship' (*ius accrescendi*). The joint tenants are 'all one person', and if one dies it is as if she had never existed: the survivors still own the whole of the land so there is nothing for the heirs of the dead joint tenant to inherit. It follows, therefore, that the last survivor of joint tenants will own the whole land absolutely.

The risk involved in the right of survivorship may seem unfair, but in fact it is quite convenient that legal ownership of trust land should not be affected if one co-owner at law dies. In equity, on the other hand, although joint tenancy is possible, the risks can be inconvenient; for this reason, equity 'leans against' this form of co-ownership.

Tenancy in common

Tenancy in common is often referred to as an 'undivided share': the land is in shares but they have not yet been divided up. Tenancy in common requires only one of the four unities – the unity of possession – and there is no right of survivorship. When a tenant in common dies, she can leave her undivided share to anyone she pleases. However, as far as a buyer of land is concerned, the interests shared in equity are 'behind a curtain': she can overreach all the beneficial interests (whether joint tenancy or tenancy in common) by paying the trustees (providing there is more than one, see 10.4 above), who will, of course, be legal joint tenants.

Creation of a joint tenancy or tenancy in common

At the start of the relationship
At law there are no problems – a joint tenancy at law arises whenever a legal interest in land is shared concurrently, that is, whenever land is conveyed into the names of two or more people, as discussed above. The difficulties arise in equity, because here there may be either a joint tenancy or a tenancy in common; it is also possible for there to be – in equity – both joint tenants and tenants in common simultaneously sharing under the same trust of land.

The starting-point in determining whether a person is a beneficial joint tenant or a tenant in common is that, although the four unities may be present and 'equity follows the law', equity tends to incline against the unpredictability of the right of survivorship. As a result, a beneficial tenancy in common will exist, not only where one of the unities is missing, but also if there is a particular reason for inferring that there was no intention to create a joint tenancy. A tenancy in common can be created expressly in the deed, which poses no difficulty. In the absence of an expressly created tenancy in common, one will be implied if there are 'words of severance' in the conveyance (words which show an intention that the owners should have shares). These words include 'equally', 'in equal shares', 'amongst' and 'share and share alike'. An example is *Barclay* v. *Barclay* [1970] 2 QB 677 (12.3 above) where land was left 'equally' under an express trust in a will to the testator's five children.

In addition, there are three circumstances in which equity *presumes* a tenancy in common. These are: (1) where there are unequal contributions to the purchase price, although this presumption can be rebutted if there has been an express agreement to create a joint tenancy; (2) where the co-owners are business partners or are using the land to run separate businesses, or for profit; or (3) where they are lending money on a mortgage.

The Privy Council has made clear that the list of special reasons for finding a tenancy in common is not closed:

> Cases in which joint tenants at law will be presumed to hold as tenants in common ... are not necessarily limited to purchasers who contribute unequally, to co-mortgagees and to partners. There are other circumstances in which equity may infer that the beneficial interest is intended to be held by the grantees as tenants in common. In the opinion of their Lordships, one such case is where the grantees hold the premises for their several individual business purposes. (Lord Brightman in *Malayan Credit Ltd* v. *Jack Chia-MPH Ltd* [1986] AC 549 at 560)

Changing an equitable joint tenancy into a tenancy in common

In what follows, it must always be remembered that, because there cannot be a legal tenancy in common, a legal joint tenancy cannot be severed (s.36(2) LPA).

An equitable owner may be a joint tenant at the start and then, at any time *before* she dies, she can change it to a tenancy in common. This change is called 'severance', and when it occurs, she becomes a tenant in common in equity with an equal share of the value of the property, whenever it comes to be sold. If an equitable joint tenant severs her interest, from that moment she no longer suffers – or gains from – the right of survivorship.

Anything which 'creates a distinction' between equitable joint tenants amounts to a severance. Equity has recognised three methods of severing a joint tenancy of personal property (listed by Page Wood V-C in *Williams* v. *Hensman* (1861) 1 John & H 546, and these are now accepted as applying also to real property:

1 By 'an act of one of the parties interested operating on her own share'.
2 By mutual agreement.
3 By a 'course of dealing' ('mutual conduct') which shows a common intention to sever.

There are, in addition, other methods of severance:

4 By notice in writing of immediate severance (s.36(2) LPA).
5 Where a joint tenant has become bankrupt and all her property is vested in the trustee in bankruptcy (see also 12.8, below).
6 Killing another joint tenant because, if the right of survivorship operated in such circumstances, the killer might be 'profiting from her own wrong'.

Some of these methods are examined in more detail below, but it should be remembered that whether severance has taken place always depends on the evidence; each case 'depends on its own facts'. Frequently, the trigger for any dispute will be the death of one co-owner, and the question may arise as to whether there has been a severance of the equitable joint tenancy before the death.

An important case on severance is *Burgess* v. *Rawnsley* [1975] Ch 429, in which the Court of Appeal considered the *Williams* v. *Hensman* methods of severance. Mr Honick and Mrs Rawnsley met at a Scripture rally. After a few months of friendship, they bought the house in which Mr Honick lived, as joint tenants at law and in equity. He thought they were going to get married; she merely intended to live in the upper flat. After a year or so, they discovered each other's error and agreed orally that he should buy her share, but they did not finally agree a price and nothing more was done. Three years later Mr Honick died, and Mrs Rawnsley claimed the whole house by right of survivorship. Mr Honick's heir, Mrs Burgess, argued successfully that the negotiations between Mr Honick and Mrs Rawnsley had amounted to a severance of the equitable joint tenancy, and so Mrs Rawnsley failed in her claim. In the Court of Appeal Sir John Pennycuick stated that there was no need for the agreement between the parties to be specifically enforceable, simply that an agreement 'serves as an indication of a common intention to sever'. As to a course of dealing between the parties, Lord Denning MR said:

It is sufficient if there is a course of dealing in which one party makes clear to the other that he desires that their shares should no longer be held jointly but be held in common ... it is sufficient if both parties enter on a course of dealing which evinces an intention by both of them that their shares shall henceforth be held in common and not jointly. (p. 439)

It is evident, therefore, that if there is a sufficient course of dealing, then there is no need for any agreement, express or implied.

The 'course of dealing' argument failed in *Greenfield* v. *Greenfield* (1979) 38 P & CR 570. Two brothers owned a house as joint tenants in law and equity; each married, and converted the house into two maisonettes, sharing the garden and some bills. When the elder brother died his widow claimed that the division of the house showed an intention to sever the beneficial joint tenancy and that she had inherited her husband's tenancy in common. The court found that the widow had 'come nowhere near' proving that there was a course of dealing showing a common intention to sever, and she got nothing.

A unilateral, unstated intention to sever will not do, and nor will 'a mere verbal notice by one party to another'. By s.36(2) LPA, however, a written notice by one joint tenant to another will suffice if the legal and beneficial joint tenants are the same people. No agreement from the other joint tenant is required, and it is not even necessary for the notice to be received. In *Kinch* v. *Bullard* [1998] 4 All ER 650, a wife, suffering from a terminal illness, was intending to divorce her husband. They were both the beneficial joint tenants of the matrimonial home and, since she no longer wanted the right of survivorship to operate, she instructed her solicitors to send him a notice severing the joint tenancy. The solicitors sent the letter by first-class post but, before it was delivered, the husband suffered a serious heart attack. The wife, realising she would lose half the house if her husband died with the joint tenancy having been severed, destroyed the letter as soon as it arrived. Her husband died a week or so later and never learned about the letter. The wife died the following year and an action was brought by the husband's executors, who claimed that the joint tenancy had been severed by the written notice and they were therefore entitled to the half-share in the property left to them by the husband. By s.196 LPA, a notice is properly served 'if it is left at the last known place of abode or business in the United Kingdom of the ... person to be served'. In this case, the court held that the notice had been properly served when the letter fell through the letter box onto the mat. The wife's destruction of the letter had failed to prevent her severance of the joint tenancy through which otherwise she would have gained the whole of the property by the right of survivorship. (See also *Re 88 Berkeley Road* [1971] Ch 648.)

Under the Forfeiture Act 1982 and as a matter of public policy, a person who unlawfully kills another should 'not acquire a benefit in consequence of the killing'. In the tragic case of *Dunbar* v. *Plant* [1998] Ch 412, two lovers, Miss Plant and Mr Dunbar attempted to kill themselves following a suicide pact. Miss Plant failed; Mr Dunbar succeeded. Although the forfeiture rule applies in cases of aiding and abetting a suicide (as here), the Court of Appeal, by a majority, was able to exercise its discretion under s.2 of the Act to modify the effect of the rule 'where the justice of the case required it'. It held that, under the particular circumstances of the case, the couple's joint tenancy of their house had not been severed and that Miss Plant was entitled to the whole of the beneficial interest in the proceeds of sale (since the house had already been sold).

Applying the rules

Problem questions on co-ownership require a step-by-step analysis of what happens to the legal and equitable ownership. This is, perhaps, most easily done initially in table form.

Imagine that a group of five people – A, B, C, D and E – buy a house as joint tenants in equity, each contributing equally to the purchase price. The first four over 18 years old become the legal owners as joint tenants holding on trust for all five. Certain events now take place, each of which may affect the legal ownership or sever the equitable joint tenancy. A description of each event and an analysis of its effect are contained in Table 12.2.

This kind of problem question often ends by stating that some of the surviving co-owners now want to sell and others want to remain in the property, inevitably requiring a discussion of the case law under ss 14, 15 TLATA (12.8 below).

Table 12.2   Applying the co-ownership rules

Event	Law	Equity	Comment
At the start	A, B, C, D (joint tenants)	A, B, C, D, E (joint tenants)	No more than four legal owners.
A dies	B, C, D (joint tenants)	B, C, D, E (joint tenants)	The right of survivorship operates for both legal and equitable joint tenants
B sells her share to X	B, C, D (joint tenants)	C, D, E (joint tenants of $\frac{3}{4}$) X (tenant in common of $\frac{1}{4}$)	No change at law unless all legal owners execute a deed. B has only dealt with her equitable title, severing her joint tenancy.
C gives written notice of severance	B, C, D (joint tenants)	D, E (joint tenants of $\frac{1}{2}$) X, C (tenants in common of $\frac{1}{4}$ each)	No change to the position at law. C has severed her joint tenancy in equity.

12.6 The Role of the Trustees and the Rights of the Beneficiaries

The trustees of a trust of land hold the legal title to the land, and their rights and duties are subject to the general law of trusts and to the particular provisions (if any) of the trust in question (s.8 TLATA). Most importantly, as stated earlier, the trustees have a power to sell the land and a power to postpone its sale (ss 4, 5).

Section 6(1) TLATA provides that the trustees 'have all the powers of an absolute owner': thus, they may sell, mortgage, lease or otherwise deal with the land. This extends their powers under the old rules of strict settlements and trusts for sale and enables them properly to administer the trust property; however, by s.8(1), the terms of the trust may restrict these powers. In addition, the powers of trustees of charitable, ecclesiastical and public trusts continue to be limited in special ways. By s.6(3) trustees also have the power (subject to the terms of the trust) to buy land with trust money as an investment, or for occupation by a beneficiary or 'for any other reason'. In exercising these powers, the trustees must 'have regard to the rights of the beneficiaries'.

Where the beneficiaries are of full age and capacity, the role of trustees may be limited or unnecessary. Thus, s.6(2) restates the old rule that if such beneficiaries 'are absolutely entitled to the land', the trustees can convey the land to them. Subject to the terms of the trust, the trustees may also have the power to divide up ('partition') the land for any purpose, but only if the beneficiaries are adult tenants in common, absolutely entitled, and they all consent (s.7). The trustees may also (again, subject to the terms of the trust) delegate their powers to these beneficiaries (s.9), thus allowing beneficiaries in occupation to carry on the routine management of the land themselves.

However, despite these apparently unlimited powers, it is still possible – as under the old law – to make dealings with the trust land subject to the consent of a particular person or persons (s.8(2)). For example if a spouse dies and leaves her property to her children, it could be a term of the trust that the property could only be sold with the consent of the surviving spouse who might well also have the right to live there, thus ensuring that the property remains unsold, at least for a time.

The TLATA also restates and extends to all trustees of trusts of land the duty to consult beneficiaries. Section 11 provides that, subject to a contrary intention being expressed in the trust:

> The trustees of land shall in the exercise of any function relating to land subject to the trust –
> (a) so far as practicable, consult the beneficiaries of full age and beneficially entitled to an interest in possession in the land, and
> (b) shall so far as consistent with the general interest of the trust, give effect to the wishes of those beneficiaries, or (in case of dispute) of the majority (according to the value of their combined interests).

This section will not normally apply to an express trust created before 1997 (s.11(2)(b)).

Normally, trustees are appointed in the trust deed, or, in the case of implied trusts, the trustees will be the persons who hold the legal title. If there is no trustee (for example if land is conveyed to a child who by s.1(6) LPA cannot own land) the court can appoint trustees. Sections 19–21 of the Act give beneficiaries a measure of control over their trustees, in that they can require the appointment of a new trustee or the retirement of a current trustee, unless the settlor has expressly specified that the beneficiaries should not have this power.

The beneficiaries of a trust of land are generally entitled to whatever the trust provides for them. Their rights under the old trust for sale depended on the original purposes of the trust, but this again posed a conceptual problem for land lawyers. Since the land was, in theory, to be sold straight away, equity saw the interests of the beneficiaries as being in the proceeds of sale rather than in the land (12.2 above): it was decidedly odd that the beneficiaries might have a right to live there. The TLATA, having abolished the doctrine of conversion, now also provides a statutory right for beneficiaries to occupy the trust land.

Section 12 states that a beneficiary is entitled to live in the house 'if the purposes of the trust include making the land available for his occupation'. This right to occupy is subject to it being available and suitable for occupation by the beneficiary. In *Chan* v. *Leung* [2003] 1 FLR 23, the Court of Appeal had to decide whether a large house in Surrey was suitable for occupation solely by Miss Leung, a university student. Jonathan Parker LJ stated that:

> 'suitability' for this purpose must involve a consideration not only of the general nature and physical characteristics of the particular property but also a consideration of the personal characteristics, circumstances and requirements of the particular beneficiary. (para. 101)

Despite its size and the expense of its maintenance, the judge did not consider the house unsuitable for Miss Leung, especially since she would only wish to occupy it until the end of her studies. Even if this had not been the case, since she had previously been living there with her partner, the judge 'would have taken some persuading' that it was unsuitable for her now he had left.

Section 13 TLATA gives the trustees certain responsibilities in cases where beneficiaries are entitled to occupy the land, as is common in trusts of the family home where adults share beneficial interests. It provides that trustees have the power to exclude a beneficiary from the land, although not 'unreasonably', and may impose on an occupying beneficiary 'reasonable conditions' (for example, to pay expenses relating to the land, or compensation to a beneficiary who has been reasonably excluded from occupation). In making such decisions, the trustees must take into account the intentions of the creator of the trust, the purposes of the trust and the circumstances and wishes of the beneficiaries.

An example of the difficulties which may arise in these situations can be illustrated by the case of *Rodway* v. *Landy* [2001] Ch 703. Two doctors in partnership bought a property together from which to run their practices. They fell out. One of the partners sought an order (under s.14 TLATA, see 12.8 below) for the property to be sold to her. The other asked the court to order that, since they were both trustees as well as beneficiaries, they could use their powers under s.13 to divide the property in two, allowing one partner exclusive occupation of one part of the property, and the other partner exclusive occupation of the other part. The Court of Appeal was of the opinion that if the building lent itself to division in this way, the trustees were entitled under s.13 to exclude the beneficiaries' entitlement to occupy all of the building, and that, under s.13(3), they could require them to contribute to the cost of the adaptation of the building. Here, of course, the trustees and the beneficiaries were the same people, and the case also serves as an example of the separation of the roles and functions of trustees and beneficiaries.

12.7 Protection for Buyers of Trust Land

A buyer of land (including a mortgagee) subject to a trust can overreach the beneficial interests; providing payment is made to two or more trustees or a trust corporation, as already explained, the buyer 'shall not be concerned with the trusts' (s.27 LPA).

Where the trust makes any sale subject to the consent of more than two people, s.10 TLATA provides that the purchaser only has to be sure that two have actually consented. In unregistered land, a purchaser is further protected since she is not concerned whether the trustees are acting in the interests of the beneficiaries or whether they have been consulted (s.16(1)). Section 16(2) provides that a purchaser will still get good title, even if the disposition is in breach of trust, so long as she does not have actual notice of it.

The same principle probably also holds good under the general rules of registered land, although Ferris and Battersby ([1998] Conv 168) have argued that dispositions by the trustees in breach of trust would result in a failure to overreach. However, the Court of Appeal decision in *Birmingham Midshires Mortgage Services Ltd* v. *Sabherwal* (2000) 80 P & CR 256 indicates that this is unlikely. The facts took place before the TLATA came into force but, when discussing its effect in registered land, Robert Walker LJ stated:

> the [TLATA] contains nothing to exclude the essential overreaching provision contained in s.2(1)(ii) of the Law of Property Act 1925. On the contrary, that provision is amended so as to meet the new terminology of the [TLATA] ... so is in effect confirmed ... by the [TLATA]. (p. 261)

12.8 Conflicts between Owners of Trust Land

If the provisions for consultation and the gaining of consents are not observed and the land is sold or mortgaged in breach of trust, aggrieved beneficiaries can, in theory, sue their trustees. However, since the land will probably by then already have been irrevocably sold or mortgaged and the trustees will probably not be worth suing, it is, where possible, far better to prevent misdealing by taking the trustees to court to decide whether the land should be sold.

The relevant statutory provisions are ss 14, 15 TLATA, which are also crucial in circumstances where a purchaser has stepped into the shoes of a defaulting trustee and seeks possession and sale against a beneficiary whose rights were not overreached. They are also important in cases where a secured creditor is seeking sale of the land but is opposed by a beneficiary's claim that she is not bound by the mortgage. If any of the co-owners are bankrupt and the application for sale is made by the trustee in bankruptcy (who represents the interests of the creditors), the case will be heard under the provisions of the Insolvency Act 1986, not under the TLATA (see below).

Section 14(1) TLATA allows any trustee or beneficiary of a trust of land, or anybody with an interest in the trust property, to apply to the court which, under s.14(2), may make any order it thinks fit:

(a)   relating to the exercise by the trustees of any of their functions (including an order relieving them of any obligation to obtain the consent of, or to consult, any person in connection with the exercise of any of the functions) or

(b)   declaring the nature or extent of a person's interest in property subject to the trust.

Section 15 TLATA expressly indicates how the court should exercise its discretion:

(1)   The matters to which the court is to have regard in determining an application for an order under s.14 include –

(a)   the intention of the person or persons (if any) who created the trust,

(b)   the purposes for which the property subject to the trust is held,

(c)   the welfare of any minor who occupies or might reasonably be expected to occupy any land subject to the trust as his home, and

(d)   the interests of any secured creditor of any beneficiary.

When the application concerns the exclusion of occupation rights under s.13, the court also must have regard to 'the circumstances and wishes' of each of the beneficiaries who might have a right to occupy (s.15(2) and see *Rodway* v. *Landy* (12.6 above)). In other applications, the court must normally take into account the wishes of the majority of adult beneficiaries currently entitled to the equitable ownership, according to the value of their beneficial interest (s.15(3)).

An important question for the courts in the exercise of their discretion is the continuing relevance of the principles developed under s.30 LPA, the forerunner to s.15 TLATA. Under s.30, the court asked two questions: (1) what was the underlying purpose of the trust for sale? and (2) has the purpose ended? It had been necessary to invent these two questions because under the old trust for sale the duty to sell was 'immediate and binding', and any power to postpone sale could only be exercised if the trustees were unanimous. Thus, the only way to block the duty of sale if even one trustee wanted to sell was to make the purpose of the trust paramount.

Therefore, if the underlying purpose of the trust was to live in the house, and this purpose had not ended, then sale would not normally be ordered. In *Jones* v. *Challenger* [1961] 1 QB 176 the house had been bought by a husband and wife as a matrimonial home but the marriage had broken down and the wife had left. There were no children and the Court of Appeal held that the house should be sold because, 'with an end of the marriage, [the] purpose [of the trust] was dissolved and the primacy of the duty to sell was restored' (Devlin LJ, p. 183). In contrast, in *Re Evers' Trust* [1980] 3 All ER 399, a house had been bought by an unmarried couple who had three children. The man left and applied for an order for sale in order to take out the money he had contributed towards the purchase price. Ormrod LJ found that the underlying purpose of the trust was to provide a family home and, since that purpose still subsisted, albeit without the man, declined at that time to make the order.

The s.30 jurisprudence had recognised that where the party seeking an order for sale was a creditor, the principles based on bankruptcy cases would apply (see below), and the creditor's interest would take precedence over the wishes of the beneficiaries to stay in the property unless there were exceptional circumstances (*Lloyds Bank plc* v. *Byrne* [1993] 1 FLR 369), even, sometimes, where a beneficiary had a s.70(1)(g) overriding interest (*Bank of Baroda* v. *Dhillon* [1998] 1 FLR 254). Now, however, the purpose of the trust is only one consideration among several in s.15 to be taken into account by the court. Even so, in the first case to be heard under s.15, *TSB* v. *Marshall* [1998] 2 FLR 769, the County Court stated that the s.30 case law would continue to provide guidance as to how the courts should exercise their discretion.

A different approach was taken by Neuberger J in *Mortgage Corporation* v. *Shaire* [2001] 4 All ER 364 (and see Pascoe [2000] Conv 315), a case in which a secured creditor brought an action under s.14 for possession of the trust property following mortgage arrears. Here it was held that the interest of the mortgagee was only one of the four factors to be considered by the court and that there was nothing to indicate that it should take precedence over, for example, the interests of any resident children. The judge was clear that s.15 was intended to enable the courts to exercise a wider discretion than formerly in favour of families as against secured creditors. With regard to previous authorities, he stated:

> there are obvious dangers in relying on authorities which proceeded on the basis that the court's discretion was more fettered than it now is. I think it would be wrong to throw over all the earlier cases without paying them any regard. However, they are to be treated with caution, in the light of the change in the law, and in many cases they are unlikely to be of great, let alone decisive, assistance. (p. 380)

Despite *Shaire*, the Court of Appeal in *Bank of Ireland Mortgages Ltd* v. *Bell* [2001] FLR 809 has recently returned to the previous orthodoxy of *Byrne*: although s.15 had increased the scope of the discretion available to the court:

> a powerful consideration is and ought to be whether the creditor is receiving proper recompense for being kept out of his money, repayment of which is overdue. (Peter Gibson LJ at para. 31)

There was no equity in Mrs Bell's property, the debt was continuing to increase, and her son was almost 18. The court found little difficulty in ordering sale.

It seems, then, that where an application for sale is made by a secured creditor, there is little practical difference between the operation of s.15 and the position in bankruptcy (see also *First National Bank plc* v. *Achampong* [2003] EWCA Civ 487 and below, 'Bankruptcy'). Despite the unfortunate consequences for the occupiers, there is a certain logic to this, since it is open to a creditor to initiate bankruptcy proceedings, then have the case heard under s.335A Insolvency Act 1986 (below) and thus avoid s.15 (see *Alliance and Leicester plc* v. *Slayford* (2000) 33 HLR 743 (7.3 above).

Bankruptcy

The major statutory exception to the principle that occupying beneficiaries may be able to prevent a sale of trust land is where any party is bankrupt; s.15(4) TLATA provides that such a case must be considered not under s.15 but under s.335A Insolvency Act 1986. Here again the court must make such an order 'as it thinks just and reasonable', having regard to the interests of the bankrupt's creditors and all the circumstances of the case except for the needs of the bankrupt. Where the trustee in bankruptcy's application relates to a dwelling house which has been the home of the bankrupt or the bankrupt's spouse or former spouse, the court will also have to take into account the extent to which the spouse contributed towards the bankruptcy, the spouse's needs and resources and the needs of any children. However, by s.335A(3), once a year has passed since the bankruptcy was declared, the court:

> shall assume, unless the circumstances of the case are exceptional, that the interests of the bankrupt's creditors outweigh all other considerations.

This reference to exceptional circumstances in s.335A(3) has given statutory effect to a principle developed in recent years by the courts. In *Re Citro (Domenico) (a bankrupt)* [1990] 3 All ER 952, a case heard under the s.30 common law jurisprudence, the Court of Appeal considered the nature of exceptional circumstances. The disruption of losing a home and changing schools is 'not uncommon', and therefore not exceptional; Nourse LJ described this in ironic Dickensian terms as 'the melancholy consequences of debt and improvidence with which every civilised society has been familiar' (at p. 962). As Brown concluded ((1992) 55 MLR 284 at p. 291):

> In the necessary balancing exercise between creditors as against bankrupts and their families, the former will always win in the end, and that end comes sooner rather than later.

Before *Re Citro*, only in *Re Holliday* [1980] 3 All ER 385 had the court postponed sale in a bankruptcy case: here the spouse had made himself bankrupt, the creditors were not pressing for repayment, there were young children and the wife would have been unable to find accommodation elsewhere in the area with her share of the proceeds of sale. As if that were not enough, the bankrupt had left his wife for another woman. Asking the question 'in all the circumstances of the case, whose voice in equity ought to prevail?', a different Court of Appeal from that in *Re Citro* had felt able to postpone sale for five years.

Under the Insolvency Act, if the court finds that there are exceptional circumstances it may postpone sale or refuse it entirely. At first instance in

Judd v. *Brown* [1998] 2 FLR 360, Harman J refused sale where the bankrupt's wife was suffering from cancer and undergoing chemotherapy; in *Re Raval* [1998] 2 FLR 718 an order for sale against a paranoid schizophrenic, for whom a move to a smaller house away from the support of her family and friends could have caused a relapse, was postponed for a year in order to allow suitable accommodation to be found for her.

In *Claughton* v. *Charalambous* [1999] 1 FLR 740 the bankrupt's spouse, who suffered from renal failure and osteoarthritis, lived in a house adapted for her with a chair lift. Finding these circumstances to be exceptional, the County Court judge suspended the order for sale indefinitely, probably also influenced by the fact that the value of the bankrupt's share of the property would have been taken up in costs so his creditors would have got nothing. Given the discussion in *Re Citro* on the nature of exceptional circumstances, it is interesting to note that on appeal in this case, Jonathan Parker J said:

> in my judgment it would be entirely inappropriate for this court to lay down what circumstances may be regarded as exceptional in any particular case when Parliament itself has not chosen to do so. (p. 744)

It appears, then, that the courts are prepared to offer a measure of protection to the family home in cases where a member of the family is suffering from a serious or terminal illness and whose health would be further prejudiced by a forced removal from her home. In seems unlikely, though, that anything else will count as 'exceptional circumstances' and the interests of the creditors will eventually defeat those of the bankrupt and her family.

12.9 Comment

The Trusts of Land and Appointment of Trustees Act 1996 provides a coherent conceptual foundation for trusts of land. It extends and clarifies the roles of trustees and beneficiaries in relation especially to partition, consultation, rights of occupation and delegation, and gives beneficiaries limited powers in respect of the appointment of trustees. It is not really possible at this stage to predict the effects of the new trust to sell or retain and how the courts will balance the matters to be taken into consideration in deciding whether the land should be sold or retained and, although it appeared from the judgment in *Shaire* that the law had changed, the decision in *Bell* seems to indicate that this may not be the case, at least in any degree.

The doctrines of joint tenancy and tenancy in common on the whole work quite well. However, the rules about severance of an equitable joint tenancy – on which so much may depend – are at times uncertain and often unjust. It has even been suggested that the equitable joint tenancy should be abolished, in order to avoid 'much troublesome and expensive litigation' (Thompson [1987] Conv 29, p. 35).

Some problems remain, not least for family members when a co-owner faces s.14 proceedings from a secured creditor or a trustee in bankruptcy. Although the Insolvency Act 1986 was designed to provide a compromise between the needs of the family and the wishes of the creditors to get at their money, in most cases the court will order the home to be sold after a year. This can be contrasted with the introduction of 'homestead legislation' in New Zealand and in North America, an approach which reflects the different priorities in those jurisdictions. Under the New Zealand Joint Family Homes Act 1964, for example, a home registered by spouses as a 'joint family home' will, in most cases, be secure in cases of bankruptcy or attack by creditors (see Gray and Gray, 2001, pp. 935–6). It is unlikely, however, that such an enlightened position will be adopted here.

Summary

12.1 Strict settlements developed as a way in which families could hold land through several generations; trusts for sale were created to hold land as a temporary investment. The TLATA abolished both for the future, creating a new 'trust of land' with power to sell or retain the land.

12.2 Under the old trust for sale, equity regarded the beneficial interest as an interest in money, not in land, although this was sometimes ignored in order to protect occupiers of land; the TLATA abolished this doctrine of conversion.

12.3 An interest under a trust of land may arise expressly, or by statute, or by a resulting or constructive trust.

12.4 Legal title to land may only be shared under a joint tenancy, and the maximum number of legal joint tenants is four. Joint tenants share the unities of possession, interest, title and time, and take the risk of the right of survivorship.

12.5 Equitable co-owners may be joint tenants or tenants in common, depending on whether there have been words of severance or on the general circumstances of the creation of the trust; tenants in common share the unity of possession.

12.6 Equitable joint tenants can sever their tenancy and become tenants in common.

12.7 Trustees of a trust of land have, subject to the terms of the trust, the powers of an absolute owner of land; this may include powers to transfer the land to adult beneficiaries absolutely entitled; to partition the land; to delegate their powers to beneficiaries. They have duties to consult the beneficiaries and to make reasonable decisions in relation to beneficiaries occupying the land.

12.8 Beneficiaries have the right to be consulted, and may have the right to occupy or receive compensation.

12.9 Under a trust of land, any trustee or beneficiary can go to court for an order of sale or otherwise, and the court may make such order as it thinks fit; where a party is bankrupt, the land will probably be sold after a year, unless the circumstances are 'exceptional'.

Exercises

12.1 Why was the doctrine of conversion abolished?

12.2 How do you know if co-owners are joint tenants or tenants in common when a trust of land is created? Why is it important?

12.3 When is a joint tenancy severed?

12.4 When do beneficiaries have the right to occupy trust land?

12.5 What should you do in order to get an equitable interest in a house?

12.6 When does land subject to a trust have to be sold?

12.7 Five friends, Denise, Michael, Florence, Jacob and Ben, who had just graduated and found jobs, bought a house, intending to share it while they established themselves in their new careers. They each contributed £10 000 to the deposit and were equally liable for the mortgage repayments.

Denise decided to leave her job and sail round the world, so she sold her share of the house to her friend Amanda who has now taken over her mortgage liability.

Florence and Michael became lovers and had a baby. Since the house is large, they want to divide it into two maisonettes, keeping the smaller one for themselves. The others want to keep it as it is.

Ben's business investments have failed and he thinks he might be made bankrupt.

Discuss the rights of all the parties and explain what might now happen to the land.

Further Reading

Brown, 'Insolvency and the Matrimonial Home – The Sins of the Fathers' (1992) 55 MLR 284

Ferris and Battersby, 'The Impact of the Trusts of Land and Appointment of Trustees Act 1996 on Purchasers of Registered Land' [1998] Conv 168

Hopkins, 'The Trusts of Land and Appointment of Trustees Act 1996' [1996] Conv 411

Miller, 'Applications by a Trustee in Bankruptcy for Sale of the Family Home'[1999] Insolvency Law and Practice 176

Pascoe, 'Section 15 of the Trusts of Land and Appointment of Trustees Act 1996 – A Change in the Law?' [2000] Conv 315

Probert, 'Creditors and Section 15 of the Trusts of Land and Appointment of Trustees Act 1996: First Among Equals' [2002] Conv 61

Tee, 'Severence Revisited' [1995] Conv 104

Thompson, 'Beneficial Joint Tenancies: A Case for Abolition' [1987] Conv 29

13 Implied Trusts and Proprietary Estoppel

13.1 Introduction

The last chapter explained how trusts of land can be created by an express declaration of trust, or by statute in cases where land is transfered to more than one person without such an express declaration. This chapter considers the circumstances in which the courts will impose an implied trust – either a resulting or a constructive trust – on the parties, and also the operation of proprietary estoppel, a doctrine discussed in Chapter 2 and which has a particular relevance here.

However sensible it might be for two people to sort out their property and financial arrangements before they buy a house, or before a person moves in to live with someone who already owns a house, this does not always happen. Certainly in the latter case, to open these kinds of negotiations at such a time might be thought to be somewhat calculating and therefore to be avoided. Equally, such thoughts might never have crossed the parties' minds at such an emotional stage in their relationship. Alternatively, there may have been some informal understanding that the person who does not own the legal title will contribute towards the mortgage repayments, or financially in some other way to their shared lives. As a result of this failure to formalise their property relationship, if they later decide to part and then try to extricate themselves from their complex financial and emotional relationships, or if a mortgage lender tries to gain possession of the land following mortgage arrears, it is the courts which will have the frequently difficult task of deciding whether the non-legal owner has any right to the land and, if so, the extent of that right. As Clarke remarked:

> In an ideal world, those who intend to own property or a share in it would do three things: they would agree what they intended to do; they would then record their intentions; and they would take legal advice to ensure that what they wanted had been achieved in a manner which the law recognises. However ... life is not like that. ([1992] Fam Law 72)

In the absence of an express or statutory trust, a person who later wants to claim a share of the beneficial interest in the land will try to establish that there was always an intention that she should have such an interest, and ask the courts to declare that she is a beneficiary under either a resulting or a constructive trust. Failing that, she may try and establish some right to the land through estoppel. (The doctrine of proprietary estoppel and its relationship with resulting and constructive trusts is considered at 13.5, 13.6 below.)

Most of the cases in this chapter concern unmarried home sharers since, when spouses divorce or separate, the courts have a wide discretion under the Matrimonial Causes Act 1973 to redistribute the family property. However, the principles of property law rather than family law apply in cases involving unmarried partners, or siblings or friends living together (or, even in cases where the parties are married, a mortgagee is seeking possession or a trustee in bankruptcy is seeking sale).

13.2 **Resulting Trusts**

If there is no other evidence of the parties' intentions, a resulting trust will arise when a person contributes towards the purchase price of land, but the legal title is transferred into the name of someone else. The presumption is that the parties intended that the legal owner owner holds the land on trust for the benefit of the contributor. Thus, when Mrs Boland (see *Williams & Glyn's Bank Ltd v. Boland* [1981] AC 487, Chapter 11) contributed to the purchase price of the house bought by her and her husband, Mr Boland, as the sole registered proprietor, was deemed to be holding the land on trust for himself and his wife through a resulting trust.

If the contribution is by way of a gift or a loan to the legal owner, the presumption of a resulting trust will be rebutted, and the contributor will not gain a beneficial interest. There is also an old doctrine called the 'presumption of advancement', by which the courts used to presume that money given by a parent to a child for the purchase of land was a gift, and that it was not intended that the parent should acquire any interest in the land. In *McGrath* v. *Wallis* [1995] 2 FLR 114 the Court of Appeal followed the modern line that this presumption is now a 'judicial instrument of the last resort' and is rebuttable by even the slightest evidence. Here, where a father had provided money to help his son buy a house for them to live in together, there was evidence (from an incomplete deed) of an intention that the land was to be held on trust for them both as tenants in common. Therefore, the presumption of advancement did not operate and, when the father died intestate, the son's sister was entitled on the intestacy to a share in her father's interest in the land.

Since nowadays people tend to depend on mortgage loans to finance the purchase of their homes, it is more common for people who do not hold legal title to attempt to establish a beneficial interest in the land through their contributions to the mortgage repayments (see 13.3 below). Gray and Gray, 2001, p. 670, argue that that resulting trusts should now be confined to those 'relatively rare' cases where there is no evidence as to the parties' intentions, but the person claiming the beneficial interest made a direct contribution towards the initial purchase price of the land.

13.3 **Constructive Trusts**

Constructive trusts are potentially much wider than resulting trusts. They do not necessarily depend on a voluntary property relationship created by the parties, but rely on a more fundamental moral principle.

During the late 1960s and 1970s, Lord Denning MR used the constructive trust as a means of achieving a fair solution to family disputes over land. They could be imposed by the courts whenever people found themselves in a situation where one would naturally trust the other because of the underlying social consensus on what was 'fair'. A constructive trust might therefore be imposed whenever a person would otherwise get 'a manifest and unfair advantage' and where it would be unconscionable for the legal owner to deny a claimant's beneficial interest. The constructive trust is currently used in this way in other common law jurisdictions.

However, over the last 20 years in Britain, the constructive trust has been more limited. An important leading case is *Lloyds Bank plc* v. *Rosset* [1991] 1 AC 107. Mr Rosset bought a semi-derelict farmhouse with money from a Swiss trust fund; the trustees of the fund insisted that his name only should appear as the registered proprietor. For six months, Mrs Rosset supervised the renovation and decorated the house. In subsequent possession proceedings brought by a mortgagee, she claimed an equitable interest under an informal trust, which, she argued, would enable her to claim an overriding interest under s.70(1)(g) LRA 1925 (see 11.5 above) and thus defeat the mortgage taken out by Mr Rosset without her knowledge. The House of Lords held that she had not shown that she had gained an interest, and therefore the bank was able to defeat her claim (see Ferguson (1993) 109 LQR 114).

Since there had been no declaration of trust and since Mrs Rosset had not contributed to the purchase price, Lord Bridge said that an equitable interest would only arise if she could demonstrate that there had been a *common intention* that she should own a share in the land. This could be shown by either:

1   An *express agreement* that the land should be co-owned, plus some act by the claimant to her detriment or some significant alteration of her position in reliance on the agreement. This would give rise to rights, according to Lord Bridge, under a constructive trust or proprietary estoppel;

or, in the absence of an express agreement:

2   *an act by the claimant from which the court may infer a common intention*, giving rise to an interest under a constructive trust. Probably the only act which would be sufficient would be the direct contribution of money (such as the repayment of a mortgage) towards the purchase of the property.

Mrs Rosset failed under the first category because there had been no agreement that she should have a beneficial interest, and under the second category because her work on the house did not amount to a financial contribution towards its purchase.

Express common intention
In *Rosset*, Lord Bridge approved the earlier Court of Appeal decision in *Grant* v. *Edwards* [1986] 2 All ER 426 in which a man and a woman lived together for about ten years and had two children. He had told her that her name should not go on the legal title of the house that they shared because this might prejudice her divorce proceedings. Although clearly he never intended that she should have a beneficial share in the house, nevertheless the Court of Appeal was prepared to find that his excuse for not putting her name on the title amounted to evidence of a common intention, since otherwise no excuse would have been needed. In addition, the couple had shared equally some money left over from an insurance claim when the house had partly burnt down. The woman had acted to her detriment in reliance on the common intention by paying all the household bills:

> In a case such as the present, where there has been no written declaration or agreement, nor any direct provision by the plaintiff of part of the purchase price so as to give rise to a resulting trust in her favour, she must establish a common intention between her and the defendant, acted on by her, that she should have a beneficial interest in the property ... In my judgment [she must prove] conduct on which [she] could not reasonably be expected to embark unless she was to have an interest in the house. (Nourse LJ at pp. 431–3)

As the claimant had established that there had been a common intention that the house should be co-owned and that she had relied on this to her detriment, the Court imposed a constructive trust on the man and awarded her a share of the beneficial interest.

In *Hammond* v. *Mitchell* [1992] 1 WLR 1127 (and see Bottomley [1994] Fem LS 83) a man and woman lived together for 12 years in a bungalow registered in his name. He had promised her that she was equally the owner of the property but said that he could not put her name on the Register for tax reasons. There were also several businesses and a house in Spain, and she claimed a half share in all of these. Waite J, in some despair at the detailed and conflicting evidence and the 19 days of the trial, finally awarded her a half-share in the bungalow.

The full flavour of the dispute can only be gained from reading the report: there was evidence of a promise that the land was half hers, of her involvement in the businesses and their sharing of whatever money they had, and of her agreement to risk any interest she might have in the bungalow as security for a bank loan for business purposes. All these taken together showed a common agreement plus an act to her detriment. She therefore satisfied the first *Rosset* category. However, the judge commented:

The primary emphasis accorded by the law in cases of this kind to express discussions between the parties ... means that the tenderest exchanges of a common law courtship may assume an unforeseen significance many years later when they are brought under equity's microscope and subjected to an analysis under which many thousands of pounds of value may be liable to turn on fine questions as to whether the relevant words were spoken in earnest or in dalliance. (at p. 1139)

In *Chan* v. *Leung* [2003] 1 FLR 23 (referred to in 12.6 above), Mr Chan formed a relationship with Miss Leung, who helped him in his business affairs while he was in prison in Hong Kong, in return for a share in the business. He also promised her that he would divorce his wife, marry her and provide her with a house. They bought a house in England in the name of a company in which they were the sole shareholders, and lived there together until the relationship broke down three years later. Miss Leung successfully claimed a beneficial share in the property, arguing that there was an express agreement that she should have half of the house, which she had relied on by helping Mr Chan with his business interests and uprooting herself from Hong Kong. Just as in *Hammond* v. *Mitchell*, the whole course of the parties' relationship was examined. At the trial there had been a lengthy rehearsal of the evidence and much had turned on whose version of the events was believed by the judge:

The judge having heard the witnesses over a considerable time, inevitably had a feel for the case which this court cannot have. (Jonathan Parker LJ at para. 89)

Inferred common intention

An earlier case, *Burns* v. *Burns* [1984] Ch 317, reinforces Lord Bridge's view that a claimant is unlikely to succeed under his second category unless there is 'the solid tug of money'. An unmarried couple lived together for 19 years in a house, legal title to which was held by the man. She brought up their children, kept house and, when the children were older, she took a job which allowed her to contribute to the housekeeping and buy various household items such as a washing machine. She also decorated inside the house. When their relationship ended, her claim to a beneficial interest failed:

What is needed, I think, is evidence of a payment or payments by the plaintiff which it can be inferred was referable to the acquisition of the house ... the mere fact that the parties live together and do the ordinary domestic tasks is, in my view, no indication at all that they thereby intended to alter the existing property rights of either of them. (Fox LJ at pp. 328, 331)

There had been indications in an earlier leading case, *Gissing* v. *Gissing* [1971] AC 886, that the House of Lords might be moving towards a more liberal approach. In that case, Lord Diplock was of the opinion that indirect financial contributions to the household expenses might be sufficient to enable a claimant to gain a beneficial interest, but only if they enabled the legal owner to make the mortgage repayments.

In the first instance decision in *Le Foe* v. *Le Foe* [2001] 2 FLR 970, a case in which a mortgagee was seeking possession, a wife who had made indirect financial contributions gained a beneficial share in the property:

> I have no doubt that the family economy depended for its function on [the wife's] earnings. It was an arbitrary allocation of responsibility that [the husband] paid the mortgage ... whereas [the wife] paid for day-to-day domestic expenditure. (Nicholas Mostyn QC at para. 10)

The law on whether indirect financial contributions should allow an inference of common intention is perhaps uncertain, despite Lord Bridge's view that they probably do not. The Law Commission is clear that they should do so (see *Sharing Homes* (2002) Law Com No 278, Part VI, para. 6(a)).

13.4 What Share of the Equitable Interest?

Once a court has found that an informal arrangement has resulted in the creation of a beneficial interest behind an informal trust, it must then go on to quantify the share of the equity to which the successful claimant is entitled. The law is somewhat confused in this area, but two approaches can be identified. In the first, based on resulting trust principles, the parties are entitled to a share of the beneficial interest in proportion to their contribution to the purchase price. However, since most property is bought with the help of a mortgage loan, or there may be continuing indirect contributions, the issue is complicated by the need to consider whether subsequent direct financial contributions can increase the claimant's share. It is in such cases that the second approach may prove more helpful.

This approach, more applicable to constructive trusts, is based on the parties' intentions as to how the property should be shared. It may be simple enough for the court to find this out if it has been made clear, perhaps through express discussions. However, if the parties' intentions are unclear, as will frequently be the case, the court must examine the detail of their relationship in order to discover their intentions. The court may be able to infer an intention to share in proportion to the respective contributions, but an alternative and more flexible 'holistic' approach to quantification taken, for example, in *Midland Bank plc* v. *Cooke* [1995] 4 All ER 562 (and see Oldham [1996] CLJ 194), allows the courts to use 'general equitable principles' to produce a fair result and do justice between the parties.

In *Cooke* the wife contributed £550 to the original purchase (her share of a wedding present) and the trial judge held that this entitled her under a resulting trust to about 7 per cent of the value of the house. However, the Court of Appeal held that once there was evidence of the common intention to share the property, then the judge has to:

undertake a survey of the whole course of dealing between the parties relevant to their ownership and occupation of the property and their sharing of its burdens and advantages ... [The court] will take into consideration all conduct which throws light on the question what shares were intended. Only if that search proves inconclusive does the court fall back on the maxim that 'equality is equity'. (p. 574)

Here, it was very clear from the wife's involvement in their complex financial arrangements that they had intended to share the property equally, and the wife was therefore awarded a half share in the equitable ownership.

In *Drake* v. *Whipp* [1996] 1 FLR, Mr Drake and Mrs Whipp bought a barn for conversion into a home. Mrs Whipp contributed 40 per cent of the purchase price of the barn, but the costs of conversion amounted to twice its purchase price, and to this she contributed only 13 per cent, although she put in a great deal of her labour. In other words, her overall financial contribution was about 20 per cent. She argued that she should have a 40 per cent equity in the property, based on her contribution to its original acquisition. Mr Drake claimed that her share should be restricted to 20 per cent in order to reflect the overall financial position. Peter Gibson LJ found that a constructive trust rather than a resulting trust existed here, since there had been detrimental reliance on a common intention that Mrs Whipp should have a beneficial interest, and that therefore the court could adopt 'a broad brush approach' to determining the shares. At the end of reviewing the whole story of their joint enterprise, including her work on the land and her contribution to the housekeeping bills, he awarded her a one-third share.

13.5 Proprietary Estoppel

Chapter 2 explained how, at times, proprietary estoppel can come to the aid of a person who has suffered detriment following a failed s.2 LP(MP)A 1989 contract to buy land. The application of the doctrine is, however, much wider than this, and has an important role to play when a person is attempting to establish some right in another's land. Lord Bridge in *Rosset* discussed rights acquired 'under a constructive trust or proprietary estoppel'. In some ways, constructive trusts are similar to proprietary estoppel (see 13.6 below), but while resulting and constructive trusts will provide a successful claimant with a beneficial interest in the land as equitable co-owner, proprietary estoppel is a much more flexible creature and the courts have a certain discretion as to the nature of the remedy that they can award.

A successful argument of estoppel can prevent a person enforcing her strict legal rights if to do so would be unfair on a claimant who has acted to her detriment as a result of that person's actions or representations. In contract law the doctrine is known as promissory estoppel and is thought to provide a defence only. In land law, the doctrine of proprietary estoppel has a greater scope and can found an action – in other words, it can be a 'sword' as well as a 'shield'.

Over the years, the doctrine has developed from a fairly strict set of requirements – the five *probanda* (criteria) of *Wilmott* v. *Barber* (1880) 15 Ch D 96 – to the more flexible modern approach of Oliver J in *Taylors Fashions Ltd* v. *Liverpool Victoria Trustees* Co Ltd [1982] 1 QB 133:

> I am not at all convinced that it is desirable or possible to lay down hard and fast rules ... [T]he more recent cases indicate, in my judgment, that the application of the ... principle ... requires a very much broader approach which is directed rather at ascertaining whether, in particular individual circumstances, it would be unconscionable for a party to be permitted to deny that which, knowingly or unknowingly, he has allowed or encouraged another to assume to his detriment than to inquiring whether the circumstances can be fitted within the confines of some preconceived formula serving as a universal yardstick for every form of unconscionable behaviour. (pp. 149, 151–2; approved by the Privy Council in *Lim Teng Huan* v. *Ang Swee Chuan* [1992] 1 WLR 113)

The question therefore is whether it would be unconscionable if someone were to go back on their assertion or encouragement. In *Re Basham (decd)* [1986] 1 WLR 1498 a man had promised his stepdaughter that if she looked after him he would leave his house, formerly her mother's, to her in his will. In reliance on his promise, over many years she had cooked for him, maintained the house and taken legal action in relation to a boundary dispute, and her husband had refused a better job elsewhere. It would therefore have been unconscionable for him to deny his promise. He died intestate, however, but as a result of the stepdaughter's successful claim of proprietary estoppel, the man's heirs were prevented from relying on their legal right to inherit. The trial judge, Edward Nugee QC, explained estoppel as:

> where one person, A, has acted to his detriment on the faith of a belief, which was known or encouraged by another person, B, that he either has or is going to be given a right over B's property, B cannot insist on his strict legal rights if to do so would be inconsistent with A's belief. (p. 1503)

The effect of decisions such as *Taylors Fashions* and *Re Basham* is that, if as a result of the defendant's conduct the claimant has an expectation that she has, or will have, rights in the defendant's land and she acts to her detriment in reliance on that expectation, then she will have raised an 'equity' in the land in her favour which can be satisfied either by the defendant or, failing that, by the award of a remedy by the court. Although arguments centre round an examination of whether the claimant has such an expectation, and then on whether she has relied to her detriment on this:

it is important to note at the outset that the doctrine of proprietary estoppel cannot be treated as subdivided into three or four watertight compartments ... [It is] apparent that the quality of the relevant assurances may influence the issue of reliance, that reliance and detriment are often intertwined ... Moreover the fundamental principle that equity is concerned to prevent unconscionable conduct permeates all the elements of the doctrine. In the end the court must look at the matter in the round. (Robert Walker LJ in *Gillett* v. *Holt* [2001] Ch 210 (below) at p. 255)

The expectation

The expectation in the claimant can be raised either by an express representation as to her present or future rights in the land, or by 'wilful silence'. In the latter case, an estoppel may be established if a landowner, knowing the true position, stands by while the claimant does something on the landowner's land in the mistaken belief that the land belongs to the her. As Lord Wensleydale stated in *Ramsden* v. *Dyson* (1866) LR 1 HL 129:

If a stranger build upon my land, supposing it to be his own, and I knowing it to be mine, do not interfere but leave him to go on, equity considers it to be dishonest in me to remain passive and afterwards to interfere and take profit. (p. 168)

In most estoppel cases, however, there will have been an express representation or an encouragement to act in a certain way. In general, there will be no difficulty with this except evidentially, but in *Taylor* v. *Dickens* [1998] 3 FCR 455, Judge Weekes QC held that a promise that a person would inherit under another's will was insufficient to amount to a representation on which to base an estoppel claim. Since a will can be revoked at any time, there must, he said, also be a collateral promise that there will be no revocation of the will.

In *Gillett* v. *Holt* [2001] Ch 210, the Court of Appeal was asked to consider the claim of Mr Gillett who, as a boy, had been befriended by a wealthy farmer. At the farmer's suggestion, Mr Gillett had left school early without any formal qualifications, had gone to work for the farmer and had continued to do so for some 40 years, giving up opportunities to develop his career. During this time the farmer gave him and his family repeated assurances that he would inherit the farm and the farm business, and he executed a will to that effect. Eventually, however, the farmer transferred his attentions to someone else, dismissed Mr Gillett from his employment and excluded him from his will. Mr Gillett argued that the farmer was estopped from doing this, since he had relied on the farmer's repeated representations that he would one day inherit the farm, rather than pursuing his own career as a farmer. The Court of Appeal agreed with him and, in finding that it was the detrimental reliance on the promise of inheriting under the will which made the promise binding, even though the will itself could later be revoked, overturned the first instance decision and criticised the judgment in *Taylor* v. *Dickens.*

The detrimental reliance

Once the claimant has shown that she was encouraged to act in a certain way, the courts will presume that her actions were in reliance on that encouragement, unless the legal owner is able to rebut this presumption (see *Greasley* v. *Cooke* [1980] 1 WLR 1306, below). The question is one of whether the acts would have been undertaken in any case as part of the relationship between the parties, or whether they were undertaken in reliance on the promise. The expenditure of money is clearly an act showing reliance on a promise. For example, in *Pascoe* v. *Turner* [1979] 1 WLR 431, a woman who had been promised that the house in which she was living and which belonged to her former partner 'was hers' established reliance by spending 'a quarter of her modest capital' – a few hundred pounds – on maintaining and improving the property.

Acts in reliance, though, as in *Re Basham,* may often be something other than the expenditure of money. In *Greasley* v. *Cooke,* a young woman went to work as a maid in a household. After some time, she formed a relationship with one of the sons and lived with him as if she were his wife. Although she was no longer paid for her work, she continued to look after the family, including a daughter who was ill, and was assured that she could live in the house for the rest of her life. Her partner, who had inherited the house, died, and the heirs attempted to evict her. Lord Denning MR held that her unpaid work in caring for the family, especially the daughter, amounted to acts in reliance on the assurances that had been made to her.

In *Gillett* v. *Holt,* Mr Gillett would hardly have acted as he did had it not been for the farmer's assurances. However, his actions would not have amounted to a detriment unless the farmer had gone back on his promises, and the question then becomes one of whether 'the repudiation of an assurance is or is not unconscionable in all the circumstances' (at p. 232). It is also apparent, therefore, that the element of detriment in proprietary estoppel only arises once the claimant's expectation is removed. Until that time, she expects that her acts in reliance on the assurance will be to her advantage.

The remedy – satisfying the equity

A successful estoppel claim has the effect of raising an equity in the property. The courts must then find a means of 'satisfying the equity', and they have considerable discretion, within equitable principles, to award a remedy. It might be thought that the obvious remedy would be to require the defendant to fulfil the promise. This 'expectation-based' approach, however, impinges on the law of contract and the doctrine of consideration, and on the rules of formality in land law, and the effects could well be unjust.

The approach generally taken nowadays is based on compensating the claimant for the detriment she has suffered as a result of removal of the expectation. The court is concerned to achieve:

a proportionality between the remedy and the detriment which [it] is its purpose to avoid (Mason CJ in *Commonwealth of Australia* v. *Verwayen* (1990) 170 CLR 394 at p. 414)

In addition:

The court's aim is ... to form a view as to what is the minimum required to satisfy [the equity] and do justice between the parties. The court must look at all the circumstances, including the need to achieve a 'clean break' so far as possible and avoid or minimise future friction. (Robert Walker LJ in *Gillett* v. *Holt* at p. 237)

In *Pascoe* v. *Turner* (above), the court ordered the legal owner of a house to convey the fee simple to the claimant. Without more, this appears to be a windfall for the claimant and unjust on the man. In fact, the man was prosperous and, according to Cumming-Bruce LJ:

determined to pursue his purpose of evicting her from the house by any legal means at his disposal with a ruthless disregard of the obligations binding on conscience. (p. 438)

The court felt that the woman could only be protected from the man's harrassing behaviour by requiring him to perfect his gift and convey the land to her. The award of some lesser right in the land, such as a licence to remain there during her lifetime, would not have been enough to achieve this.

The daughter-in-law in *Re Basham* was awarded the house that had been promised to her. In *Yaxley* v. *Gotts* [2000] Ch 162 (see 2.6 above), Mr Yaxley received a long lease of one of the flats in the building he had been renovating.

In *Campbell* v. *Griffin* [2001] EWCA Civ 990, a man who had initially been a lodger in the house owned by a retired couple, gradually took on responsibilities as their carer and they came to rely on him completely and treated him as their son. They assured him that he had a home for life and, indeed, the husband changed his will in order to leave him a life interest in the house. The husband died before the wife, who took the property by right of survivorship as the sole surviving joint tenant. She, however, was unable to make a will in the man's favour because she was suffering from senile dementia. The man established that he had an equity in the property through estoppel, but the Court of Appeal was unable to give effect to the promise of a life interest, since this would have been disproportionate to the detriment he had suffered and unfair on others who were to benefit from the estate. He was awarded £35 000, charged on the property.

Similarly, in *Jennings* v. *Rice* [2003] 1 FCR 501, an old woman's part-time gardener became, over the course of a number of years, her unpaid full-time carer, even sleeping on the sofa in her sitting room during the last three years of her life. Despite promising him that the house would be his one day, she never made a will. After her death, the man made a claim on her estate for the house. Although his argument of estoppel was successful, the court again emphasised the need for proportionality between the expectation and the detriment and, instead of fulfilling his expectation by ordering the transfer of the house, awarded him £200 000, less than half its value.

In *Gillett* v. *Holt*, the court did not require the farmer to fulfil all his promises to Mr Gillett, who instead was awarded the freehold of the farmhouse and some land, along with £100 000 to compensate him for his exclusion from the farm business.

On occasion, this approach, being essentially based on restitution, may result in no award at all being made, even though the claimant is successful in her estoppel claim. In *Sledmore* v. *Dalby* (1996) 72 P & CR 196, Mrs Sledmore sought possession of a house she owned against Mr Dalby, her son-in-law, who had lived there for many years. He had undertaken some work on the property in reliance on an assurance that his wife would be left the property after her parents' death and on the assumption that, since his wife had since died, he would be able to live there for the rest of his life. However, Mrs Sledmore had little money, was liable to lose her present home and had a greater need for the house than did her son-in law, who could afford to pay for his own accommodation and, indeed, was living elsewhere at the time. Granting possession to Mrs Sledmore, Hobhouse LJ recognised 'the need for proportionality between the remedy and the detriment' and the need to do justice between the parties. Mr Dalby had already had his remedy and so got nothing.

13.6 Constructive Trusts and Proprietary Estoppel Compared

It is probably clear from the discussion above that there is a degree of overlap between constructive trusts and proprietary estoppel. In *Yaxley* v. *Gotts*, Robert Walker LJ stated:

At a high level of generality, there is much common ground between the doctrines of proprietary estoppel and the constructive trust ... [a]ll are concerned with equity's intervention to provide relief against unconscionable conduct, whether as between neighbouring landowners, or vendor and purchaser, or relatives who make informal arrangements for sharing a home, or a fiduciary and the beneficiary or client to whom he owes a fiduciary obligation. (p. 176)

In *Jennings* v. *Rice*, Robert Walker LJ was of the view that:

Sometimes the assurances, and the claimant's reliance on them, have a consensual character falling not far short of an enforceable contract ... [and] the proprietary estoppel may become indistinguishable from a constructive trust. (para. 45)

This indication that, at times, there is little or no difference in the criteria required to establish a constructive trust or a proprietary estoppel was approved by Jonathan Parker LJ in *Chan* v. *Leung* (13.3 above), who was of the opinion that this was the position in that case.

In both constructive trusts and proprietary estoppel there is detrimental reliance on a common understanding between the parties that the claimant will gain an interest in the land. However, an estoppel claim does not necessarily require a common agreement since the doctrine will not permit a legal owner to stand back while the other party acts in reliance on a mistaken belief as to her rights.

A further difference arises when considering the nature of the remedy a successful claimant might obtain. Under a constructive trust, she will have a beneficial interest in the land which will arise at the time of the performance of the acts in reliance on the agreement, and the only question will be the extent of the share to be awarded by the court. In proprietary estoppel, however, these acts give rise to what has been described as an 'inchoate equity' in the land. The nature of the right is not known until the court gives its decision and, as discussed above, can range from the award of the fee simple, as in *Pascoe* v. *Turner*, to nothing at all, as in *Sledmore* v. *Dalby*.

It is also necessary to consider whether rights arising under a constructive trust or a proprietary estoppel are binding on third parties – later mortgage lenders or purchasers of the land. The rules on the circumstances in which a beneficial interest is binding are now well-established and have been considered earlier (see 10.4 and 11.5, above). Case law also indicated that an equity arising from proprietary estoppel could bind a purchaser of registered land under s.70(1)(g) LRA 1925 (see *Lloyd* v. *Dugdale* [2002] 2 P & CR 13 (2.6 above), and this is now confirmed by s.116 LRA 2002. In registered land, therefore, such an equity can now be protected by the entry of a notice on the Register (which is unlikely to happen, since the person in whose favour the equity has arisen will probably not know that it should be formally protected). However, when coupled with actual occupation, it is an interest overriding subsequent dispositions. The difficulty with this is that the precise nature of the right will not be known until a remedy is awarded by the court.

13.7 Comment

The present law on the acquisition of interests under implied trusts is particularly unsatisfactory. The law is based on finding that the parties had a common intention to share the beneficial ownership of the land. There are real evidential difficulties in establishing that an express agreement existed sufficient for Lord Bridge's first category in *Rosset* – see, for example, the comments of the judge in *Hammond* v. *Mitchell* (13.3 above). Lord Bridge's second category of a common intention inferred from the conduct of the parties is based on a fiction, since there may well have been no such common intention, the non-legal owner claiming an interest in the land only when her possession is threatened, either by a mortgagee or when the relationship ends.

The law operates to discriminate against female cohabitees – the likeliest claimants – for two reasons. Firstly, while the traditional role of a man is seen to be to earn money which would go towards the purchase of the house, that of a woman is generally considered to be by no means wholly financial. As well as less well-paid employment outside the home, a woman is more likely to be responsible for the day-to-day care of children and the home. In taking only money into account as an 'act referable to land', the judges have adopted a commercial definition of the contribution necessary to gain an equitable interest which denies the realities of family life.

Secondly, the reliance on agreement and common intention is based on a contractual and property-based analysis which is often inappropriate when exploring family relationships based on trust. For judicial decisions in this area to rest on a contract (a private law voluntarily created by two equally placed individuals), rather than on the wider communal understanding of the nature of a trust relationship, is as inappropriate as was the old trust for sale applied to modern family land. The same criticism can be levelled at proprietary estoppel which, while being in some ways a much more flexible doctrine, still generally requires an assertion from the legal owner that the claimant has or will obtain an interest in the land.

It can be argued therefore that this contractual and commercial basis does not go far enough, and that domestic law should adopt the wider understanding of constructive trusts, based on unconscionablity, found in other common law jurisdictions. In Canada, for example, the constructive trust is based on the doctrine of unjust enrichment rather than intention. A 'remedial' constructive trust there will arise in circumstances where the legal owner has been enriched by some benefit, not necessarily financial, conferred on him by the claimant, providing there is no 'juristic' reason for this, such as a contractual obligation or a gift (see, for example *Sorochan* v. *Sorochan* (1986) 117 DLR (3rd) 257.)

In its 2002 discussion paper, *Sharing Homes* (Law Com No 278), the Law Commission reviewed what it described as the 'unfair, uncertain and illogical' law on the property rights of unmarried couples. Recognising the need for reform, it considered the proposal that, where a home is shared and the non-legal owner makes a direct or indirect financial contribution, or contributes in terms of domestic work on the home or towards the relationship, that person might gain a share of the home under a statutory trust proportionate to her contribution (unless, of course, the non-legal owner is a tenant or a lodger, or unless the contribution is intended as a gift or a loan). In the end, however, the Law Commission concluded that such property-based reform would be too difficult to achieve because:

the infinitely variable circumstances affecting those who share homes have rendered it impossible to propose the scheme as a viable and practicable reform of the law. (para. 1.27)

Summary

13.1 Resulting and constructive trusts are trusts which are created informally.

13.2 A resulting trust requires a direct contribution to the initial purchase price of the property or to the mortgage.

13.3 A constructive trust will be imposed on the legal owner when there has been an express agreement that the claimant should have a beneficial share in the property, and as a result has significantly altered her position.

13.4 Under resulting trust principles, the beneficiary will gain a share in the property proportionate to her contribution to the purchase price.

13.5 Under a constructive trust, the courts may well now adopt a 'broad brush' approach to the quantification of the beneficiary's interest, seeking, through an examination of their whole relationship, to establish how the parties intended the property to be shared.

13.6 Proprietary estoppel has many similarities to a constructive trust. A successful claimant will establish an equity in the property through detrimental reliance on an expectation, encouraged by the legal owner, that she will get an interest in the land.

13.7 In order to satisfy the equity raised by a successful estoppel claim, the courts aim to achieve proportionality between the remedy and the detriment suffered and will award the minimum remedy necessary.

Exercises

13.1 What do you have to do to get a beneficial share in land under an informal trust?

13.2 How do you know what share you will get?

13.3 What is proprietary estoppel, and how does it differ from a constructive trust?

13.4 Is the law in this area satisfactory?

13.5 Jerome, who used to be a prosperous businessman, was the sole registered proprietor of a house which he bought in 1993 for £200 000, paying for it with £20 000 from his savings and the rest by means of a mortgage. Two years later, he asked his student girlfriend, Lena, to move in with him, telling her that she would always have a home there. Lena looked after the house and garden, and carried out any maintenance on the property. In 1996, Jerome's business failed and he took paid employment, but did not earn enough to cover all the outgoings. Lena, therefore, gave up her studies and took a job, and her contributions to the household budget enabled Jerome to pay the mortgage. Two months ago, Jerome was killed in a road accident. In his will he left everything to his mother, who has told Lena to leave the house, now worth £400 000, since she wants to sell it. Advise Lena.

Further Reading

Battersby, 'Informally Created Interests in Land' in Bright and Dewar (eds), *Land Law Themes and Perspectives* (Oxford: OUP, 1998)

Bottomley, 'Production of a Text: *Hammond* v. *Mitchell*' [1994] Fem LS 83

Bridge, 'The Property Rights of Cohabitants – Where Do We Go From Here?' [2002] Fam Law 743

Bridge, 'Sharing Homes: Property or Status' in Cooke (ed), *Modern Studies in Property Law, Volume 2* (Oxford: Hart, 2003)

Clarke, 'The Family Home: Intention and Agreement' [1992] Fam Law 72

Ferguson, 'Constructive Trusts – A Note of Caution' (1993) 109 LQR 114

Law Commission Discussion Paper: *Sharing Homes*, (2002) Law Com No 278

Nield, 'Estoppel and Reliance' in Cooke (ed), *Modern Studies in Property Law, Volume 1* (Oxford: Hart, 2001)

Oldham, 'Quantification of Beneficial Interests in Land' [1996] CLJ 194

Pawlowski, 'Beneficial Entitlement – Do Indirect Contributions Suffice?' [2002] Fam Law 190

Pawlowski, 'Sharing Homes – Legislation Down Under' [2003] Fam Law 336

Probert, 'Sharing Homes – A Long Awaited Paper' [2002] Fam Law 834

Probert, 'Trusts and the Modern Woman – Establishing an Interest in the Family Home' [2001] CFLQ 275

Siddle, 'Cohabitation' [2002] Fam Law 727

Thompson, 'An Holistic Approach to Home Ownership' [2002] Conv 273

Thompson, 'Estoppel: Reliance, Remedy and Priority' [2003] Conv 157

Thompson, 'The Flexibility of Estoppel' [2003] Conv 157

Wong, 'Rethinking *Rosset* from a Human Rights Perspective' in Hudson (ed), *New Perspectives on Property Law, Human Rights and the Home* (London: Cavendish, 2003)

Part V

Licences in Land

14 Licences

14.1 Introduction

A person who has a licence to be on another's land has that person's permission to be there – in other words, a licence prevents someone from being a trespasser. In a different context, Chapter 5, on leases, examined those situations in which a person who was unable to establish that she had a lease, perhaps because there was no exclusive possession, may instead have had a licence to be on the land. Similarly, someone who fails for lack of formality in a claim to have an easement may well hold a licence to go on to her neighbour's land.

This chapter aims to examine the nature of licences and, in particular, the extent to which they might be interests in land – property rights – or whether they are merely personal rights. The distinction is important, since property rights attach irrevocably to the land, are sold along with the land and, if protected in the appropriate way (see Chapters 10, 11), will bind a purchaser of the burdened land.

Licences cover a huge variety of activities. A fan at a football match is a licensee, as is a secretary in an office, a customer in a shop, a paying guest in an hotel, and perhaps a cohabitee sharing her lover's house. Licences may last for a few minutes or for life, and can be created within a family or a commercial setting. It is hardly surprising that there are several types of licence and that the rights and remedies of licensees differ widely.

Licences can be divided into the following categories:

1 Bare licences.
2 Licences coupled with interests in land.
3 Contractual licence.
4 Licences by estoppel.

14.2 Bare Licences

A bare licence arises when the landowner gives permisssion for another person to be on her land. This may be express, such as an invitation to a friend to come in and have a cup of coffee, or implied, such as for a postal worker delivering letters. Such licences are gratuitous – given without consideration – and can lawfully be revoked whenever the landowner wishes; the licensee must then leave within a reasonable time or she becomes a trespasser and may be physically removed. This kind of licence cannot be transferred by the licensee to another person, and neither can it bind someone who buys the land from the licensor.

14.3 Licences Coupled with an Interest in Land

When a person owns a *profit à prendre*, the right to take something from another person's land (see Chapter 8), she will be unable to exercise the right without a licence to go on to the land. So, for example, the owner of a profit of piscary, the right to take fish, automatically has a licence to cross the servient tenement to get to the river. The licence cannot be revoked and will continue for as long as the interest exists, binding third parties in the same way as the profit.

14.4 Contractual Licences

A contractual licence is created wherever a person has permission to be on another's land as part of a contract between them, such as the fan at the football match and the paying guest in the hotel, who are both contractual licensees. Contractual licences are common and will generally arise expressly.

In the 1970s, however, the Court of Appeal used the device of the implied contractual licence as a solution in cases of disputes in certain kinds of family relationships, such as the one which arose in *Tanner* v. *Tanner* [1975] 1 All ER 776. In this case, a woman moved from her Rent Act protected tenancy into a house bought by her married lover for her to live in with their twin children. When he later formed a relationship with another woman and tried to evict her, the Court of Appeal held that she had a contractual licence which could not be revoked until the children were of age. However, since she had already been rehoused following the first instance decision which went against her, she was awarded £2000 to compensate her for her loss. This contractual analysis is problematic when applied to family and domestic arrangements, especially when taking into account the traditional contractual requirements of consideration and the intention to create a legal relationship, and nowadays it is likely that such cases would be argued on the basis of estoppel (14.5 below).

The rights of a contractual licensee depend upon the terms of the contract. Lord Greene MR stated that:

> A licence created by a contract ... creates a contractual right to do certain things which otherwise would be a trespass. It seems to me that, in considering the nature of such a licence and the mutual rights and obligations which arise under it, the first thing to do is to construe the contract according to ordinary principles. (*Winter Garden Theatre (London) Ltd* v. *Millennium Productions Ltd* [1946] 1 All ER 678 at p. 680)

It is often assumed that a contractual licence is worth less than a lease, and this may be true in regard to the licensee's security if the land is sold and, in general, licences do not attract the statutory protection afforded to leases. However, there are occasions when it is more beneficial to be a licensee than a tenant under a lease. For example, in *Wettern Electric Ltd v. Welsh Development Agency* [1983] 1 QB 797, a company held the licence of factory premises which were so badly constructed and became so unsafe that the licensee company had to leave. It successfully sued for breach of an implied term that the premises would be fit for their purpose; this term could not be implied into a contract for a lease, not being one of the 'usual' covenants (6.3 above), but in a licence the ordinary rules of contract law applied:

> The sole purpose of the licence was to enable the plaintiffs to have accommodation in which to carry on and expand their business ... If anyone had said to the plaintiffs and the defendants' directors and executives at the time when the licence was being granted: 'Will the premises be sound and suitable for the plaintiff's purposes?' they would assuredly have replied: 'Of course; there would be no point in the licence if that were not so.' The term was required to make the contract workable. (Judge Newey QC, p. 809)

Revocability

There has been a continuing debate on whether a contractual licence can be revoked by the licensor. In *Hurst* v. *Picture Theatres Ltd* [1915] 1 KB 1, for example, a cinema customer was physically removed because the owner (wrongly) believed he had not paid for his ticket. The Court of Appeal decided that the licensor should not have turned the licensee out and he was entitled to damages for false imprisonment and breach of contract. The decision was based on the argument that the equitable remedies of specific performance of the contract and an injunction to prevent the breach would, in theory, have been available to the customer, who therefore was seen by equity as having a right to remain in the cinema and thus could not be a trespasser.

In the *Winter Garden Theatre* case (above), the theatre owner attempted to revoke a licence allowing a theatre company to produce plays and concerts in its theatre, although there was no provision in the contract for him to do this. The House of Lords stated that whether a contractual licence could be revoked depended entirely on the construction of the contract. In this case, the licence was not intended to last forever and could therefore be determined by the theatre owner on reasonable notice.

Verrall v. *Great Yarmouth BC* [1981] 1 QB 202 is a clear example of a case in which a contractual licence could not be revoked. Following a change in its political control, a local council tried to revoke a licence to use a hall for a two-day conference which it had previously granted to an extreme right-wing political organisation. It was held that the council could not do so. Damages for breach of contract would not be sufficient remedy since no alternative venue was available, so the Court of Appeal unanimously held that the contract should be specifically enforced. Lord Denning MR said:

An injunction can be obtained against the licensor to prevent [the licensee] being turned out. On principle it is the same if it happens before he enters. If he had a contractual right to enter, and the licensor refuses to let him come in, then he can come to the court and in a proper case get an order for specific performance to allow him to come in. (p. 216)

Effect on buyers of land

If it is correct that in some circumstances a licence cannot be revoked, then a relevant question is the effect of such a licence on a purchaser of the land from the licensor. Has an irrevocable licence now become an interest in the land to which it relates, thus binding third parties, or does the traditional view prevail, that a licence is merely a personal right?

King v. *David Allen & Sons Billposting Ltd* [1916] 2 AC 54 is an example of the traditional approach. The licence in this case was to fix advertising posters to the licensor's wall. The licensor then granted a long lease of the building, a cinema, and the leaseholder prevented the licensee from fixing the posters. The House of Lords held that the licensor was liable to pay damages for breach of contract. Although the cinema leaseholder was not a party to the case, Lord Buckmaster LC several times referred to the licence as a purely personal right and not an interest in land. Had the alternative view prevailed, the licensor would not have been in breach.

However, in *Errington* v. *Errington & Woods* [1952] 1 KB 290, a father paid the deposit on a house and told his son and daughter-in-law that, if they continued in occupation and paid the mortgage instalments, the house would be theirs. When the father died, the son moved in with his mother, who had inherited the house, and she sought possession against her daughter-in-law. The Court of Appeal held that the arrangement was a contractual licence: if the licensees had paid the whole of the mortgage, the father, had he lived, would have been ordered to transfer the house to them. This contractual licence could not be revoked so long as one of the licensees kept to their side of the bargain, and it would bind a purchaser with notice:

> The couple were licensees, having a permissive occupation short of a tenancy, but with a contractual right, or at any rate, an equitable right to remain as long as they paid the instalments, which would grow into a good equitable title to the house itself as soon as the mortgage was paid ... contractual licences now have a force and validity of their own and cannot be revoked in breach of contract. Neither the licensor nor anyone who claims through him can disregard the contract except a purchaser without notice. (Denning LJ, pp. 296, 298)

In later years it was Lord Denning's view that equity would enforce a contractual licence against anyone who ought fairly to be bound by it. In *Binions* v. *Evans* [1972] Ch 359, for example, a contractual licence permitting a widow to remain in a cottage for the rest of her life bound, under a constructive trust, buyers of unregistered land who had agreed to take the land subject to her rights:

> Wherever the owner sells the land to a purchaser, and at the same time stipulates that he shall take it 'subject to' a contractual licence, I think it plain that a court of equity will impose on the purchaser a constructive trust ... It would be utterly inequitable that the purchaser should be able to turn out the beneficiary. (Lord Denning MR, p. 368)

Although the view of Denning LJ in *Errington*, that contractual licences can bind third parties, was discredited in *Ashburn Anstalt* v. *Arnold* [1989] Ch 1, the Court of Appeal in that case approved his later imposition of a constructive trust in *Binions* v. *Evans*, since it was necessary to protect the licensee against unconscionable dealing by the new legal owners who had expressly agreed to uphold her rights. However, the court took a restrictive view on the use of constructive trusts in such situations, since:

> [t]he court will not impose a constructive trust unless it is satisfied that the conscience of the estate owner is affected. The mere fact that that land is expressed to be conveyed 'subject to' a contract does not necessarily imply that the grantee is to be under an obligation, not otherwise existing, to give effect to the provisions of the contract. (Fox LJ, p. 25)

14.5 Licences by Estoppel

Chapter 13 considered how detrimental reliance on an expectation encouraged by the legal owner gives rise to an equity which may be satisfied by a remedy designed to do justice between the parties and compensate the claimant for the detriment she has suffered. This remedy may sometimes be the award of an estate in the land, as in *Pascoe* v. *Turner* (13.5 above). It is frequently something less, and the award of a licence for the claimant to remain on the land is not uncommon.

In *Inwards* v. *Baker* [1965] 2 QB 29, a son was encouraged to build a bungalow on his father's land by the father's promise that the son could remain on the land. The son built the bungalow but when the father died his heirs claimed the land. The Court of Appeal held that, since the father would have been estopped from going back on his promise and the heirs were in the same position as the father, the son's equity should be satisfied by the award of a licence to stay on the land.

In *Greasley* v. *Cooke* (13.5 above), the former maid who had lived in the house for many years was awarded an irrevocable licence to continue to occupy it for as long as she wished.

Effect on buyers of land

It is evident that Lord Denning felt that estoppel rights were capable of binding a buyer of the land. In *Inwards* v. *Baker*, for example, he said, 'any purchaser who took with notice would clearly be bound by the equity'. He followed this in *Ives (ER) Investment Ltd v. High* [1967] 2 QB 379 (for the facts, see 10.3 above): since the earlier owner of the flats would have been estopped from denying the garage owner a right to use the drive belonging to the flats, successors in title to that earlier owner were also bound.

In *Re Sharpe (a bankrupt)* [1980] 1 WLR 219, a woman lent £12 000 to her nephew to buy a maisonette on the basis that they would live there together. He became bankrupt, and the trustee in bankruptcy, having contracted to sell the maisonette, sought a possession order against her. Although the case was decided on the basis that the woman had a contractual licence to remain in the property until the loan was repaid, Browne-Wilkinson J said:

> If the parties have proceeded on a common assumption that the plaintiff is to enjoy a right to reside in a particular property and in reliance on that assumption the plaintiff has expended money or otherwise acted to his detriment, the defendant will not be allowed to go back on that common assumption and the court will imply an irrevocable licence or trust which will give effect to that common assumption. (p. 223)

This licence was binding on the trustee in bankruptcy, and although the judge was not required to express a view on the position of the purchaser from the trustee, he stated:

> It may be that as a purchaser without express notice in an action for specific performance of the contract [the purchaser's] rights will prevail over [hers]. As to that I have heard no argument and express no view. (p. 226)

Whether a licence by estoppel does bind a purchaser is therefore not entirely clear. In unregistered land, as in *Ives* v. *High*, it may depend on whether the purchaser had notice of the equity. In registered land, as discussed earlier (13.6 above), case law indicates that under the LRA 1925 the equity raised by the estoppel might have been sufficient, when coupled with actual occupation, to amount to an overriding interest under s.70(1)(g), and s.116 LRA 2002 has now confirmed that an equity by estoppel is capable of binding purchasers.

14.6 Comment

If one thing is clear about licences, it is that there is not one answer to the questions, 'Are licences interests in land?', 'Are they property?'. The probable conclusion to be drawn from the brief summary in this chapter is that some contractual and estoppel licences are, but that most licences are not.

A few years ago these issues were the subject of frequent investigation by academics, some embracing the idea that twentieth-century land lawyers had produced a new interest in land, perhaps equivalent to the development of the restrictive covenant in the nineteenth century.

> The courts seem to be well on their way to creating a new and highly versatile interest in land which will rescue many informal and unbusinesslike transactions, particularly within families, from the penalties of disregarding legal forms. Old restraints are giving way to the demands of justice. (Megarry and Wade, 1984, p. 808)

From this viewpoint, some licences were symbols of a new form of property, a right to share, which would take its place beside the traditional private and exclusive property rights. After *Ashburn Anstalt* (14.4 above), however, this seems no longer to be the case. The 'old restraints', such as the need for certainty of conveyancing and its formal processes, appear to have reassumed their importance, although it should be noted that, in registered land at least, that the equity raised by a proprietary estoppel seems now to have some of the features of a proprietary interest.

Summary

14.1 A licence is a permission to be on land: it may be a bare licence or one coupled with an interest in the land such as a *profit à prendre*, or may arise through contract or estoppel.
14.2 A bare licence can be revoked at any time.
14.3 A licence coupled with an interest in land will last as long as the interest in question.
14.4 Whether a contractual licence can be revoked depends on the terms of the contract.
14.5 An estoppel licence may be awarded by the court when a person acts to her detriment in reliance on a promise that she will gain an interest in land.
14.6 Licences by estoppel and licences that give rise to a constructive trust may bind a buyer of land.

Exercises

14.1 What is an 'interest in land'?
14.2 Can contractual licences be revoked on reasonable notice?
14.3 Are licences property?
14.4 John and Linda are the registered proprietors of a large house. When they bought it 15 years ago, it was very run-down and they did not have the time or money to renovate it by themselves. They therefore agreed with Hannah and Joshua (Linda's sister and brother-in-law) that they would move in and help with the work; they said Hannah and Joshua would be able to make their home there. Hannah won £15 000 in the lottery and lent it to John and Linda so they could pay for a new roof. Joshua gave up his job to work on the house and look after John and Linda's children. He has been in hospital since falling off a ladder when mending one of the chimneys last year.

John and Linda are now going to separate. They have transferred the land to Damien who has been registered as proprietor. Advise Hannah and Joshua.

Further Reading

Anderson, 'Of Licences and Similar Mysteries' (1979) 42 MLR 203
Dewar, 'Licences and Land Law: An Alternative View' (1986) 49 MLR 741
McFarlane, 'Identifying Property Rights: A Reply to Mr Watt' [2003] Conv 473
Megarry and Wade, *The Law of Real Property*, 5th edn (London: Stevens, 1984)

Index